Tying & Fishing TERRESTRIALS

All photographs by the author
Line Drawings by Karen Almy

Tying & Fishing TERRESTRIALS

By Gerald Almy

STACKPOLE BOOKS

TYING AND FISHING TERRESTRIALS
Copyright © 1978 by
Gerald Almy

Published by
STACKPOLE BOOKS
Cameron and Kelker Streets
P.O. Box 1831
Harrisburg, Pa. 17105

Published simultaneously in Don Mills, Ontario, Canada
by Thomas Nelson & Sons, Ltd.

Printed in the U.S.A.

Library of Congress Cataloging in Publication Data
Almy, Gerald, 1951-
    Tying & fishing terrestrials.

    Bibliography: p.
    Includes index.
    1. Trout fishing. 2. Insects. 3. Flies,
Artificial. I. Title. II. Title: Terrestrials.
SH687.A53 1978   799.1'7'55   78-17309
ISBN 0-8117-1746-1

Acknowledgments

Many fine fishermen and writers lent their thoughts and insights for the preparation of this text; moral and material assistance flowed freely from family, friends, and editors. Special thanks go out to the following people:

My parents, Gerald and
  Maria Almy
Karen Almy
Rebecca Almy
Neil McAleer
Jerry Hoffnagle
Charlie Fox

Dave Engerbretson
George Harvey
Ed Sutryn
Dave Whitlock
Mike Fong
Chauncy Lively

Dave Johnson
Tom Wendelburg
Al Troth
Bill McIntyre
Mathew Vinciguerra
Charles Meck

CONTENTS

THEORY   Part I

FISHING THE TERRESTRIALS   Part II

TYING THE TERRESTRIAL PATTERNS   Part III

INTRODUCTION

Nature is not kind to her children. A life wipes out a lesser one in the endless, hazardous, and cruel game of hunter and hunted. It is ironically true that while the angler is a natural lover of nature, he capitalizes upon such small tragedies for his very sport. That is the tactic Ernie Schwiebert advises in *Matching the Hatch* and that Vince Marinaro examines so closely *In the Ring of the Rise*. And in fact, the more attuned the angler is to the deadly game of life in the stream world, the better prepared he will be to enter it.

By necessity, trout as predators depend upon a varied diet. It has been demonstrated to me that trout are individualistic creatures, not all responding in the same way to the same situation, not all desiring to live in the same type of water or general location. So trout fishing demands that the angler approach with an open mind, not overly bound by traditions that may not fit the situation at hand. It is especially true in our day, in which the angler must often "invent" his fishing.

The greatest teacher of all is the trout itself, but angling time is so limited that the student of fly fishing must depend upon recorded experiences and ideas of others. Fortunately, no other sport, spectator or participant, can boast of such a volume and quality in its literature as fly fishing for trout. Neither can any other sport boast of such a horde of well-read patrons. The fact of the matter is, we anglers depend upon and cherish the words of our predecessors and fellow fishermen. Reading becomes one of many ancillary pleasures of the sport.

The great literature stemming from the scholarly anglers of the English chalk streams produced in the decades preceding the turn of the century centered around the drifting mayfly and its imitations. So it was that the lore of fly fishing began to revolve around the Ephemera, even though they are not the only insects trout feed on. The special qualities of dry fly fishing with mayfly patterns took hold in these early writers' work, and was transmitted to succeeding generations as the gospel. Later writers in England and especially in this country, such as Charlie Brooks and Ernest Schwiebert, have followed the logic of fly fishing to perfect underwater patterns and techniques that are quite deadly, and expanded our repertoire to include caddis and stonefly representatives. But still the magic of dry fly fishing holds its spell.

It is not surprising. The floating fly offers great suspense and anticipation, the heart of any game. What is surprising is that the earlier authors and most dry fly anglers today do not think of dry fly fishing with any forms other than the aquatics. Perhaps the appeal of casting a delicately hackled fly at a rise form was so great that we wanted too much to preserve it. No one bothered to look at how the basic principle can be applied to catch fish using patterns other than the cherished mayflies and the lately popular caddis imitations. But trout do not limit their surface feeding to select species, even if we prefer that they do. So it was up to recent generations of anglers to invent terrestrial fishing. It has been a unique contribution by many individual anglers, and in many ways a truly American one.

Still, for a long time it seemed there was no room on the mayfly pedestal for grasshoppers and crickets. Then fishermen began to realize, sadly, that the aquatic hatches were deteriorating—mainly the vaunted and cherished mayfly—and yet trout continued to surface feed. Either by choice or necessity they were taking the land-born insects. And not unpredictably, the fish took flies that were eventually tied to imitate them. On an occasion several years ago I referred to them as "the terrestrials," and the name stuck. Encompassed are: ants, jassids, hoppers in the main, and in varying degrees, the oak worms, beetle forms, true flies, treehoppers, the stingers, termites, and the larva of moths.

As the author of this book notes, even though these insects surround us numbering in the millions, they have almost been overlooked in the angling literature. A few articles, a few illustrations, a few book chapters are all that is available on the subject. We have needed a complete study in book form which binds together all the scattered terrestrials lore. That brings us to the present time, and another enterprising angler-author who is willing to share some very valuable experiences with terrestrials which otherwise might remain unavailable. Gerald Almy fills the void in an eminently satisfactory way with this book, which he chooses to entitle *Tying & Fishing Terrestrials*. I have both enjoyed and benefited by reading his work; I am sure you will experience the same.

CHARLES K. FOX

PREFACE

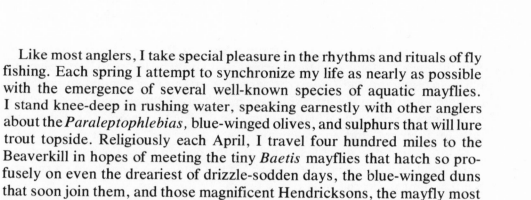

Like most anglers, I take special pleasure in the rhythms and rituals of fly fishing. Each spring I attempt to synchronize my life as nearly as possible with the emergence of several well-known species of aquatic mayflies. I stand knee-deep in rushing water, speaking earnestly with other anglers about the *Paraleptophlebias,* blue-winged olives, and sulphurs that will lure trout topside. Religiously each April, I travel four hundred miles to the Beaverkill in hopes of meeting the tiny *Baetis* mayflies that hatch so profusely on even the dreariest of drizzle-sodden days, the blue-winged duns that soon join them, and those magnificent Hendricksons, the mayfly most cherished of all by Beaverkill browns.

But when I think back over recent seasons, the most successful dry fly fishing that I have enjoyed was almost always with terrestrials—patterns that imitate the common beetles, crickets, hoppers, and ants teeming in the streamside habitat. The hatches of mayflies and caddis sometimes came as predicted in the books, sometimes not; occasionally, even when the aquatics came, the trout inexplicably refused to rise. And when the mayflies did emerge on cue, the trout rose well, and my delicate dry fly patterns proved successful, I still had the bulk of the day left to fish. Who wants to go home after the hatch when home is two, three, or more hours away? In these situations it was the terrestrials, almost without fail, that made the day's fishing.

On a damp evening on the Beaverkill last June I fished through a phenomenal spinnerfall of blue-winged olives, *Ephemerella cornuta.* It was an unusually productive hour and a half of fishing, with trout lined up shoulder to shoulder, feeding at a frantic pitch. Easily over a hundred fish were porpoising in famed Hendrickson's Pool.

But over the entire three-day visit, it was black ants and beetles that provided the most reliable dry fly fishing. Fur ant patterns and deer hair

11

beetles produced steady day-long action on the surface. Eighty browns succumbed to the land-based patterns, including half a dozen fish in the fifteen to nineteen-inch class. Never have I done this well during a mayfly or caddis hatch over many years of fishing this wonderful river.

Yet on the Beaverkill, as on many other fine public trout waters, terrestrials are by-and-large ignored. When the "white fly" (*Ephoron leukon*) hatches on Pennsylvania's popular Yellow Breeches Creek at dusk and spinners fall, anglers crowd together like herrings in a dip-net, flicking mayfly imitations blindly in the dark. And what do they take? Perhaps two or three trout per angler on the average—often less. A good terrestrial fisherman working this same water along the shoreline during the day can easily catch twenty or thirty fish or more with ants, beetles, jassids, and crickets—with elbow room, too.

Visit the sparkling waters of Falling Springs Run in Pennsylvania from July through September in the morning and you'll be lucky to find a place to park, so popular is the *Tricorythodes* hatch on this tiny, fecund stream. Yet at lunchtime, when the little spinners have finished their mating dance, it's as if someone blew the whistle at the end of a factory work day: Everyone puts up their rod and zooms away.

In fact, the petite mayflies signal just the beginning of the day's feeding. Terrestrials will offer excellent sport for the same fish over the next twenty hours—right up to the next day's hatch.

It was on these and other classic limestone waters of south-central Pennsylvania that I received my education in the ways of terrestrial-feeding trout. As my wanderlust grew, I traveled to new and decidedly different streams throughout the East and South and eventually the Midwest and Rocky Mountain states. The patterns which had proven so successful in Pennsylvania were not discarded, even though it occasionally meant being an oddball on the river. Casting hoppers along the Stephan's Bridge stretch of Michigan's Au Sable drew stares from the elite local entomologists, puffing aloofly on briar pipes as they waited patiently for tiny *Pseudocloeon* duns to appear. On broad western rivers, fishing tiny leafhoppers in preference to humpies and goofus bugs is an Easterner's peculiarity. On southern mountain trout waters there is often a surprised cock of the head, a tone of incredulity in the voice when I reveal that I've been catching fish on an ant, a cricket, or a jassid instead of the touted Royal Coachman.

So far I have endured it and "listened" instead to the fish. And without a doubt, the tone, pace, and atmosphere of fishing the terrestrials has its own allure. Most obvious is the slow, smooth tempo of the fishing. Intense hatches of aquatics offer exciting sport. But they have a way of getting anglers tightened up like overwound alarm clocks, and the results are very often disappointing, for one reason or another.

Fishing the terrestrials is a more relaxed affair. There is no rush to put your fly over as many fish as possible, as quickly as possible before the hatch dissipates. The insects are literally always "emerging" on land nearby, and to a greater or lesser extent, some are always finding their way into the stream and the gullets of trout. We can take the time to make accurate casts, tie properly-snugged knots and leaders, and approach the fish in a systematic way.

It would be misleading, however, to suggest that terrestrial angling is always sedate and soothing. At times it can be quite as frenetic as any hatch, particularly when large browns charge flies that land ten feet or more from their holding stations, clamping down on the fly with wide-stretched jaws. This is not relaxing! Nor, for that matter, is the sight of a heavy trout sipping in a tiny ant on a 7X tippet amid a labyrinth of weed beds. But it can be argued, as I have attempted to do in *Tying & Fishing Terrestrials*, that there is enough that is unique about fishing terrestrials to warrant a close look at the way these varied insects fit into our increasingly sophisticated approach to catching trout on flies.

For some reason—partly because of the romance of the mayfly and partly because of the terrestrials' reputation as special, summer-only flies—these patterns have been overshadowed by the accumulation of angling literature and gadgetry based on aquatic insects. Whatever the reasons, the open-minded angler will quickly acknowledge the obvious facts about the place terrestrials occupy in the trout world. For what we actually have in our cricket, hopper, jassids, ants, caterpillars, and bees are flies that imitate insects abundant throughout the entire country, in both freestone and limestone streams, found in the East and in the West, on forest and meadow waters, from early spring through fall—virtually the entire fishing season for most anglers.

We have patterns that are effective not only during some brief emergence time-span, but potentially the whole day long, from dawn to dusk and later, if the angler likes fishing in the black of night. We have flies that imitate naturals consumed avidly by all common species of trout, appealing especially to large fish. We have patterns that imitate a group of insects whose members are thriving in streamside habitat, while aquatic insects, regrettably, wane in numbers and importance in the diet of trout. We have flies that are productive during those daily and seasonal time stretches when the angler has access to broad, fertile reaches of water virtually for himself, time and space to enjoy that increasingly rare phenomenon of solitude astream. And we have flies that are sorely neglected by a great many dry fly fishermen. I hope this book will begin to rectify that.

Part I

THEORY

. . . I am beginning to think that the presence or absence of mayflies on American trout streams is highly overrated as a factor in angling success. The bread and butter in a trout's larder are, in my opinion, being neglected.

I visited a fish camp where all the guests were on the front lawn playing baseball. Inquiry revealed that the 'mayfly was off,' and believing that the trout wouldn't feed until it was on they had dissolved into a group so corrupted as to be entirely unrecognizable. Great trout were feeding regular as clockwork just beyond their outfield.

A.J. McClane, "Mr. Botz and the Beetle,"
Fishing with McClane

chapter
one

THE GREAT HORDE

The terrestrial insects—insects born and bred on land—are everywhere about us. They surround us in numbers and varieties that defy comprehension. Close to *one million* known species of terrestrial insects inhabit the earth; new species are being discovered at the rate of over five thousand per year. Some entomologists say the total figure will soon be doubled. Over eighty-two thousand kinds of terrestrial insects are found in North America alone.

They are everywhere. In the fields, in the forests, in the meadows, in deserts and swamplands, on mountaintops and seashores, in wildernesses and city lots, rare is the acre of land that does not harbor large numbers of terrestrial insects, from minute species that can crawl through the eye of a needle to fiendish longhorn beetles measuring up to eight inches in length. The diversity of life styles involved is equally stunning. There are vegetarians and carnivores, predators and parasites, farmers and marauders, dairymen and slavemakers, fliers and walkers, leapers and crawlers—every rogue and worker the imagination can conjure up.

For the trout—and for the trout fisherman—this phenomenal and widespread abundance of terrestrial insects is a happy circumstance, for the land-based insects provide a steady and substantial source of food over the bulk of the yearly cycle. Not only are the insects plentiful and rich in caloric value, but they apparently have a unique taste appeal to the fish. It is not at all uncommon for a wise old brown trout to interrupt steady feeding on hatching mayflies to inhale a black ant struggling to free itself from the grip of the water's surface film. On several occasions, I have seen selective rainbows that were sipping midges suddenly clamp down viciously on a Japanese beetle that plopped into the water. I once watched a small native brook trout wrestle a huge cicada down its tiny gullet. It took two or three charges, but there was something so determined about the little trout's gluttony that I found myself silently cheering the fish on.

Terrestrial insects outnumber the aquatics by such a wide margin that the term "insect" is virtually synonymous with *terrestrial* insect in everyday usage. Even fly fishermen fail to comprehend that, by comparison, the aquatic insects comprise a tiny category—barely five percent of all insect species inhabit the water (though the early ancestors of all insects were once marine). A mere fifteen hundred species of mayflies have been discovered; over two hundred times this many species of beetles exist.

But ironically, the typical dry fly fisherman's boxes probably contain ninety-five percent imitations of aquatic insects and five percent terrestrials—exactly the opposite of the ratio in nature.

It may seem, with the stupefying variety and quantity of insects involved, that to attempt to write about the "terrestrials," then, is a bit ambitious. Certainly true, if one were proposing a detailed entomological study.

But the terrestrials important to the trout fisherman can, for all practical purposes, be singled out of this buggy horde and treated as a group bound by their similar ties to a life on the solid ground. Fortunately, not all the eighty-two thousand varieties found in North America need be imitated by the angler. Many never find their way into trout streams in sufficient numbers to warrant imitation. However, both the number and the variety that *do* enter the aquatic realm of the trout is far more than most anglers realize.

RIPARIAN HABITAT

Both the quantity and diversity of land-bred insects found *in* trout waters is a direct result of the lush habitat found along virtually all trout streams—the fertile strip of land adjacent to the water. The exceptions to this rule are the migration, dispersal, and mating flights that may originate miles from water and still deposit tens of thousands of land insects within grasp of the trout. However, day-in and day-out, the bulk of the food trout receive from land originates from the stream banks.

The bushes, trees, and grasses along our trout streams harbor a microcosm bristling with insect life, supporting a multitude of overlapping insect communities, each encompassing dozens, even hundreds of individual mini-habitats.

But unless you stoop to look at the small scuttlings going on beneath your feet, this wealth of life is not readily apparent. Even the fly angler, normally more aware than the average citizen of the minute creatures carrying on their lives about him, tends to concentrate on the stream itself. The dry fly fisherman often struggles to capture and identify a tiny *Baetis* mayfly floating the currents in sparse numbers, yet may fail to notice ants dropping like clockwork from shoreline foliage into the same waters.

The broad divisions of habitat along trout streams are obvious—there are woodlands, grassy fields, rocky shoreline stretches, and shrubby edge areas between forest and meadow. Less discernible are the countless subdivisions among these broad habitat types where the different terrestrial species

---

A few astute anglers have taken note of the relationship between shoreline habitat and the abundance of land insects. Some of these individuals have gone so far as to plant particular weeds along the stream—not just to prevent erosion or provide shade, but to create an abundant supply of terrestrial insects as well. Among these fishermen is one who stands out as a modern angling legend—Charles K. Fox of Carlisle, Pennsylvania—Letort Creek country. Ever-observant, on a muskie trip to Opossum Lake Charlie noticed that a certain weed seemed unusually attractive to a broad array of land insects, including the coppery Japanese beetles. "The insects were all over these plants," Charlie said. "Some were eating the leaves, others the purple blossoms. At first I didn't know what it was, but I found out later it's called loose froil. It's pretty rare, really, but we dug some of it out of those swamps and planted it here along the Letort and it's done real well. Now the insects are attracted to these weeds and a lot of them get into the stream for the trout."

The land surrounding trout streams such as the Brodheads Creek, shown here, features hundreds of overlapping mini-habitats—both forest and meadow—where land insects thrive.

stake their territorial claims on their inch, foot, or yard of space.

Seldom is a square foot of territory left unexploited. The terrestrial insects are the ultimate opportunists; this is the secret to their overwhelming success. About half the terrestrial species, for example, eat green plants. Very few plants, grasses, or trees exist without a full share of insects living in, on, and "off" them. Several species chew the tender green leaves of plants with grinding mandibles. Certain beetles slip between the bark and inner trunk and live on the rich, soft food between the two layers. Other terrestrials go deep into the heart of plants with needle-sharp proboscises to suck free their nourishment. The hardy consume the tough stem tissue itself. Some herbivores eat only seeds, while underground species eat only roots. When the host plant dies, there are over two hundred thousand species that eat only decaying plant material, just waiting.

They are specialists all, each consuming its narrowly defined portion of the plant, each sticking to its precisely mapped-out territory. This specialization reduces direct competition and allows phenomenal numbers and varieties of land insects to coexist in dense populations in the same plant habitat.

In addition to the herbivore population, the territory of the carnivorous insects overlaps with that of the plant-eaters that form their diet. While the herbivores have evolved to take advantage of every conceivable source of plant food, parasites and predators have kept pace, feeding on and keeping in check the millions of vegetarians. Complementary relationships permit maximum saturation of the earth and its vegetation. Each insect has its nook of shelter, parcel of food, and natural enemies.

Dense, varied populations of terrestrial insects can exist on a single plant species—whole interdependent communities on an individual shrub. More often than not, the plant survives in spite of the heavy burden of animal life it supports. The intricate web of checks and balances keeps a tight grasp on such overlapping communities. If a particular insect threatens to wipe out a plant species on which it lives, parasites and predators will multiply to match the expanding food supply and keep the plant consumers from tilting the delicate ecological balance. Of course man, in his well-intentioned but short-sighted efforts, frequently tips this balance himself, often with disastrous consequences. And then blames it on the insects!

In southern England, Waloff, Dempster, and Richards studied the intricate relationships existing between insects that live on Scotch broom plants. A total of thirty-five different species of herbivorous insects ate the various parts of this single plant type. Additionally, seventy species of parasites lived off these thirty-five species of herbivores. And some sixty predatory insects preyed upon the Scotch broom eaters. A total of one hundred sixty-five different species supported by one type of plant!

The richness and abundance of riparian habitat in terms of terrestrial insect life does the trout precious little good if these land-dwelling insects do not make it into the water. The fact is that insect populations are so dense along waterways that sheer numbers alone insure that, over the course of a day, many of these creatures, going about their daily routines on vegetation overhanging the water, will slip, fall, jump carelessly in the wrong direction, or be chased by larger insects to a watery doom.

Wind is a chief factor for depositing terrestrial insects in the water. It doesn't take much of a gust to blow a tiny leafhopper or a miniscule orange ant from its perch. Most terrestrial insects are equipped with wings at one stage or another of their life. But many are notoriously poor fliers, hard set to make it across a wide trout stream. Adding to the peril is the fact that insects have no rational conception of water as dangerous. Their leap or flight may land them in a stream as easily as a meadow.

In addition to these sporadic splashdowns, land insects often find their way into trout waters from miles away. For some species, flight is the central means of locomotion. They are equipped with wings from the moment they obtain their adult form and use the wings in their daily search for food. In other species winged forms appear only when mating or dispersal of the species is on the agenda.

Whatever the motive for flight, many of these insects, especially the lighter, smaller species, are caught in powerful wind gusts that carry them dozens and hundreds of miles, heedless of the efforts of their tiny wingbeats to change their direction or make a safe landing. The breezes ultimately deposit tens of thousands of the wind-blown terrestrials in trout streams and lakes.

Once in flowing waters, crosscurrents, riffles, curves in the stream's course, and wind distribute the floundering insects over the entire surface of the water—if the trout give them that much time! For the fish often sense where the majority of terrestrials come from and line up along shore like bank patrons on payday, waiting to cash in on the bounty of the land.

And there are many other day-to-day dangers in the life of riparian insects. Larger predators such as birds, mammals, and reptiles also unintentionally chase many terrestrial insects into the realm of the trout. Leafhoppers, aphids, and cicadas, as well as certain beetles, have an instinctual

SPANNING THE BRIDGE

This short stretch of Kettle Creek features grassy band on right side of photo, log jam in foreground, gravel bar on left, deciduous trees on left bank, and conifers further upstream—all provide habitat for different land insects that may enter the stream.

response that causes them to immediately drop from their perch when touched or approached by suspected danger. Some drop at the mere sight of movement near them. This is undoubtedly a valuable behavior trait for the species as a whole since it enables them to escape the darting beaks of birds and tongues of predatory animals. But those individuals who happen to live along a trout stream or lake may find this survival tactic backfiring on them when they drop from their perch into the water near a hungry trout.

Rain is clearly an important means by which terrestrials enter trout streams. Imagine individual raindrops the size of a calf and weighing a hundred pounds pelting the earth, and you will have a vivid impression of the force a mild summer shower represents to a typical terrestrial insect. When tiny rivulets begin forming as rainwater rushes off the slopes of rocks, tree trunks, and leaves, thousands of hapless land insects are washed like so many floundering flood victims into the treacherous world of feeding fish. And the trout, as any astute angler can confirm, are well aware of this plentiful food supply during a rain.

Dave Whitlock notes still another manner in which trout in streams below dams receive a daily allotment of land insects in their diet. "Most trout tailwaters through the summer months have enormous chum lines of terrestrials develop each day as water fluctuations occur." The Smith in Virginia, the Lackawaxen in northeastern Pennsylvania, and the White River below Bull Shoals Dam in Arkansas (which Whitlock says "is as fine a terrestrial fishery as any in the country for eight- to twenty-inch rainbows") are examples of rivers where daily water releases wash countless thousands of insects from streamside vegetation into the realm of the trout.

With all these possibilities for an immense variety of insects to become meals for trout, the next question for the thinking dry fly man is, *When?* When do terrestrials enter the water? Unfortunately, he won't get as pat an answer as he is used to getting for, say, *Ephemerella subvaria*. While we can't pinpoint the terrestrials to regular emergences, there are two general time frames that will help the dry fly man approach terrestrial fishing with the greatest chance of success. These are seasonal availability and daily availability: how many months of the year they are present on the water, and what times of day the insects are most likely to become accessible to trout.

KEY TO AVAILA- BILITY

The seasonal availability of terrestrials to trout hinges on the presence and activity of adult insects (with some significant exceptions which will be treated later). Larvae and nymphs represent relatively inactive life-phases, often played out in hidden recesses far from the water.

Adult stages, on the other hand, represent extremely active life styles. The chores of housekeeping, hunting, food-gathering, care of young, reproduction, dispersal, and migration are among the typical behavior patterns of mature land insects. It is this rapid-paced, bustling life style that makes these adults such likely candidates to end up in the gullet of a trout.

Here the comparison with the mayfly is revealing. A mayfly is available to trout as a surface food (where the dry fly fisherman is concerned) during its winged stages of existence as dun and spinner, and only, of course, during those brief periods when it is actually on the water.

In terms of the twelve-month cycle, hatching may last in such rare cases as the *Tricorythodes* for several months. More commonly, as with the quill gordon (*Epeorus pleuralis*), or the green drake (*Ephemera guttulata*), duns will hatch over a few days, perhaps a week. Looking at the mayflies as a group, peak emergences occur almost without exception in the spring, concentrating prime dry fly fishing with ephemerids to a period of one or two months.

The mayfly's accessibility to trout is reduced even further when one looks at the second aspect of temporal availability, i.e., the twenty-four hour daily cycle. Justification for fishing the mayflies in terms of opportunity during a typical day astream is brief, to say the least. Duns and spinners enact their phases on the water's surface in a matter of a mere one, two, or three hours. Of course it is this very ephemeral nature of the mayflies and the concentration of adults on the surface over brief time spans that makes mayfly fishing such a fascinating and frenetic affair. Nevertheless, the same characteristic dooms mayfly fishing to be short-lived in both the hourly and seasonal sense, and it's frequently more appetite-whetter than belly-filler for the dedicated dry fly fisherman.

What a striking difference in both seasonal abundance and availability over the twenty-four-hour daily cycle one finds when considering the terrestrials.

From the annual standpoint, terrestrials are active over much longer periods of time than most people realize. Ants, crickets, snowfleas, leaf-hoppers, houseflies, and numerous species of beetles can be seen poking their heads out and wandering about on warm, sunny winter days. When the headwaters of Pennsylvania's legendary Big Spring Creek were opened for fishing several years ago after a lengthy closure, it was the middle of winter. Anglers found deep-girthed brooks, browns, and rainbows lined shoulder-to-shoulder—all stream-bred beauties. For dry fly men, even in the midst of a harsh Pennsylvania winter, black and cinnamon ants were among the most productive flies.

Spring is a time of abundance among the aquatic insects. But as we've seen, from the standpoint of a day's fishing these hatches are often confined to a few hours in the afternoon. The terrestrials are generally hardier critters, and even in April, May, and June many will be active from mid-morning through twilight. While many terrestrial insects hatch in the spring after wintering over as eggs or larvae, others, the ants for example, pass the winter in the adult stage. These insects are already beginning their spring cleaning, food-gathering, house repair, and sometimes mating even as the early Hendricksons are popping out on the quickened currents.

Summer is the season traditionally associated with terrestrials, and it is indeed a time of superabundance of land insects. Late-hatching beetles, hoppers, moths, crickets, treehoppers, and sundry land flies bring the meadows and woods alive with sound and movement. But it is certainly a mistake to consider this the only significant period of terrestrial insect activity. (Indeed, some insects are actually *less* active during the hot months of July and August—a phenomenon known as estivation, which is basically the opposite of hibernation.)

Fall continues summer's plenitude, with populations of many species, especially those of the woodlands, rising to their peaks. For those varieties of land insects producing more than one generation per season, the offspring increase and age groups overlap, reaching peak abundance just prior to the onset of killing frosts. Even after numerous subfreezing nights, some hoppers, beetles, ants, treehoppers, crickets, and other land insects will be encountered in streamside habitat. Their movement slows with the falling temperatures, but some still find their way into the bellies of trout, as late-season stomach analyses repeatedly bear out. As the food supplies dwindle in autumn, trout seem to relish each morsel more dearly, as if sensing the imminent coming of winter and leaner times.

The availability of terrestrial insects to trout over a twenty-four-hour cycle is even more astonishing. They are not available only during midday, as some believe. Too many variables are involved to pin the land insects down to a neat, specific time slot—species, season, locality, humidity, and wind velocity all influence daily activity patterns significantly. Indeed, any attempt to say "this is the hour when terrestrials are active and become trout foods" must be doomed to failure, for one or another of the terrestrials is typically bustling and flitting about at various times throughout the *entire* twenty-four hours of a day.

This ceaseless activity is a result of the density of insect life in small, tightly packed areas along streams. The riparian land literally bristles with insect life: To allow for such density and variety of creatures, specialization has evolved to decrease direct competition among species to tolerable levels.

This same rationing tendency is apparent also in the insects' schedules of activity—both seasonal and daily. Insects have arranged themselves over the millennia so that not everyone will be wanting to use the highway of the plant stem at the same peak "rush hour." Each has his slice of time when he is to be active—his slice of year-time and his slice of day-time. Some overlapping is unavoidable: Indeed, predator and prey must overlap if the carnivore is to survive.

Unlike the aquatics, night is a time of great activity for the terrestrials—a time of danger and hazards for many, as predators like the fearsome ground beetle scuttle hurriedly about in quest of caterpillars and other soft-skinned victims. Moths, notoriously active at night, provide large, meaty meals for heavy trout emboldened by the mask of blackness.

Such complexity and varietal richness is lacking in most aquatic envi-

---

In the bitter-cold weather of central New York, where Paul Needham did much of his ground-breaking research on trout streams, leafhoppers were found in the stomachs of brook trout on December 11. So much for the myth that terrestrials are summer flies!

ronments. The diversity and abundance of species is not as great, and hence the competition for space has not developed to such a pitch. The insects' activity needn't be spread out over time to avoid conflict. Mayflies can all hatch at once; on rich streams, two or three species may emerge simultaneously. Indeed, due to their vulnerable position to trout, birds, and other predators during emergence, it is to the mayfly's advantage to hatch in large numbers over a brief, concentrated time span. By virtually covering the surface of the water with duns, some will surely escape the heavy attrition by predators.

All this is to say that it can be sensibly argued that terrestrials can and often should be given the status of "workhorse" dry flies for the vast majority of trout fishing situations, to be replaced on the tippet only when significant selective feeding on aquatic insects takes place. Terrestrials, often in many varied forms, are active over the entire day cycle for virtually the whole fishing season, along the entire length of most trout streams. And as we've seen, the transition from "along" to "in" the trout stream is accomplished in many constantly recurring ways.

ERRATIC ENTRANCE

Even when they do not become the dominant food in the diet of the trout, the terrestrials still often represent the best dry fly choice. This statement stands partly on the relatively long life-phases of adult terrestrial insects, their abundance and availability over long periods of the day and season, but equally on another factor: the erratic manner in which the terrestrials become available to trout.

Wind gusts, rain, a careless step or jump—the countless ways in which terrestrials enter the stream—coupled with the diverse, overlapping periods of activity of the various land insects, teach trout quickly that these are foods to be taken randomly, any time and place they make their appearance.

The trout, like the terrestrials it consumes, is above all an opportunist. While there are definitely periods and situations where a trout will feed selectively on a particular land insect, much in the manner he feeds on hatching mayfly duns, this is *not* typical terrestrial fishing. The trout learns early in its life to accept the terrestrials as they come—virtually any time of day or night, in a wide assortment of shapes, sizes, and colors.

So there needn't be a swarm of ants on the water for a trout to take an interest in your imitation ant, or an abundance of Japanese beetles for him to sip in a deer hair beetle fly. Usually just a few of these insects falling into the water is enough to prime the fish.

The random, erratic availability of the terrestrials actually works in the trout's favor in one respect. Since the land insects generally come on periodically over a drawn-out time span, the fish can capture a great many of the ones that do fall into the stream—just the opposite of the situation with the mayflies, which overwhelm the trout with numbers so that many escape to mate and continue the species.

The accidental, staccato appearance of the terrestrials in the aquatic realm explains why typically we see only sporadic rises when land insects are being taken. The food comes erratically; hence the rise forms are erratic. But it should not be assumed that the fishing will likewise be sporadic.

On the contrary, the trout rise to the occasion, so to speak. When an insect plops in from shore, they grab it; when your imitation plunks in, they will do the same. It only takes one rise of a fish to your fly to hook the fish. It doesn't matter that it hasn't risen thirty times in the last ten minutes, so long as he rises the one crucial instant when the fraud floats over him! So in this sense, the erratic appearance of terrestrials—and the fact that trout have adapted to it—also works in the angler's favor. This sporadic feeding activity, which extends throughout the entire fishing day under most

Many terrestrials spend the bulk of their lives on the undersides of leaves where they escape the attentions of all but the most observant fishermen.

circumstances, is an especially welcome happenstance for those of us who have to drive several hours to reach good trout water and want to get in a full day's dry fly fishing, not just the pleasure of an hour-long hatch which may or may not materialize.

The terrestrial angler feels no great remorse over the fact that the land insects might not be the predominant food in the fish's stomach. The random way the insects present themselves makes them acceptable foods to the trout even when proportion-wise they may not be most important in the fish's diet at that particular time. I have seen fish break off feeding in flush hatches to take ants, as if they were taking a bite of salad in the middle of the main course.

This fact should not be taken to imply that terrestrials never do become the predominant food for trout. Indeed, many times they are the top item on the menu, and during these periods the terrestrial angler's chances are enhanced even further. It is in one sense unfortunate that these situations are becoming increasingly common with the decline of mayfly hatches.

At this point it might seem astonishing that terrestrial insect activity and the excellent fishing opportunities it provides are by and large ignored by the majority of fly fishermen. But even though the land insects are numerically and varietally superabundant adjacent to and *in* trout streams, it is not to be expected that most people would notice them. There are several reasons for this. First, they do not actually live in the water and so unless one pauses to reflect upon the various ways these insects might enter the stream, the terrestrials would not seem an obvious choice, especially when we all have Ephemera dancing in our heads.

Once this leap of logic is bridged, one has to consider the physical nature and behavioral characteristics or life styles of the terrestrials. Many are extremely small. Most are decidedly cryptic and secretive in their habits and habitat. Often they are dull and well-camouflaged, and almost always they utilize some form of cover, hiding in some crevice or resembling some inanimate object. The chinch bug, for example, like many other herbivorous insects, lives out its life on the *underside* of leaves. Few anglers examine the tops of leaves for potential trout foods, let alone the bottoms. Treehoppers, the "brownies" of the insect world, appear as thorns or buds on the woods of the forest.

Of course, certain of the larger, more obtrusive terrestrials are easily noticed—most notably the grasshoppers—when large adults are abundant. But for every terrestrial the typical angler observes on shoreline vegetation, hundreds go undetected.

Even in the water, where most of us are trained to look for trout foods, the land insects are less visible. Most lie inert, flush in the water's surface film—a far cry from the highly visible mayflies with their erect wings. Even the tiniest emphemerids, such as the *Tricorythodes* and ubiquitous *Baetis* species with their silhouetted upwings, are easy to spot compared to the terrestrials.

Yet another factor contributing to the disregard of terrestrials among anglers is their general neglect by the authors of major fishing books. Compared to the reams of printed material on the mayfly, the land insects are minor characters in the annals of trout fishing.

THE LITERATURE

Though Charles Cotton mentions several land insect patterns, in *The Compleat Angler*, including a "Horse-flesh Flie," "ant-flie," and grasshopper, Alfred Ronalds was the first writer to fully recognize the large role terrestrials play in the diet of trout. His brilliant *Fly-fisher's Entomology*, which first appeared in 1836, went through five printings in his lifetime. A dozen editions have come out since the book was first published, though it is now well-nigh impossible to obtain.

Ronalds' work was done on the English Midland rivers of Staffordshire and Derbyshire, such as the Dove and Blythe, a fact that makes his conclusions very much applicable to the typical American trout stream. The waters were not as fast and infertile as steep-gradient mountain brooks, nor as rich and uncommonly fertile as the chalk streams Frederick Halford was to fish. It is perhaps partly because the rivers he fished were not extraordinarily rich in aquatic insect life that Ronalds took such a keen interest in the terrestrial insects in the diet of trout.

Ronalds meticulously studied the stomach contents of fish caught through all seasons and found that, in addition to aquatic insects, the trout's bellies were stuffed with caterpillars, leafhoppers, houseflies, spiders, millipedes, earwigs, beetles, and ants. He observed the total environment of the trout—including the surrounding land—and catalogued dozens of important terrestrial food forms. From an observation hut built on the water he experimented with feeding trout and studied their reaction to the various insects, including houseflies and bees, which he tossed to them through a tube leading from his hut to the river. Ronalds first recognized the terrestrials as major trout foods throughout the fishing season, with some forms prevalent in spring, others in summer, and still different land insects entering the stream in significant numbers through fall.

It's true that in Ronalds' time all fishing was with the wet fly, and many of his patterns are rather vague resemblances of the insects found on streamside vegetation. But Ronalds stands alone as the first angler-writer to

The Letort; even on a super-productive limestone creek, terrestrials play an important part in year-round angling.

recognize the full importance of terrestrial insects as trout foods. What is mystifying now is how these land-based foods could have become relegated to an inferior, almost insignificant status over ensuing years.

Part of the explanation may be that the next most influential fishing writer of nineteenth-century England, Frederick Halford, developed most of his theories on the classic chalk streams of the southern portion of the country, where aquatic insects were so abundant that the terrestrials apparently were unimportant food sources for the well-fed trout. Halford devoted little attention to the land insects compared to his extensive coverage of the aquatics.

On the other hand, Edward R. Hewitt, master American angler of the twentieth century, had a great appreciation for the attraction terrestrial insects exerted on trout. During a fishing expedition on the Neversink River in New York State, he opened his mouth at an unpropitious moment and several flying ants flew in. Rather than spitting the insects out immediately, Hewitt tasted them. The experience led him to theorize that trout rose to the ants "on account of this taste," which was "bitter with formic acid."

Hewitt also observed that trout consumed other land insects such as moths, butterflies, and grasshoppers. His Bivisibles were recommended to readers as impressionistic representations of land insects. In *A Trout and Salmon Fisherman for Seventy-Five Years* he says of these patterns: "Such flies seem to attract trout when there is no hatch on the water. The trout must take them for land insects settling on the water, and not expecting a hatch of them, take any that come along" (p. 139). The Neversink skater, another classic Hewitt fly, was first tied to imitate butterflies.

Preston Jennings included a brief chapter on the order Hymenoptera (ants, bees, and wasps) in his *A Book of Trout Flies*, but relegated even the ants to a very lowly importance and suggested that the flies be fished wet.

Alvin R. Grove, whose excellent work *The Lure and Lore of Trout Fishing* was published in 1951, formed his fishing theories in a time when aquatic hatches on nearby Pennsylvania streams were rich and the tradition of imitating mayflies was deeply entrenched in the angling literature. Nevertheless, Grove includes many references to the terrestrials as trout foods in his book. He points out in particular that land insects are especially important on freestone streams.

Then in the interval between the publication of Grove's book and its reissue in 1971, a drastic change in the ecology of many trout streams took place. In the preface to the reissue Grove addresses this transformation and stresses the ever-increasing importance of terrestrials in the diet of trout: "The loss of fly hatches during the past twenty years is almost beyond belief. . . . Terrestrials have become more important. While no one who knows would have downgraded the grasshopper, ant, cricket, or other terrestrials at anytime in his fishing career, it seems that they may now make up a rather significant part of the diet of trout and are represented by more and better fly patterns than in the past" (p. xiii).

But the renaissance of terrestrial fishing as we know and practice it today had its wellspring in one classic work of genius—*A Modern Dry Fly Code*, by Vince Marinaro. Though much of Marinaro's text concentrates on the aquatic insects, the most significant contribution of the work is in the realm of the terrestrials. With Charles Fox, author of *This Wonderful World of Trout* and *Rising Trout*, and other skilled anglers from south-central Pennsylvania—Ed Shenk, Ernie Schwiebert, Russ Trimmer, Ed Koch, and Bill Blades—the small coterie of Letort Creek regulars developed land-insect fishing to a fine and deadly art.

For the angler interested in taking a serious approach to terrestrial fishing, Vince Marinaro's *Code* is the place to start. Though the terrestrial theories and patterns direct themselves mainly toward the challenging trout of one particular stream—the Letort—many of the insights and imitations developed are effective on the more typical freestone waters the majority of anglers fish. *In the Ring of the Rise*, Marinaro's latest work, adds further to the pioneering work of the *Code*.

The terrestrials have appeared in supporting roles in many of the books published since the *Code* was reissued in 1970. Doug Swisher and Carl Richards direct a brief chapter to the land insects in their *Selective Trout* and in *Fly Fishing Strategy*. The imitations are, however, still recommended for specialized time spans. Leonard Wright in his two books, *Fishing the Dry Fly as a Living Insect* and *Fly Fishing Heresies*, revives a number of neglected trout tactics and includes some observations on the feeding of trout and terrestrial fishing.

Charles E. Brooks is a strong proponent of terrestrial fishing. In *The Trout and the Stream* he remarks that "all of the largest trout I've ever taken on floating flies, save one, were taken on artificials designed to imitate terrestrial creatures" (p. 125). Brooks also cites drift net surveys showing that more terrestrials were eaten by trout over the stretch of a season than aquatic insects. He treats a number of important terrestrials, including crickets, hoppers, and caterpillars, and has some very useful suggestions for the western dry fly angler.

Gary La Fontaine, another fine western writer, turned some of his attentions to the terrestrials in his *Challenge of the Trout*.

Doubtless there have been other books that have focused briefly on the terrestrials, but these are the major ones that come to mind. Except for *A Modern Dry Fly Code*, no modern work devotes the bulk of its space to the terrestrial insects. The majority of fishing literature that has come out in recent years, as in the past, has concentrated on the aquatics. Of late, the caddis has joined the mayfly on the pedestal, thanks mainly to the work of Leonard Wright, Larry Solomon, and Eric Leiser. But in spite of the work of Marinaro, Fox, and other Cumberland Valley innovators, and in spite of such lone voices as Al McClane, who more than once proclaimed the land insects equal if not *more* important than aquatics, the terrestrials have yet to gain a wide acceptance among anglers.

The aquatics are a fitting symbol of the "spirit" of fly fishing, as well as a link to its traditions and a symbol of the timeless, special world of angling. Mayflies will, I hope, always be there when we first limber up a rod in April. But it is well to gain a broader viewpoint of the trout's world—one that encompasses the total environment of the fish, including the water and surrounding land and air. The current fascination with strict, detailed imitation of aquatic flies has spawned a myopic vision that has kept too many anglers from observing the dense populations of insects thriving covertly in the stream*side* arena.

Terrestrials are the ardent dry fly angler's ace-in-the-hole in the face of waning mayfly populations. Their resiliency and adaptability to changing environmental conditions is truly phenomenal. If a forest is wiped out and weed grasses take over in typical vegetative succession, the mere passage of a single season will see the grasses again teeming with those bustling opportunists, the terrestrial insects. From adjacent meadow areas they will fly, be blown, crawl, or hop to get to the new habitat. Grasshoppers will filter in, dropping into the unutilized cover; diverse species of beetles will waddle in from crowded neighboring fields; a queen ant with her precious commodity of fertilized eggs will alight and begin the arduous task of founding a colony. And as the brushy stage of plant succession takes over, still another group of land insects will stake their claim to the changing habitat. By contrast to the aquatics, the terrestrials are a tough and durable lot—too tough, a farmer might say.

In no sense should an acknowledgment of the mayfly's decline be construed as a defeatist's response to the assaults on our precious remaining trout streams. With increasing environmental awareness and the growth of such conservation organizations as the Federation of Fly Fishermen, Trout Unlimited, and the American League of Anglers, among others, the destruction of trout waters is abating. In some cases, aquatic fly life is actually burgeoning with it. But the fact remains that mayfly hatches on most waters are a pale shadow of what they were in Gordon's time, or even the recent date of 1950, when the pathbreaking *Modern Dry Fly Code* appeared.

There may of course be a small number of purists who simply feel earth-bound flies lack the dignity, grace, and tradition of the revered mayflies. Frankly, it always seemed such characters were more mythical than real, but a story that John Crowe recounted in *Pennsylvania Angler* magazine would suggest there actually are such figures flitting about. After describing the capture of a large trout at Fisherman's Paradise (Spring Creek) in central Pennsylvania, he relates the following encounter: "As soon as I let the big trout go, a man who had been watching came down the honeysuckle covered bank. 'Nice fish,' he said. 'Do you mind if I look at the fly?' Of course I didn't mind. In fact, I gave him the bedraggled beetle, plus a couple of new ones. He looked doubtful. 'Are these legal in here?' he asked. 'I thought this place was restricted to *fly fishing*!' "

A.J. McClane, the stalwart of creative approaches to fly fishing, offers the best rebuttal to such elitists in his *Practical Fly Fisherman*: "Normally, the air will be full of insects, mayflies and caddis flies, beetles, grasshoppers, crickets, and whatnot. What rule of priority makes the mayfly more important than the beetle, or the caddis more charming than the cricket? If you examine a trout's stomach it will be evident that whatever the air is full of the trout is full of. Fish are like vacuum cleaners working on a stone floor and a liquid ceiling'' (p. 135).

Still, chances are if you live in any state other than Pennsylvania, you hear and read precious little about the terrestrials, which in itself contributes to their neglect. Rather, the imitations of non-aquatic insects are delegated to certain very specialized situations and time slots. The naturals themselves do not stand out like a soaring mayfly or a fluttering caddis, and so they're easy to ignore. We struggle madly to match any stray ephemerids we see popping up because mayflies are what dry fly fishermen are *supposed* to imitate. And oh, so often the results are meager in terms of numbers and size of trout at the end of the day.

Even among those who are not constrained by any blind loyalty to the mayfly, there are often misconceptions harbored regarding terrestrial fishing that discourage anglers from turning to these flies in time of need. One of the most prevalent mistaken beliefs is that terrestrials are only important trout foods on limestone or spring creeks, of which there are relatively few in the country. Nothing could be further from the truth. I heard this theory bantered about on a recent July afternoon on the Beaverkill in New York State. I was chatting with one of the most skilled and knowledgeable dry fly fishermen I've ever seen in action. I was telling him about the flies I commonly used that time of year (ants, beetles, etc.) when he interrupted me—"just on limestone streams, though, right?"

Most assuredly not. In fact, I had taken eleven trout that morning on ants in the very pool we were gazing down on as we spoke—the classic Hendrickson's Pool.

The origins of this myth probably sprang from the fact that Marinaro's *Modern Dry Fly Code*, the only book to date to pay detailed attention to the terrestrials, was based exclusively on his experiences on the gentle limestone creeks. Thus when many anglers think of terrestrial fishing, they immediately conjure up images of serene, vegetation-choked spring creeks, delicate cane wands, tiny jassids, and 7X tippets—not the average fishing situation.

Terrestrial fishing is bound by no such narrow horizons. It is wrestling bright cutthroats from a roaring western river with a muscular graphite rod, luring speckled brook trout from babbling mountain brooks bordered with fir and spruce, or flicking grasshopper imitations off shoreline grass in a coldwater reservoir. Fishing the terrestrials encompasses the spectrum of water types, tackle, and tactics; touches all bases of mood, place, time, and tempo.

Virtually all streamside habitat in both acidic and alkaline, freestone and limestone streams is rich in insect life. Indeed, in many cases, due to the fertility of the limestone waters in generating vast quantities of aquatic foods such as shrimp, sow bugs, and mayflies, the terrestrials are actually *less* important than on comparatively infertile freestone streams. And, at some times of the season on some freestone streams, there may actually be more available food on the banks than in the stream itself.

A related fallacy is that meadow-bordered stretches of water are the only good places to fish terrestrials. While the forest streams may not have quite the abundance of terrestrial insects found along meadow waters, they still produce large quantities of land insects and, in fact, a greater variety than the typical grass-bordered stream. The species are usually different from those in meadow waters, and the tactics for fishing them may vary, but the terrestrials are present and form an important part of the diet of forest stream trout.

There is also much confusion over the sacred cow of selectivity. This is an oft-misunderstood term. Basically, there are two types of selectivity that the fly fisherman may encounter in his quarry. The first is a universal skepticism among "educated" trout. The other is a short-lived attitude that occurs for only very brief periods among this first group of smart trout when one food form becomes available in large quantities.

The first, most basic type of selectivity is displayed by virtually all wild trout over a year old with some exposure to anglers under their belt, as well as holdover stocked trout. These are the "smart" trout; they exhibit the selectivity of *discrimination*. These fish are often downright meticulous about sorting out what they will and will not eat. Potential food items are scrutinized; any item which does not look just right—including many perfectly healthy natural insects—is rejected. Artificials designed under the "attractor" theory, tied to pique the fish's curiosity or excite him into striking, will rarely fool these trout.

Species has little to do with this quality of discrimination. It is a complex factor of individual intelligence, age, exposure to fishing pressure, and fertility of the water, among other things. If you think brook trout are pushovers, as has been the maligning myth over the ages, come try for the fourteen- and fifteen-inch natives in Big Springs Creek in south-central Pennsylvania. If you consider rainbows "easy," try the pink-striped beauties of Henry's Fork of the Snake River. Cutthroats are perhaps the closest thing to a truly naive trout species, but even these fish can be meticulous in choosing their food. Thus while they are the most discriminating of the trouts, browns are not the only fish to display this form of selectivity.

Trout that exhibit this initial type of selectivity are also the ones that, under very specific and limited conditions, manifest the second, less common form—that of exclusive selectivity. This term is fairly self-explanatory. Trout displaying exclusive selectivity feed on one insect species to the exclusion of all other varieties passing over them. This form of discrimination is not exceedingly common, as anyone who has done more than a few autopsies on trout has discovered. Rare is the trout gullet stuffed brimful with a single variety of insect. Exclusive selectivity, when it occurs, is almost always associated with the brief, intense appearance of an insect—often but not always aquatic—in great quantities. It is a function of abundance.

Fishing to trout rising selectively to a particular species of insect, be it mayfly, caddis, or ant, is challenging, rich angling. But it just isn't all that common an occurrence, based on a realistic look at angling time. In terms of hours on the stream, probably ninety percent of the time we fish for trout they are not feeding exclusively on any *one* insect species. For ninety percent of the time there simply isn't any one insect abundant enough to encourage such specialization. Even after the frenetic rising characteristic of a heavy hatch, when anglers wade to shore and compare notes, it's often found that everybody was taking their fish on different patterns!

It's all too easy to become trapped in an overly systematic, scientific approach to trout fishing and matching the most abundant fly on the water, especially those flies we are familiar with. Paradoxical as it may sound, the practice often leads to the danger of oversimplifying trout behavior. Trout, particularly the larger ones, are too individualistic and whimsical to be pigeonholed. "There's a trout feeding on *Ephemerella cornuta*," one may say, "A good hatch." But if this happens to be a trout that relishes black ants or succulent field crickets, and one drifts down amid the flotilla of mayflies, the fish will likely gulp it down.

Many terrestrial insects like this June beetle are quite large, and are capable of attracting very large trout to the surface.

When I'm fishing terrestrials and a mayfly hatch develops, if I've been taking fish consistently I often continue to fish the land-insect imitations to see how long the trout will keep striking them, to determine just how heavy the hatch must get before the fish become "exclusively selective" to that one insect. Many times they never do stop taking them. The exceptions are those increasingly rare situations where the hatch becomes truly intense and the fish can afford to be so discriminating. Exclusive selectivity must always take a back seat to survival, and survival means a full belly—whether it's stuffed with Hendricksons or ants.

The sight of trout breaking their "selective" feeding patterns to intercept a different form and color of fly is such a frequent occurrence as to be considered virtually commonplace. Midge-feeding trout sometimes seem to sip in the tiny insects for lack of more substantial fare. Many will quickly abandon their single-mindedness for a more satisfying, belly-filling beetle or grasshopper if it presents itself. And the converse is also true—trout feeding on large food forms will often break their pattern to take their favorite terrestrial.

An extremely fat sixteen-inch brown came my way recently on the lovely Little Juniata River in central Pennsylvania on a #18 black ant. The fish had three very large crayfish and one or two ants stuffed in its gullet. Clearly, this trout wanted some variety in his menu. Crayfish literally carpet the floor of this rich river, and the heavy-paunched fish could easily have had its fill of crustaceans. Instead, he chose for his last meal a tiny black ant.

Of course it's not the frivolous affair of reaching for either a can of roasted almonds or a bag of chips. For trout, it's a battle for survival. In addition to providing a different treat, grabbing a beetle while actively feeding on a *Baetis* hatch will fill a fish's belly quickly and give it strength and calories to grow and endure.

So much for selectivity. Another common, tradition-nurtured myth is that trout must be seen actively rising to fish for them with dry flies. This foolish purism leads many anglers to while away priceless hours astream waiting for steady rising activity or resort to nymphs and streamers, thinking dry flies futile because no rises are visible.

The fact is that the sporadic manner in which most terrestrials enter the stream seldom incites frenzied rising activity. Rather, the trout respond with staccato, widely distributed rise forms that can easily go unnoticed without close observation. If a gust of wind blows half a dozen ants into an eddy, you may see six quick rise forms. But unless another ant then gets chased or slips into the stream, it may be five minutes before the next swirl appears. But the trout are there, waiting for the terrestrials. A properly presented ant imitation is virtually assured to take them.

"Pounding them up!" purists may taunt.

"Ah, pity I haven't your refined sense of scruples," the unsophisticated terrestrial angler will retort over his shrieking reel.

Even Frederick Halford recommended fishing likely spots when rises were not apparent. "Some dry-fly fishermen are such purists that they will not under any circumstances whatever make a single cast except over rising fish, and prefer to remain idle the entire day rather than attempt to persuade the wary inhabitants of the stream to rise at an artificial fly, unless they have previously seen a natural one taken in the same position. Although respecting their scruples, this is, in my humble opinion, riding the hobby to death, and I for one am a strong advocate for floating a cocked fly over a likely place, even if no movement of a feeding fish has been seen there." [*Dry-Fly Fishing*, P. 43]

A final myth we might look at is not quite as common as some of the others discussed but is nonetheless believed by many novice fly anglers. This is the impression that terrestrial fishing is a particularly difficult form of fly fishing and that it involves almost exclusively tiny flies and ultra-fine tippets.

The first point can be quickly dismissed. Productive terrestrial fishing lies well within the grasp of any angler who can throw an accurate, neat cast thirty-five or forty feet with most any light- or medium-weight fly outfit. Far more important than great skill as a caster is keen knowledge of trout behavior and feeding habits backing it up.

Secondly, terrestrial fishing is *not* by definition small fly fishing. Certainly there are times when only a #24 cinnamon ant or a #22 brown treehopper will take a particular fish. But the bulk of terrestrial fishing involves flies in the #8 to 20 size range. Fishing with this size fly is within the grasp of any angler.

A good many terrestrial insects are rather large creatures, and if imitations are to realistically represent them, they must be tied on correspondingly large hooks. This works to the angler's advantage in several ways. The size of these chunky land insects often brings fish surprisingly long distances to intercept them. Their bulk also makes them particularly attractive to big trout that like their meals in great mouthfuls. If you are angling in waters that hold heavy fish, terrestrials will more than likely prove the best flies for bringing these lunkers to net. Dave Whitlock, who has probably caught as many big trout on a fly as any other angler, says that "almost without exception most of the larger trout I've examined with stomach pumps have contained various terrestrials."

Part II

FISHING THE TERRESTRIALS

". . . The contents of my fly box, for fishing my home waters, would look rather strange to a fly-fisher of an older generation. He would see jassids, ants, beetles, crickets, grasshoppers, and the like. My box of mayfly imitations is reserved for those trips to blessed lands and waters where it is still possible to fish to a fine hatch of aquatics" (p. x).

—Vincent Marinaro, *A Modern Dry Fly Code*

chapter two

STREAM STRATEGY

Two basic conditions must be met before I normally turn to the terrestrials. First, spring must have progressed to the stage where fish begin to rise regularly and the water and air temperatures consistently reach fifty to fifty-five degrees during the day. Although there are times when trout will consume terrestrials in the winter (particularly on spring creeks), as a general rule we can consider the land flies as spring through fall imitations—the time when most of us do our dry fly fishing.

Secondly, I check the stream to see whether there is *significant* aquatic insect activity drawing rises from trout. It may be midges, caddis, stoneflies, or mayflies. If there is a hatch progressing, and trout are feeding on the insect, clearly this is the fly to mimic. All too often, however, there will be no such significant hatch in progress, and I can feel reasonably assured that the proper terrestrial fly will bring action.

Choosing the best pattern is the first order of business. At its best this decision is a process of careful observation and the calculation of experience and the present stream situation—and lots of experiments. Any number of variables can influence my fly choice. Some of the most important considerations include nature of the streamside habitat, time of day and season, variety of terrestrials active on land or present on the surface film of the water, presence or absence of rising fish, nature of the rise forms, water type being fished, strategic considerations in delivering the fly, size of fish, fishing pressure the water receives, location of the trout in the stream, and past experiences on a particular stretch of river.

Clearly, fly choice is a complex decision. These items are not intended, however, to be a simple check list. Rather, these are factors that the thinking fly fisherman will instinctively include in formulating his choice. Often many of the items will be sifted through on a subconscious level, and indeed, sometimes it may seem that a virtual sixth sense is determining fly choice.

There is no substitute for experience astream in determining the most productive terrestrial pattern for a given situation—with the *least* amount of experimentation. However, a close examination of a few of the factors influencing fly choice will be of great value to the new angler and to the veteran on an unfamiliar stream.

Streamside Research

Let's face it: Most of us are more avid anglers than we are entomologists. But by forcing ourselves to do a little streamside research, we can often save fruitless casting. Examining the shoreline habitat for insect activity is the first step in determining which terrestrial may be effective. With this preliminary step, a pool of possible flies from which to choose can be isolated.

It takes but a few minutes to study the vegetation, look over a rotting log or two, and check for caterpillars dangling from gossamer threads, ants scurrying recklessly up and down shoreline tree trunks, leafhoppers bristling in streamside grasses. Any terrestrial found in fair numbers within a dozen yards of the stream's edge is a candidate.

A caution: Don't draw sweeping conclusions from what you see on your initial examination of the bank habitat. Different terrestrials are active at different times. If you arrive at dawn, a few straggling moths, crickets, and an eager ant or two may be the only insects about. As the morning sun warms the earth and penetrates into rocks and logs, more and more species will be drawn out. At the same time the nocturnal insects will be turning in for the day. The cast of insect characters is in constant flux, and re-checking is required throughout the day. A fly that produces at dawn may be useless by 9 A.M.

Grasshoppers, for instance, are notorious late sleepers. When the first fingers of dawn creep over the horizon, they slowly tilt their bodies at right angles to absorb the full rays of the sun's warmth. Only by midmorning will they begin the restless movement that will put them into the reach of trout. Their relatives the crickets, on the other hand, are most active at dawn and dusk.

While most terrestrial insects are best sought out individually by poking and peeking in leaf litter, rocks, bark, and debris, there is another useful method for sampling the riparian population. This involves sweeping the shoreline foliage with a heavy-framed insect net; it is particularly effective in flat meadows along streams with heavy grass and weed growth. Take a strong, long-handled net and move quickly through the grass sweeping the upper half of the vegetation. The mesh will soon bristle with a motley collection of insects. The most abundant specimens will be likely trout producers at some point in the day.

Terrestrial insects can frequently, of course, be found *in* the water, as well as along shore. Locating and identifying these can be a more time-consuming procedure, but it often yields the most pertinent clues of all to selecting the right fly. This sampling can be accomplished by holding a fine-meshed seine across the current angled slightly upstream at the bottom. Since all terrestrials are buoyant, those with good eyes can also use a small, hand-held aquarium net and scoop up bugs spotted floating awash in the surface film.

These investigations will give you a census of which insects are active along that particular stream and a group of flies from which to choose in sampling the preferences of the trout. The fisherman who studies the streamside habitat and learns the behavioral characteristics and vegetation preferences of the major terrestrials will eventually be able to predict with some accuracy what insects will be found at a particular time of year along a given stretch of water.

An autopsy of the first fish we take will certainly tell us what we want to know about the feeding preferences of trout under a given set of circumstances. But killing trout to find out what they're taking is a technique most of us use less and less often with the passage of time. There are simply too many anglers and too few trout to afford this luxury on a regular basis. For some, also, there is the queasy feeling that this method of sampling the trout's taste preferences may be too easy. It reduces the intensity with which we must approach the environment and external behavior of the trout, the mental effort we must exert to unlock the puzzle each fishing trip poses.

As a compromise, a few experienced anglers use stomach pumps to sample the preferences of the trout without killing it. But again one almost feels as if he is invading the privacy of the trout by forcing the fish to cough up its breakfast so that we may increase our fishing pleasures. And even in the hands of the experienced angler, the stomach pump has inherent dangers for the fish.

But fly choice can seldom be dictated solely by the findings of our streamside research anyway. Trout fishing would be a game for the scientist if this were the case. It is not, as we all know. The decision is at the same time more complex and less precise. And no angler would deny that it is more fun to learn by fishing.

Tactical Considerations in Delivering the Fly

The physical nature of the stream being fished can play a vital role in the decision of which fly to use. An obvious example is the heavily wooded stream where roll casting is the only really effective manner of presenting the fly. Here an imitation that is highly buoyant is preferable, since false casting to dry the imitation is difficult, if not impossible. Cork bugs, deer hair flies, and quill body imitations are perhaps the very best flies for such casting conditions.

Heavily fished Yellow Breeches Creek in south-central Pennsylvania is a classic example of the situation where the physical characteristics of the stream dictate fly choice. Many fishermen wade and cast from midcreek positions toward shore. The fish line up shoulder to shoulder along the banks, sipping in the multifarious assortment of land insects that tumble off the trees leaning over the milky green water.

The most successful local anglers on the Breeches, however, do not wade; they stalk their fish from the banks and roll cast perhaps only ten or twenty feet. Sometimes they simply dap the fly cautiously from their hidden position behind a pale-barked sycamore trunk.

These anglers use the stream banks' advantage of height to allow them to see down and watch the fish. It requires stealth in approach and slow, subtle movements; and it gets results. But in this situation a backcast is impossible; tree growth is heavy along the shore directly behind the fishermen. The banks rise sharply, threatening to snag even the highest of backcasts, and so roll casting is the only method that produces consistently. Flies that need little or no drying between presentations are the most effective here.

Position of Trout in the Stream

The specific area of a stream you are fishing can also have a direct bearing on fly choice, at least as far as size is concerned. Big, bulky, non-flying insects such as roaches and crickets seldom get far from shore before they are inhaled by waiting fish. These imitations are especially good choices for fishing the edge of a river. On the other hand, prolific insects such as small ants and leafhoppers may be blown out into the middle of a stream or carried there quickly by crosscurrents. These flies often produce best on trout showing in midstream.

The Value of the Unexpected

When casting "blind" (that is, without seeing the fish or his rise form), a larger land-insect imitation is generally more effective. This is sometimes labeled "pounding them up" by purists, but actually it is a technique that requires some skill to execute properly, as well as a strong knowledge of where trout naturally lie in the stream. It is little short of amazing how many trout a skilled angler can catch with this method. All would be passed up by our purist, who would wait steadfastly for dimpling trout before casting.

Interestingly enough, casting blind with these larger flies is often particularly fruitful on the slow, griddle-slick pools—waters that have the reputation of being tough during summer months. Conversely, flicking delicate little jassids out into a churning riffle (where big, bushy flies are usually recommended) can lead to extraordinary fishing. Never underestimate the value of the unexpected.

This maverick attitude is especially telling on our better public trout streams in the East—waters that take a heavy pounding throughout the season. The majority of anglers fishing these streams follow the dictates of tradition and literature and use large, cumbersome flies in the rough water and minutiae on gossamer tippets in the clear pools.

The angler who does just the opposite can often fool some exceptional trout. A big beetle or large carpenter ant can sometimes draw excellent results when the experts are casting #24s and #28s.

I was fishing a large northern trout stream recently when this tactic proved highly effective. The midday July sun beat down harshly, and only a few fish were showing in the main section of the pool. Two anglers were casting #28 White Dots on midge sticks, taking a few trout, and of course missing many on the tiny hooks. The trout they were catching were running only eight to ten inches; otherwise I might have joined them.

I knew the pool held good fish, however, and felt they could be coaxed up with the proper offering. Dull black ants were scurrying over shoreline rocks, so I clinched on a #16 fur ant with deer hair legs. Dabbing the fly with Mucilin, I eased out into the current a polite distance below the two midge fishers and worked out the three-weight line. Gently the ebony fly descended onto the currents and began a free float at the tail of the pool.

With a loud slurp a heavy fish smacked the ant and hooked himself solidly. The trout ran wild on the 6X tippet, bulling hard towards the sharp, gray bottom rocks. Eventually it succumbed to the pressure of the seven-foot Orvis and lay spent and gasping at my feet. I slipped the barbless hook out of its mouth and held the 16½-inch brown loosely in the flow while he regained his equilibrium. With a flick of a powerful caudal fin the trout vanished into the pool.

Later, in conversation with the other two anglers one asked what fly I'd taken the fish on.

"Black Ant."

"What size?"

"Sixteen."

"*Sixteen*! We're fishing #28s!" he said in an accusative tone.

I must confess I felt a bit sheepish using such a "cumbersome" fly when midges and 8X tippets were recommended by the experts' formulas. But the ruse has proven so productive over subsequent seasons that I seldom suffer pangs of conscience anymore.

If it is considered odd to fish big, heavy flies on low summer pools, it is downright heretical to drift tiny #22s and #24s through churning riffles at the heads of pools. The traditional logic suggests the big fly here so the angler can see it and so the trout will be sufficiently inspired to come up in the heavy flow. This reasoning often pays off. But again, if you are fishing a stream that receives much pressure, choosing the *un*obvious has decided benefits. Trout can easily detect a size #22 leafhopper or a minuscule brown ant floundering in choppy riffles. Often they will rise to such tiny morsels floating through a heavy riff.

An unlikely strategy, yes. But oh, so effective is the tiny fly in heavy flow.

Rises

Careful scrutiny will usually reveal some rising trout even during the hottest summer months. When rises are apparent, they can often yield vital clues to the proper fly.

As a general rule, larger insects elicit heavier, louder strikes from trout. This is particularly true when the insect is capable of struggling visibly on the surface. Big grasshoppers, roaches, and moths seem to excite fish. Smaller flies, on the other hand, are more often sipped in with only the tiniest of dimples. Many inexperienced fishermen mistake these quiet rise forms for "humping" trout—fish taking food forms just beneath the surface. Close observation will reveal the fish's snout actually breaking through the surface when he takes ants, leafhoppers, or small true bugs (Hemiptera).

The exception to this rule often shows up in quiet backwater eddies of streams, where big trout cruise like colorful submarines patrolling their home territory. These fish *know* their food will drift helplessly in the eddy for some time. They may inhale large crickets and small pinhead-sized beetles with the same barely perceptible dimple.

During an idle moment on the Letort one evening I witnessed a fine brown displaying this very subtle rise form while taking a large land insect. It was nearly dark, and I had just rolled in from a day's angling on the Lackawaxen in the Poconos. I hadn't planned on fishing. Walking down to the stream, I paused some distance from the shore and watched for rises.

Crickets were creaking loudly in the streamside grasses. The damp, foggy evening was much to their liking. But excitement leads to careless errors, and with an audible splat a black form appeared on the water. What looked like a cricket drifted into a placid eddy. A tiny dimple disturbed the water and the black shape vanished.

"Probably a young trout," I told myself. But the rod was still rigged from the Pocono trip, so I hastily returned to the truck and attached a #12 cricket to the 5X tippet.

Cautiously I crept on my knees to the water's edge and dapped the fly gently to the surface where the natural had so recently met its end. Again a tiny dimple broke the water's surface. I lifted, fully expecting to winch a thrashing little fingerling from the water as I raised the tip. Instead, a great, bucking weight met my movement and a lively fight ensued. Several precarious minutes later, I twisted the sodden fly from the white roof of the mouth of a subdued seventeen-incher. Thus while quiet rise forms in the main current usually signal trout feeding on small terrestrial forms, the rule of thumb does not always apply in backwater eddies.

The pace or frequency of the rise forms can also give hints as to what fly to tie on. The big-bodied land insects seldom enter the water in great abundance, and rises to these insects are generally at a more staccato pace. Fish rising steadily, at a more or less regular tempo, are more than likely taking smaller terrestrial forms that enter the water in large quantities and allow such rhythmic feeding.

Trout consuming these minute land insects will also generally take a set feeding station and rise in one place. Fish feeding on big June beetles or hoppers dropping randomly in the water may move several feet to grab these large insects. There is no one stationary feeding position—the fish stalks any chunky terrestrial that falls within hearing range like a hunter. Thus the mobility of a rising trout—his reluctance or willingness to move out of a set feeding lane—can also yield pertinent information on what the fish might take.

The following, then, are a few of the things that should be considered when deciding which terrestrial pattern to use: nature of the streamside habitat; variety of terrestrials active in the riparian foliage or present on the water; presence or absence of surface-feeding trout; pace, distribution, and size of rise forms; time of day and season; tactical considerations in presenting the fly; pressure the water receives; and position of trout in the stream. But there are no shortcuts to day-in, day-out success with terrestrials. Fishing experience on different trout waters, and particularly experience repeated over the flow of seasons on the same streams, often figures heavily. The angler who fishes his home waters over the seasons can many times predict what land fly the fish will likely take before he arrives at the water.

Falling Springs Run courses sparkling and dapper through the fertile farmlands of south-central Pennsylvania. Pheasants are plentiful in the rich corn fields, and black and white cattle dot the gently rolling countryside. For many years I have fished this limpid stream. It has faltered from misuse, its waters silted, its banks eroded from unfenced cattle. But Falling Springs has not succumbed. Recent work by dedicated local anglers has improved several stretches of water, and fish-for-fun regulations insure a healthy head of trout in the stream.

Sulphurs and olives still ride the crystalline limestone currents in spring. And in summer there is the legendary *Tricorythodes* hatch that sends clouds of transparent-winged spinners dancing in streaks of silver over the water's surface. But it is the terrestrial fishing that satisfies my unquenchable appetite for dry fly fishing most fully. The season runs long, stretching from late March through much of November.

First to appear are the black-skinned Formicidae, the fleet-footed carpenter ants and the harvester ants that roam the shoreline in search of fodder and fall with uncanny frequency into the creek. And soon their brown- and yellow-coated relatives are joining them in the gullets of trout.

By early July it is the turn of the Japanese beetles, which provide perhaps the most exciting fishing of the season for experienced beetle anglers. By mid-July grasshopper nymphs and adults that have begun entering the stream offer yet another tempting morsel to the plump rainbows and browns. With them come true bugs living on shoreline bushes and tiny leafhoppers thick in the meadow grasses. And fat ebony crickets are maturing rapidly as the summer progresses. From the first warm days of spring through the early frosts of autumn imitations of these land insects will produce fine catches of the difficult limestone trout.

It is never a totally predictable game, of course. But the angler who fishes a stream regularly will have a strong inkling for two or three flies that are likely to produce under a given set of stream conditions. "Stream conditions" for terrestrials fishing are likely to include more elements than season, water temperature, and the charts from a book. They may include wind, *shoreline* conditions, humidity as well as air temperature, and a number of variables that could recur at any time on many different streams in different parts of trout country. As the experience of the fisherman broadens over new waters, particularly intriguing terrestrial fishing opportunities can be penciled in on the calendar, much in the manner that we look forward to a certain hatch on a special river each year.

But there is a major difference. With the terrestrials there is seldom the same precariousness inherent in the gamble of hitting an aquatic insect hatch "just so"—at precisely the proper date, under just the right weather conditions. There is a gratifying sense of dependability to the terrestrials for the angler who is willing to take a few extra moments to observe and experiment.

Even for the experienced angler on home waters, all too often the first instinct is to get into the water and start casting. In our haste, too little attention is given to fly choice. And *which* terrestrial used is often the vital decision, not necessarily because of the exclusive selectivity of terrestrial-feeding trout, but rather because of the complex tactical and entomological considerations discussed above.

The type of water you wish to fish, how you plan to fish it, and the appropriate fly for that time and season should all be calculated *before* laying out the first cast.

The need for cautious observation runs right through the approach to terrestrial-feeding trout. When terrestrials are on tap, streams are often low and critically clear. The approach to the water is extremely important, in many situations even more significant than fly choice. A spooked trout won't even take a natural insect, let alone your imitation.

APPROACH

Yet even as fly fishing has become more sophisticated in its body of technique (not to mention tackle!), many anglers have grown increasingly sloppy and careless in their approach to the stream. Much of the disrespect for the wariness of trout can be traced to the preponderance of hatchery fish in today's waters, fish that have become accustomed to the presence of man during their early lives in concrete troughs. Over the years these artificially propagated fish have lost some of their native wariness and especially fear of humans.

Unfortunately, anglers who accept this state of affairs as rationale for lumbering crudely up to the stream end up catching just that—small, thin-paunched hatchery trout recently dumped into the water. The holdovers and wild fish have either fled wildly at their approach to the stream or sunk slow and majestically into deeper water.

Truly wild trout are extremely nervous fish, attuned to the threat of predators, ready to flee at the slightest alarming movement. In the thin, clear water of summer months the spookiness is compounded. Holdover fish that have lived in the natural habitat of a stream for a season or more regain much of this inherent wildness lurking in their genes.

Falling Springs Run: this stream is not unusual in the fact that it has a regular sequence of terrestrial "appearances" that can be followed through the season.

Sight and Sound

The trout's senses of sight and hearing are his two early warning systems. Both must somehow be circumvented. The fisherman must avoid being seen at all wherever this is feasible. Drab clothing that blends with the shoreline vegetation is very helpful. If you are in view of the quarry, move with slow, fluid motions. Both animals and fish alike seldom interpret such slow movement as approaching danger. It is the sudden lumbering up of a human form into the window of the trout, the rapid flashing of the rod tip high in the air that spooks fish. Both the profile of the angler and the motion of the rod must be kept low. Side arm casts are called for within the realm of the fish's vision, and the fewer the false casts, the better.

Sound is equally important: Avoiding being heard by the trout is an absolute prerequisite to success. The fish's lateral line hearing-sensing system (and to a lesser extent, its inner ear) enables it to detect even slight vibrations from shore or wading fishermen. The astute terrestrial angler will approach the stream itself so that vibrations do not carry through the earth and alert the quarry. Casual observers might find it amusing to watch a skilled fisherman creeping and crawling like a weasel as he approaches a stream. Those who laugh are generally the same people you see treading loudly up to the edge of the stream, sloshing boldly into the water, and sending wakes ahead of them as frightened trout flee to the safety of an undercut bank or a sheltering logjam. Eyes locked resolutely on midstream, they are seemingly unaware of the fish they are spooking right below their feet!

Part of the explanation for this crude behavior may be indirectly related to the increasingly popular fish-for-fun projects. They are highly commendable management policies and provide some of the best fly fishing for trout available today. If there is a problem, it is that there are too few of them, and too many anglers on the ones that exist. The trout see scads of flies each day and waving fly rods by the dozens. Many of these heavily pounded fish have grown tolerant of the presence of fishermen, and certain fish will even remain in position as the angler approaches what he assumes is an unaware target.

But this apparent lack of fear is a trap that fools many anglers. Even though the fish may stay in its lie, a trout that has seen the angler generally is alert and much more discriminating than one that has not caught sight of the fisherman. It's impossible to speculate what is going through the fish's head, but he is a poor prospect to take a fly, even though he may remain plainly in view and patiently allow you to cast over him. He generally takes a supercritical attitude toward his food when under surveillance, if he shows any inclination to rise at all.

Failing to respect the vision of the trout is perhaps the greatest pitfall for the inexperienced terrestrial angler. Remember that a trout is actually able to see a fisherman farther back on the bank than would seem logical because water is a denser medium than air; refraction causes the light rays entering the water to bend downward and carry the angler's image to the trout, even though the fish may be undetected by the angler. Alfred Ronalds covered this subject succinctly in his *Fly Fisher's Entomology* nearly a century and a half ago with well-executed line drawings. (They are also reproduced in Chapter Two of Vince Marinaro's *In the Ring of the Rise*.)

Clearly, kneeling and crouching along a trout stream are not pleasurable undertakings. Many a day I've staggered back to the car at the end of a trout fishing day spent on my knees. But they are very effective ways to catch fish—sometimes the only way.

The stand-up fisherman can take his share of trout, *if he is careful*. The fundamental rule most stand-up fishermen neglect, however, is that as your stature increases from the kneeling to the standing posture, you must simply stay that much farther back from the stream to avoid spooking trout.

I watched a lanky old-timer with a tattered gray vest use this stand-up approach recently to take a fine brownie sipping terrestrials right next to shore. He was fishing a grassy stretch of water on a small Maryland creek. Cautiously the angler walked the shore, thirty feet back from the water's edge. When he saw a dimple next to shore, he didn't try to sneak up on the fish, but began stripping line from that distance. Only half of his leader touched the water on the cast, and none of the fly line, which piled softly on the ground. The brown sipped the small fly in nonchalantly, and the angler set the hook with a snap of his wrist. Only then did he work his line back onto the reel and walk up to the stream to finish the fight. Would that more fishermen had this old-timer's respect for the vision and wariness of trout. In their careless approaches to the water, incautious anglers often end up spooking some of the finest trout in the stream, particularly during prime terrestrial fishing season.

Shore Huggers

Once the early aquatic hatches peter out, many trout gravitate toward shore. More often than not, the big, bright-colored holdovers from seasons past are the ones that take up these prime feeding lies edging the bank. Fish of eighteen and twenty inches may be found lying in water barely deep enough to cover their backs once the first terrestrials begin tumbling into the water.

These shoreline holding positions offer a number of enticements. Undercut banks, shoreline log jams, bushes, and tree branches all provide cover and shelter from the harsh sunlight. The friction of the stream's flow with the shoreline means reduced current. This is a particularly compelling attraction for those big, lazy trout.

The foremost appeal of shoreline holding stations, however, is the bountiful supply of food that enters the water from the adjacent land. Fish are aware of where grasshoppers, crickets, beetles, and other tasty land tidbits come from. They line up greedily to be the first at the table. Even on a broad, fecund stream such as Henry's Fork of the Snake in Idaho, a great many of the 18 to 22-inch fish will be lined up along the banks waiting for insects from land to make a mistake.

Of course these large fish are the first to flee when someone trudges carelessly up to the edge of a stream. The canny fisherman always assumes

A cautious approach is demanded for terrestrial fishing. Here an angler fishing the Letort works from a kneeling position with rod low.

from the outset that there are fine fish lying within inches of the nearest shore until experience proves otherwise. In this caution lie the seeds of a successful approach to terrestrial-feeding trout.

From all this it should be clear that wading is a tactic that comes into play only after much fishing has been done, if at all. The shore-hugging trout on the side of the stream that the angler fishes deserve his first attention, then fish in midstream that can be cast to from the bank. Only when trout show beyond the reach of a shore cast should the terrestrial angler enter the water.

The fact is that few fishermen have the patience to wade as quietly and as stealthily as desired. So, if it can be avoided entirely, so much the better. Brush-bordered streams and large rivers usually require wading, but here again all water that can be fished from shore should be attended to first.

Fish the Rise, Or Blind?

Whether to fish the rise or fish blind is really not a question that comes up on good waters with a healthy population of trout. If, on the one extreme, no fish are rising, obviously the angler must fish blind, concentrating on what appear to be likely lies for the fish. If, on the other hand, many fish are rising within casting range, the targets are clear.

More often than not, *some* fish, sooner or later, will betray their position by rising; others will be sighted in the water, though not actively taking surface foods; still others will be discovered by casting blind to likely holding spots. All of these fish hold the potential of taking the appropriate land insect if given the chance. The successful terrestrial fisherman will concentrate on all three sources of trout on a day astream. He won't ignore signs of fish present beneath the surface, he won't ignore even the tiniest of dimples that may spell feeding trout, and he won't ignore beautiful holding lies simply because no fish is discernible in the flow.

The last point is particularly critical in fishing terrestrials. As Hewitt put it in *A Trout and Salmon Fisherman For Seventy-Five Years*: "In our American streams there is quite a long time at the end of the season when the water gets very low and there are very few [aquatic] insects. At this time a fisherman may spend a whole day on the stream and not see a fish rise naturally, and yet it is then that some of the best and most enjoyable trout fishing takes place.

"The trout are hidden under the stones, banks, roots, or ledges, and are rarely seen in the open water" (p. 178).

If the proper terrestrial is presented near them, these fish will often come up for it, even though they may not be actively feeding. Anglers who pass up these choice lies simply because no fish is visible may miss their best chances for lunker-sized trout on a dry fly.

I once encountered such an intriguing lie on the Smith River, a large tailwater stream with wild brown trout in southwestern Virginia. The current wafted into a deep hole against shore with a decaying log breaking the flow. No fish were rising, and shade made it impossible to spot a fish from my position. I felt certain a trout was in position under this log, however, and cast a #16 beetle around the lie at several locations. On the fifth delivery a handsome fifteen-inch brown of very wild origins sucked in the fly.

If you are fishing on water with a good head of trout, the only wise decision normally is to cast to all likely holding locations. Rocks, log jams, overhanging banks and branches, depressions in the stream bed, eddies, tails of pools, and deep channels of glides may all harbor trout.

Spotting a rise or two on the opposite shore is not a signal to rush headlong toward these dimpling fish. During a mayfly hatch this might be justifiable behavior if done with restraint. The peculiar nature of terrestrial-feeding trout (i.e., the erratic, staccato pace of food consumption) makes it extremely important that the fisherman does not neglect trout that apparently are *not* rising. Shown the right fly, these trout can be prompted to take. Trudging toward distant risers will likely result in spooking many unseen fish along the way.

During drought conditions such as those experienced during the summer of 1977, when waters become low and dangerously warm, many trout will congregate around areas where springs provide cool spots in the flow. Pocket water and riffles are also sought out at this time due to the high oxygen content of the water at these locations.

Gradually, as one fishes a particular stream over the seasons, it becomes possible to predict where fish will lie. This may be done gracefully by catching the trout and returning it to the water—or we may spook it in our haste to get to a different fish. In either case the information should be stored in the memory bank for use on future fishing trips.

Which Direction to Fish

W.C. Stewart's injunction in *The Practical Angler* (1857) to cast dry flies upstream has stood well the test of time. A century and a quarter later Stewart's advice still applies to the great majority of dry fly fishing situations. It is almost always the best approach for delivering terrestrials.

For beginners the upstream cast is the easiest to execute properly with a dry fly, and the easiest way to achieve a drag-free float. The fisherman casting upstream (or preferably, quartering up and across) can also hook trout more effectively than the downstream caster. The reason is easy to visualize: The hook is being pulled back *into* the mouth of the trout, instead of *away* from his jaws. The current is also pulling line, leader, and fly downstream, a fact that aids in the hooking process.

Most trout hooked from the downstream side can be played back towards the angler, away from the other fish in the pool. It is harder to keep a trout from alarming its companions when fishing downstream, since the fish has the leverage of the current to assist in its rush downriver. Thus more trout can be taken from a pool or glide with the upstream method before all fish are spooked or caught.

The upstream approach is also preferred for terrestrial fishing because it allows the angler to sneak much closer to the trout than if he works downstream in full view of the fish. By stalking from *behind* the fish and keeping a low profile, you can get in range to punch out short, accurate casts.

As we've seen, terrestrial-feeding trout often take up positions right next to shore. Scant water is required to accommodate such fish. I've found two- and three-pound brown trout during summer months in water three or four inches deep. Most anglers can recall similar discoveries. Yet a fisherman working downstream is not likely to get within sixty feet of these trout. The wise old holdovers and native fish we long to do battle with are particularly susceptible to spooking from a downstream approach.

Certain terrestrial fishing situations, however, dictate the downstream cast or quartering down and across. One obvious example is when fishing flies such as skaters and spiders. These imitations can be most effectively danced and skimmed over the surface with a long rod and light line, worked downstream or down and across.

Downstream casts are sometimes the only way that we can deliver a drag-free float to a trout. One situation that comes to mind is a trout sheltered by trees obstructing an upstream cast. By taking the time to go above the fish and drift the land insect down to the lair beneath the tree, such trout can often be secured; and they are likely to be heavy trout.

The downstream cast is the only real option at the tail of pools where the flow gathers and funnels rapidly to white water below. When a cast is delivered from downstream in this situation, the line is caught up by the fast water, and the fly drags almost instantly. By working from an upstream position or a forty-five-degree up-and-across angle, these tail-of-pool fish can be tricked into taking.

Rapids and fast pocket water often dictate a quartering down and across cast. Even an iron-muscled angler will rapidly wear himself to a frazzle casting up in swift water and stripping line frantically to keep control of the fly as it shoots down on the waves of white water. Quartering down and across is a more practical and efficient method of fishing these riffles. The drifts will be short ones, but they are fished out quickly, and the fly can be shown over the whole rapid in short order with tight control kept over line and fly.

On New York State's Battenkill River many trout hold in breaks in the flow where they can escape the fast, relentless pressure of the water. By casting down and across a riffle to a rise form there I was able to fool a handsome thirteen-inch brookie with a bright orange belly. It took four drifts to provoke a strike, but using the downstream method made this a quick and easy task.

One final and rather unusual circumstance calling for a downstream delivery is encountered on the stream where up is actually down. This is found where the current swirls back in an eddy and the stream flow in that backwater actually reverses its course, moving *upstream*. Fish, as would be expected, face *downstream* to the major flow in these topsy-turvy micro-cosms. Actually, of course, they are facing upstream in the flowage where they are holding. The incautious angler working upstream will almost always spook these fish, for they will be looking him right in the eyeball as he approaches from below!

A splendid little limestone stream I fish regularly has many such downstream-facing trout positioned along its course. It is always a great pleasure to take these trout with the downstream approach because so few anglers ever take the time to try for them properly; most spook the fish as they approach. Others try from downstream, casting up with generally poor results because the trout see their every movement.

Particularly familiar with this stream, I know where such fish will usually be lying and cautiously check for their presence when working upstream. If they are there, I circle perhaps sixty feet back around through the meadow and come down upon them from above. The fly is then cast from upstream. Since so few anglers bother to take this approach, the fish are almost guaranteed to strike if the cast is executed properly.

PRESENTATION

With fly choice attended to and a stealthy approach to the stream undertaken, the third and final element of successful terrestrial fishing comes into play: the delivery of the fly.

An angler needs to master basically only three casts to fish the terrestrials effectively—the check or slack cast, the roll cast, and dapping. If you can throw all manner of fancy casts in addition to these, so much the better. But you can catch ample numbers of trout using terrestrials and these basic deliveries.

The slack cast is a useful presentation under any circumstances where drag would catch the leader and pull the fly unnaturally with a traditional cast. This point is especially important on small, fast streams when you are fishing from the tail of a pool and water begins to pull at the line soon after the fly drops to the surface. The cast is also good for downstream presentations and other situations where slack line is necessary to deliver a drag-free float. It is very useful on spring creeks where aquatic vegetation creates a maze of conflicting crosscurrents that can spell instant drag.

To execute the check or slack cast, aim slightly high on the final cast and stop the final power stroke abruptly at the high noon position. The line will fall in serpentine waves on the water. Another way to make this cast is to shake the rod tip gently back and forth to the sides as you halt the power stroke.

To execute the roll cast, strip line from the reel and shake it through the rod tip. Next, raise the reel hand almost up to ear level and move the rod tip back close to the two o'clock position. Hesitate here for just a second. A quick, sharp, down and forward motion of the rod now creates a loop in the line that carries the fly out on the momentum of the unfurling line. This cast must be made with a fast snapping motion to be effective. A fairly stiff rod is best and a double taper line is most efficient.

Dapping is not really a cast at all, but over the seasons it has accounted for some extraordinary trout while terrestrial fishing. Few books or articles discuss it unless you go way back in fly fishing literature. In *The Compleat Angler* Charles Cotton discusses the technique as employed with natural mayflies in his time. Little has changed in the method of dapping since these early days, and his comments are still germane. Speaking of fish hugging the shoreline, he writes: "These are to be angled with, with a short line, not much more than half the length of your Rod, if the air be still; or with a longer very near, or all out as long as your Rod, if you have any wind to carry it from you, and this way of Fishing we call Daping . . . , wherein you are always to have your Line flying before you up or down the River as the wind serves, and to angle as near as you can to the bank of the same side whereon you stand. . . . If you are pretty well out of sight, either by kneeling, or the Interposition of a bank, or bush, you may almost be sure to raise, and take him too." [Pp. 264–65]

Cotton also advises the angler to use a heavy tippet, "three good hairs next the hook," for this type of fishing, because "You are in this kind of angling, to expect the biggest Fish [and] not an Inch of your Line [should] be suffered to touch the water in [dapping anyway]" (ibid.).

Many times dapping will be the only way you can present your fly to a trout lying next to the shoreline. Obstructions such as trees, fences, or cattle may block traditional backcasts; or weeds, shrubbery, or a stone wall may prevent the angler from using a traditional cast without hanging up on the shoreline obstacles.

Entrance of the Fly

While these casting techniques are useful for carrying the fly out to the fish, the actual entrance of the imitation on the surface of the water—the goings on at the business end of the leader—is also a vital factor in terrestrial fishing. How, precisely, should the fly land on the water and float over the trout? Little attention has been devoted to this subject in the past, due mainly to mayfly chauvinism. Most of these ephemera emerge in the water and are sucked up by the trout before leaving the surface. The object was thus to put the fly in quietly above the trout's field of view and let it drift down to him.

Sometimes this is the most natural and appropriate way to deliver terrestrials as well. In many situations, however, it is entirely *in*appropriate and fails to duplicate the natural impression the land insects make when entering the water. Often the impact made on entering the water is the most important element in deceiving terrestrial-feeding trout. Where the mayflies appeal solely to the trout's sense of sight in tempting him to rise, the terrestrials can alert the trout to their presence via both sight *and* sound.

The same watchdog senses that the trout uses to protect itself from higher predators are also its tools as a predator for capturing land insects that tumble into the water. So, while the angler must learn to get past the trout's sense of sight and sound in the approach, we must appeal to these very senses with our fly.

With a hatch of mayflies, the trout is in complete control. It is a virtual slaughter of the innocents, and the trout knows it. Calmly he takes his lie beneath the surface and tips and sips his victims with such ease that one wonders if he might not become bored with these easy pickings. The terrestrials often present a more elusive quarry for the trout. Not in mobility—the surface film is a virtual prison from which scant numbers escape—rather, it is the erratic nature of their appearance and haphazard availability that poses the greatest challenge to the trout. Except in cases of extreme abundance of a land form, such as when a mating flight of ants sets down on the water or a blustery wind deposits large quantities of leafhoppers into the stream, the trout must feed as the opportunity presents itself in the form of a foundering individual insect. A steady feeding rhythm is difficult to establish. It is more of a hunt, in essence, than the round-up that characterizes a good aquatic hatch. The fish must strike out and range wide in quest of land insects floating well out of his direct line of drift.

Sound and Terrestrial Feeding

Figuring prominently in this "search and destroy" mission is the trout's sense of sound. In many terrestrial feeding situations, the lateral line hearing-sensing system of the trout may be more important to him than his eyesight. Just as the sharp crackle of a breaking twig may alert the hunter that a whitetail is near before the deer is actually spotted, the trout often detects the presence of his quarry by the sound it creates. Like the spider responding to vibrations in his web, the trout reacts to the surface disturbance of a victim falling into the tenacious surface film. I have seen trout charge over ten feet to intercept a splashy fly when they were on the lookout for terrestrials.

Large, heavy terrestrials—the Orthoptera order, with its chunky grasshoppers, crickets, and cockroaches, as well as some true bugs, moths, cicadas, caterpillars, and beetles—have sufficient density and heft to make a significant sound when entering the stream. But smaller insects, such as the ants and treehoppers, can also make sounds that get the attention of trout. It is supremely satisfying to deliver a fur ant in a silky calm eddy with just the tiniest of splashes to draw the trout's attention.

There is most certainly a very thin line here between spooking the trout and exciting it. Only experience and practice will tell the angler exactly how much sound is necessary to attract the fish without frightening it . . . it is a distinctly variable factor. The weight and density of the insect being imitated must be considered and matched in the delivery as closely as possible; the skittishness of the trout should be taken into account; the presence or absence of wind and the nature of the water all influence the force with which the fly should land. Depth of the trout in the stream is also important. The deeper the trout are holding, the louder the entry of the fly must be to provoke a strike.

The technique of the sound cast is not difficult to master. It should be emphasized, however, that it is the *fly* which should make the noise—not the line or leader. This is best accomplished by using a fly of heavy construction. Spun or wrapped deer hair, cork, and certain other components help the fly dresser achieve this density, which simulates the natural heft of the big land insects. In a wind these flies may have to be "driven" with an extra-hard final power stroke to make a significant impression on the surface. Normally, just stopping the forward delivery higher than usual above the water will allow these flies to drop with a thud to the surface while the line and leader flutter quietly down. If you try to do it with a light fly, you'll end up slamming the line and leader down, and the fly will still descend softly to the surface—usually spooking the fish.

Where to Use the Sound Cast

This sound-appeal form of delivery is usually most effective when casting near the shoreline—from an inch to ten feet from it. This is where the bulk of hapless tumbling and leaping land insects fall, and it is here that the trout line up waiting for them.

Many land insects, including big, bulky critters such as beetles, are notoriously weak fliers. They may set down with a plop in the middle of a hundred-foot-wide river if their energy or bearings let them down. Chances are they will be snatched up immediately by alert trout. On heavily wooded streams branches may lean thirty or forty feet out over the water like terrestrial diving boards, depositing careless insects far out into the flow with a thud. Thus while shore-hugging trout may present the premier opportunity for the sound cast, the tactic can pay off in midstream as well under the right conditions.

Exploiting the trout's sensitivity to sound is an especially effective way to fish blind along attractive-looking shorelines. If shade trees, brushy vegetation, or grasses border the banks, and reasonably deep water lies nearby, some huge fish can often be enticed in this manner. The fly should be dropped at periodic strategic spots along the shore, from tight against the bank out perhaps a dozen feet. Undercut banks are particularly productive, since the trout can hide under the bank where it is shady and the current is reduced, yet still dart out to grab morsels that tumble in from land above.

This method of fishing the large terrestrials has one distinct advantage over other dry fly fishing presentations that is particularly useful when rises are sparse. It allows a maximum coverage of the water in a minimum amount of time. The more fish that see our fly, the more trout we catch. The noise of a large terrestrial entering the stream has drawing power. If a trout does not come to the fly within six or seven seconds after the cast is made, a take is very unlikely and the fly can be retrieved and cast again a foot or two upstream or to the left or right.

Floats with this technique are so short that usually no false casting is required to get the length of line in the air needed for the next delivery. The rapid manner in which this technique allows you to cover the water is particularly valuable when fishing long, flat pools that crawl along at the pace of a snail. Delivering big flies with the sound cast will allow you to cover such difficult slick water in perhaps half the time normally required. Chances are you will tussle with far more larger trout in this manner as well, since it is primarily the big fish, those twelve to twenty inches, that charge these flies when they land with a telltale plop on the surface.

The sound the insect makes when entering the water is such a vital key to the trout in this type of feeding that I've often watched fish ignore real grasshoppers, caterpillars, and crickets simply because they fell into the water out of the fish's hearing range. It's as if the sound of the insect hitting the water was the calling card the trout looked for in identifying the object as food. Insects that tumbled in upstream and were drifting sedately in the flow were passed up; those that fell with a plop into the water were gobbled up greedily. Sight was used only secondarily to authenticate the genuineness of the insect after the sound tipped the fish off to the creature's appearance in the water.

When the precise location of the fish is known, a peculiar aspect of succeeding with the sound cast can be exploited fully. To wit, this cast is often most effective when the fly is presented *behind* the trout.

Just as it is so often from behind that the deer-stand hunter first senses the approach of his quarry by the sound of a crackling branch, so the trout relies heavily on its highly developed sense of hearing to alert it when large land insects enter the water behind it. Like the deer hunter, the trout can see in front of itself. If a beetle or grasshopper plops in above it and floats down, the trout will see it. A hunter on a deer stand can likewise often spot a buck approaching him. It is in the area behind us, where our vision won't reach, that predators depend most upon the sense of hearing.

Often by plopping the fly down in back of the trout you can evoke an almost instinctive slashing charge and strike. The fish has a much shorter time to inspect the offering. Since the fly enters the water below the trout's normal taking position, it is losing ground that will take precious energy to regain after consuming or rejecting the insect. Thus the reaction is often a quick, hard swipe and an unhesitating take. Another important advantage of the behind-the-fish sound cast is its ability to draw fish out of inaccessible cover to take the fly. Though this situation may only come about a few times each season, when the need does arise, it is especially satisfying to have an ace up one's sleeve that will solve the problem. For often as not, the fish involved will be of trophy proportions.

Some trout, I think, simply become tired of having flies cast over them and of having to sort out the genuine from the ersatz. To outfox fishermen, the trout often seek out the most inaccessible spots where a cast cannot be delivered in any manner whatsoever. Most anglers never even notice these trout. Those who see them generally sigh and concede victory to the sly old devils.

But there is another approach, a presentation that will often take these fish. Such lunker-sized trout often display a penchant for big land insects. Often as not the snag, bush, or log jam they reside beneath is inhabited by succulent beetles or true bugs, or maybe a weed growth nearby harbors hoppers and crickets. By casting an imitation of such an insect as close behind these tangled lies as we can get, big trout can often be enticed out of their snag.

On gentle Falling Springs Run in Pennsylvania there was a handsome brown that spent its summers beneath a thorny wild rose bush. Why such an inhospitable abode? To discourage anglers, for one thing. Its head nestled snug beneath the low-hanging branches, eliminating even the possibility of dapping a fly over its lair. Added to this was the appeal of a bottomless larder of scrumptious Japanese beetles that were systematically devastating the foliage on the bush above it—and falling regularly into the water where the brown shrewdly snatched them up.

Over several trips my only response to this problem was to watch the trout sipping in beetles and lament that I couldn't place a cast over the fish. Then one day I watched as the brown trout turned and grabbed a beetle that plopped into the water a foot behind its lie.

Here was the answer! Quickly I knotted a #12 black deer hair beetle onto the 6X tippet and punched a cast up toward the trout's tail sticking out from beneath the rosebush. The cast was short of my chosen spot, but close enough for this hungry fish. He whirled, charged on the floating black dot, and clamped down on it viciously. I hesitated a second before tightening firmly. The fish was on. Fighting it gingerly to avoid shearing the tippet or bumping against the electric cattle fence behind me, I eventually worked the trout in and twisted the mangled beetle free of its maw. The brown was close to twenty inches and would have weighed easily over three pounds. A memorable fish, but typical of the neglected trout you can pull out of inaccessible lies with a properly executed sound cast.

Where to Deliver the Fly

It is a highly engaging pastime to experiment with an assortment of terrestrial patterns on a good stretch of water by varying the delivery of the flies while studying the trout's reactions. One factor to vary is how far from the fish the fly is cast.

We know trout will travel remarkable distances to consume terrestrial insects that they hear fall into the water. However, as a general rule of thumb, the farther behind the fish the artificial is tossed, the less likely it is that the fish will ultimately take it. This statement has some exceptions and will vary with speed of the current, type of fly, and nature of the stream you are fishing. But the trout seems to lose interest in the chase when it must waste energy pursuing its quarry downstream. It is a function of the time between alerting the predatory instincts of the trout and the caution of an animal that is also itself preyed upon. Caution and skepticism appear to grow with each additional inch the fish must swim to reach the fly.

The lighter, quieter insects such as ants must of course be cast closer to the fish if the sound cast is used at all. The impression of a treehopper or small true bug dropping a foot downstream will not even be sufficient to alert a trout, let alone to draw it that distance.

Beetles, cicadas, and the large hoppers, on the other hand, may move fish two feet or more. Usually six to eighteen inches behind the fish is a very productive region to aim these bulky imitations. This delivery may be directly behind the fish or at an angle to the side and behind. Some fish will only charge the fly if it is dropped to the left side; others, the right. If a fish is positioned off from shore, dropping the artificial behind and toward the shore is often better than the streamside.

Occasionally fish should literally be bopped on the head with the fly. This gives the least time for the trout to become suspicious and often ensures a quick take. These on-the-head casts cannot be hard, of course, or the trout will flee panic-stricken instead of striking the intruder.

Like any trout fishing strategy, the sound cast is not a cure-all. Primarily it is a method for fishing the shoreline with large, bulky imitations because this delivery imitates the natural entrance of the terrestrials into the stream.

In some streams, particularly those with a moderate to fast flow, such as the Battenkill and Letort, the technique will rarely produce. In rapids the behind-the-fish cast seldom works at all. For one thing, sound is a less prominent feeding factor in this water. The current tends to dampen the vibrations of insects falling into the water. Also, fish must expend more precious energy to venture downstream and fight back up against the current. It is primarily in the placid pools and shallow flats where the behind-the-fish sound cast with large terrestrials produces—precisely where most authorities recommend use of the tiniest flies and delicate deliveries.

Delivering the Minute Terrestrials

Fishing small flies quietly above the trout is equally fascinating angling. For the bulk of terrestrials sized #16 and smaller, and sometimes with larger insects as well, this is the most effective strategy. When using light patterns such as jassids and tiny ants, it would be difficult to manage a cast in which the fly produced noise, even if you wanted it to.

The smaller terrestrials are cast above the trout and drifted quietly over him because this duplicates the low-key appearance of the bantam-weight insect species. They are light in body, delicate in motion, and come down gracefully with little or no impact on the water's surface. Imitations should behave likewise, alighting well above the trout and floating serenely into his window.

The insects are too small and offer too little in caloric value for the trout to hunt them down in the active manner that they seek grasshoppers and large beetles. The smaller terrestrials are often so numerous on the water that there is no need for such flamboyant feeding. Many times they will be plentiful enough that the fish can stay in one narrow feeding lane and sip in the tidbits in a fashion reminiscent of an aquatic hatch.

Sight is the key sense employed by trout feeding on the smaller insects. We appeal to this sense by delivering the fly so that it floats within inches of the fish's station. It is a far different approach than plopping heavy-bodied flies with a splat behind shore-hugging trout, but the sport is quite as appealing and rewarding.

Movement of the Fly

Another aspect of fly presentation, in the past stressed by A.J. McClane and lately popularized by Leonard Wright, is movement—the activation of the fly with a well-timed, subtly executed twitch. Oddly enough, this tactic is of comparatively minor value in terrestrial fishing.

The terrestrial makes its major impact upon the stage of the trout during its entry into the water—with a thud if it is large and clumsy, the gentlest plit if smaller. True, once in the water certain land insects such as the leafhoppers skitter frantically trying to escape the clutching grasp of the surface film. But once on the water most terrestrials are incapable of making sufficient disturbance to warrant imitating.

Two notable exceptions would be the grasshoppers and crickets. Hoppers kick and squirm sometimes; other times they drift as quietly as a leaf. Crickets are good swimmers, but the more actively they try to reach land, the more vicious the strikes they elicit from trout. Activating these large, dark flies can be deadly, particularly in the evening.

The manipulation of the fly must be gentle, however, to entice strikes. And there lies the problem—keeping the movement subtle enough to be natural and realistic. Usually, the fly is barely twitched; and in most cases I "activate" terrestrials only as a last resort. If a fish examines the fly, but appears ready to slink away without striking, this is the time for a very gentle twitch. Most of the time it fails to provoke a strike, but it works often enough to make it worth trying. The astute fly fisher will have something akin to a sixth sense functioning inside him. This instinct will ever so often influence him to twitch a leafhopper or some other fly as a trout looks on skeptically. Occasionally this ploy will make the difference.

I usually prefer to be fishing a fly upstream when I twitch it. This way you can allow it to continue its natural drift after moving it. If you are fishing downstream and the trout does not respond immediately to the twitch, drag will likely set in and the game is lost. If you are casting upstream and move the fly, you can let it renew the drag-free float afterwards. Often fish that refuse to take immediately after the fly is twitched will come back and grab the imitation several seconds later as it floats unimpeded.

The exception to this upstream approach would be the spiders and skaters. These flies are best fished down and quartering across with vigorous dancing of the rod tip. They are more impressionistic flies, and it is actually their movement that provokes takes, not their form.

TACKLE NOTES   With a few exceptions, the terrestrial angler's tackle is the standard-issue dry fly equipment. Few of us can afford to maintain separate fly fishing outfits for each kind of fishing we do, even if we wanted to, so the requirements of terrestrials fishing must simply enter into the best compromise outfit.

For the average stream, a compromise between so-called "midge" and the long rod—eight or nine feet—is often best. Also, if you want to restrict yourself to one rod for virtually all trout fishing, the "medium" rod is the answer. These average rods may measure seven-and-a-half to eight feet and take 5 or 6 weight lines. They can toss a #8 hopper into the teeth of a wind and also deliver a #24 Jassid on a twelve-foot leader without rippling the surface. The rods will shoot casts forty to fifty feet without strain and prove reasonably light and untiring over a long day astream.

Lines

There are basically two choices of line for fishing with terrestrials: weight forward (abbreviated "WF" by manufacturers) and double taper ("DT"). These two line styles have see-sawed in popularity since the weight forward first came out, and of course there are advantages and disadvantages to both types.

Weight-forward lines as the name implies, concentrate the weight in the front section. This might suggest that the heavier line up front, closer to the fish, would be prone to cause noisy casts that would spook trout, but such is not the case. What scares fish is not the line itself, ten or twelve feet from the fly, but the *manner* in which the line comes down onto the water: whether it falls with a splat or lays out smoothly and quietly. The weight-forward design helps insure that the line will come down smoothly. The momentum of the heavy section of line, which is in the air working during the cast, carries the lighter shooting section of the line forward efficiently and lays out the tapered tip section with finesse.

On longer casts, when the heavy part of the double taper actually gets into the air, it is still pulling an almost equal weight shooting line through the air—much less efficient than the weight-forward design. The superiority of the weight-forward design stands out especially when large flies such as hoppers, caterpillars, and moths are on the leader. Here the efficiency of the final power stroke is critical, since weight and wind resistance are added to the leader.

Long rods are best on big, windswept waters; this is the Yellowstone River. Long rods with a "fast" action are also easier to roll cast.

Double tapers do offer an economic edge, since they can be reversed on the reel when they show signs of wear. And they are superior designs for roll casting. Since this cast gains its momentum not from the backcast, but from the snap of the rod down and forward, the line adjacent to the tip should ideally be heaviest in this cast because this is the section that shoots forward first. The heavier section has more energy to cut through the air and carry the gradually tapering tip of the line forward efficiently.

So, if one were trekking through a buzzing meadow in anticipation of a day's hopper fishing for Yellowstone cutthroats, an eight-and-a-half- or nine-foot rod throwing a 5 to 7 weight-forward line would be an excellent combination of tackle. Roll casting to trout from the banks of the Yellow Breeches, though, would call for a double-taper line and 7½-foot rod.

One final suggestion on lines: Experiment with a line one step lighter than that recommended by the rod manufacturer. A lighter line won't always prove to be an advantage, since the light line may not draw the full power of the rod. Sometimes, however, the light line will allow a slower casting cycle, lending more control over the fly and time for pinpoint, thought-out casting. Less speed will be required to keep the line from slipping down while false casting. When casting from a stooping or kneeling position, a drop in the backcast can mean a snagged fly.

Leaders

The proper leader is a variable determined by on-the-stream factors. For short casts on small waters, the leader cannot be longer than eight or nine feet, and still retain its casting efficiency. As casts lengthen to the thirty- to thirty-five-foot range, leaders up to ten or twelve feet can be punched out straight.

On windy days a shorter leader is better. Wind blasts can dissipate the forward stroke energy sharply, and so the less line to unfold, the better. Attendant problems of wind knots are also kept to a minimum with shorter leaders.

A short, fairly stiff leader is vital for efficient roll casting. This cast relies on such a limited thread of energy that there is simply insufficient power to turn over a twelve-foot taper, no matter how forcefully you snap your arm. A leader of seven-and-a-half to nine feet is superior for this cast.

Fly size must also influence leader length. Casting such large, wind resistant bugs as hoppers, roaches, and crickets requires a short leader to deliver the energy of the cast to the fly before the air friction pulls the bug down. Seven- to nine-foot leaders are best for this reason alone.

But length is only one factor in leader choices. Leaders must be stiff enough to maintain the momentum of the cast in the forward uncurling motion of the power stroke. On the other hand, a too-rigid leader is prone to cause drag on the fly in the water and reduce its natural appearance to the trout. So we compromise: Stiff butts and midsections to insure full delivery of the energy of the cast, and light, supple tippets to allow a natural drift.

Leader butts that are too limp, too small in diameter, or too short can break the fragile chain of energy carrying the fly forward. As a general rule, a leader butt should be two-thirds to three-fourths the diameter of the line end. This will typically mean somewhere between .018 and .024. Any further narrowing of the leader butt results in a breakdown of the energy from rod and line. The heavy, long leader butt will not scare fish. It *will* deliver the energy of the cast to the midsection where the leader tapers rapidly to the final tippet. A.J. McClane recommends a leader design of sixty percent butt section, twenty percent rapid gradation, and twenty percent tippet for most situations. This makes an efficient leader design for most terrestrial fishing situations, though minor variations in the proportion of leader devoted to tippet can be useful at times.

Tippet size can be very important in terrestrial fishing for a number of reasons, most of them painfully obvious when fishing in low, crystalline waters. More significantly, too heavy a tippet can reduce strikes by causing the fly to act unnaturally and drag on the water. Generally speaking, the longest and lightest tippet a particular combination of line, leader, and fly can handle effectively is the best tippet. This may dictate a tippet of thirty inches in some circumstances, such as when fishing a tiny ant, which offers little air resistance. The extra long tippet here allows a longer drag-free float; it can mean the difference between a take and a refusal. In other situations, where trout prove leader shy but want a large fly, a tippet as short as ten inches may be necessary to deliver the fly effectively and yet keep the

Six to seven-foot rods are optimum for small brush-choked streams such as the Rapidan River in Virginia.

final connection invisible. Proper tippet length and diameter is best determined on the stream by watching the way your fly and leader behave and the reaction of the trout.

Below you will find a table with uncommonly liberal recommendations for matching fly size to tippet. It is loose purposely because the traditional recommendations do not fit the special needs of the terrestrial fly fisherman using today's high-strength tippet materials. Often the best fish in a stream want a large mouthful when feeding on land insects. At the same time, the water may be gin clear and the big trout leader shy. What to do? The traditional charts recommend 2X or 3X tippets for #10 flies. Yet I have fished #10 beetles on 6X tippets with telling success when water clarity and spookiness of the fish called for it; #14 ants on 7X. There are limits here, of course, beyond which the fine tippet cannot function effectively and will not carry out a large, bulky fly. But by using a short tippet, some of the inherent problems of big flies on fragile points can be overcome. Fortunately, one of the major headaches (which no doubt led the chart-makers to suggest such heavy tippet sizes) does not occur when fishing terrestrials: the nemesis of the twisting leader. The design of virtually all terrestrial patterns—chunky, compact, and lacking upright wings—eliminates this problem.

Either knotted or knotless leaders may be used for terrestrial fishing. When angling in weed-infested waters, the knotless variety is preferable

A spare leader, tippet material, and flotant are standard gear in the terrestrial angler's vest; polaroids and a hat or a visor are essential for spotting fish and following the cast on bright days.

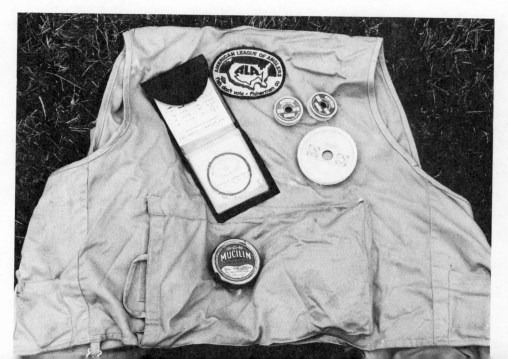

because it is less likely to catch on vegetation when a large trout rampages through its garden.

MATCHING FLY SIZE TO TIPPET

TIPPET SIZE	DIAMETER	FLY SIZE
4X	.007	6, 8, 10, 12
5X	.006	8, 10, 12, 14
6X	.005	10, 12, 14, 16, 18
7X	.004	14, 16, 18, 20, 22, 24
8X	.003	18, 20, 22, 24, 26, 28

Ancillary Gear

"Now look at that fellow wading over there," Harvey Smith said with a sly grin. "You know he doesn't know what he's doing—doesn't even have a hat on!"

The tradition of hats on fishermen is so deeply ingrained that it's almost a breach of decorum to fish with a naked scalp. And there are practical reasons for this tradition. During cold weather hats keep body warmth from escaping. In the rain they keep us dry. But most important, hats with brims help cut the glare from the water and enable us to see both fly and trout. An excellent hat for hot weather terrestrial fishing is the topless, long-billed variety worn by tennis players. They provide a substantial brim to cut the glare and, being open on the top, trap no heat under the crown.

A good pair of polaroid glasses will help you spot trout and see your fly. Seeing fish is half the battle in many terrestrial fishing situations, and polaroids are of inestimable value on a sunny day.

Part III

TYING THE TERRESTRIAL PATTERNS

"Modern terrestrial imitations are an angling event of near-legendary stature. The frustration of casting to terrestrial-smutting trout has been ended."

Ernest Schwiebert
Remembrances of Rivers Past

chapter three

TYING THE LAND FLIES

Many motivations have been advanced as justification for tying your own flies. "The deep satisfaction of catching a trout with a fly you've tied yourself" is one of the favorites. "The joy of creating a miniature work of art with one's hands" is another. Unfortunately, these usually turn out to be rather ephemeral attractions. The enduring appeal of fly tying must come on a more humble and practical level. There are two basic reasons for dressing your own imitations: (1) to get exactly the type of fly you want whenever you need them, in the numbers and sizes required, and (2) to save money. In short, fly tying is convenient and cheap.

There are those who have tried to refute the economic appeal of tying one's own flies, saying in effect that you don't really save money in the long run. I can only suspect that these individuals have succumbed to the addiction of the collector and buy every new gadget, synthetic material, and rare feather that comes on the market. A basic collection of tools for fly tying needn't cost over twenty-five dollars. Add another thirty-five dollars for hooks and miscellaneous materials, and you'll be equipped to tie thousands of trout flies for years to come.

One of the great attractions of tying the terrestrials in particular is that they require very few materials. Almost all of the items required are inexpensive, plentiful, and available at many sources. In terms of individual flies, the average terrestrial probably costs four to eight cents if you tie your own, compared to eighty cents to a dollar for store-bought models.

75

When we look specifically at the terrestrials, one additional reason for tying your own flies stands out: They are, with but a few exceptions, simple to construct. The erect wings, which prove a nemesis for so many beginning mayfly tiers, are absent on land insects. Patterns for beetles, ants, leafhoppers, and the like can be constructed in seven or eight minutes by any tier after a bit of practice. If your time for tying is tight, this can be a major attraction.

For those just delving into the craft of tying, terrestrials offer an excellent place to start. A beginner should be turning out fish-catching flies with a mere hour or two of practice.

THEORY FOR DRESSINGS

Exact realism is impossible to achieve in the fly dresser's craft—nor is it necessary. More often than not the result is a very realistic fly that either does not catch fish or one that fails to hold up under the rigors of casting and mauling in the jaws of trout.

All flies must be compromises between practicality and aesthetics. From the standpoint of realism, they must include the dominant structural features of the natural insect that are visible to the trout. On the practical side, the imitations should not twist leaders; they should float well for extended periods and be relatively easy to tie; they should be light enough to cast without strain; and finally, the flies should not turn into a shapeless blob after catching one or two fish.

The terrestrials are primarily flat in shape, almost two-dimensional compared to the mayfly dun. Even the tiny, lightweight terrestrials that float *on* the film of the water do not pose major problems in terms of refraction (by which the trout *might* see the upper parts of the natural, like a mayfly's wings, etc.), since for all intents and purposes they are flat. While the impression the trout receives of these light insects floating on the film will be hazier than that of larger insects that break through the water surface, it will be essentially the same. True, legs and such appendages will not be distinctly visible, but the opaque body form of the high-riding insect will still appear as an area of darkness; that is, the silhouette of the insect's body will be visible to the trout where the fly blocks out the sun's light.

The majority of terrestrial insects will, in fact, partially penetrate the surface film of the water. The underside of their abdomen, thorax, and head, as well as their legs, will become distinctly visible to the trout, while the back and folded wings remain high and dry above the waterline.

Body shape thus becomes the fundamental concern of all terrestrial patterns—high floaters and low floaters alike. Many times it is worthwhile to accentuate a particular body characteristic, such as the thin waist of ants or the prominent legs of a particular beetle, to exploit the trout's reliance on such structural keys in identifying the object as food. Realistically presented, duplication of the body form represents nine-tenths of a strike.

STRUCTURE

Terrestrial insects exhibit nearly every shape conceivable, from triangular humps (treehoppers) to asymmetrical rectangles (grasshoppers) to perfect circles (ladybird beetles). For the fly fisherman, it is critical to duplicate the specific body shape of the insect being imitated as precisely as possible. Indeed, mimicking the silhouette of the insect—as opposed to exact imitation—is *the* most important element in virtually all terrestrial imitations.

But while the shape of terrestrial insects varies widely, the structural components of their bodies remain basically the same. All insects have six legs and three main body parts: head, thorax, and abdomen. All possess eyes, antennae, and mouthparts. Most terrestrial insects sport two pairs of wings, though some such as the true flies (Diptera) have only one pair. Others, including the worker ants, have no wings at all.

In some insects such as ants and wasps, the divisions between head, thorax, and abdomen are distinct. In others, notably the treehoppers, cicadas, and some true bugs, the divisions are not readily visible. This lack of division usually results from a thorax that extends back over the abdomen as a protective covering to shield the internal organs in the abdomen.

Head

The insect's head contains the eyes, mouthparts, and antennae. (Curiously, the "ears" are often found elsewhere, such as on the front legs.) Insects commonly have two types of eyes—compound and simple—but they are still generally nearsighted. Two types of mouthparts are typical among terrestrial insects: those for biting and chewing and those for sucking. The latter is the more advanced form. None of these smaller parts warrant inclusion in fly patterns, though the thread where it is tied off at the eye of the hook can represent those details.

Antennae, often called "feelers," are found on virtually all insects. They aid the senses of hearing, taste, and smell. Among ants antennae are used frequently for communication. Many tiers are fond of including feelers in their patterns for added realism and aesthetic appeal, but it's doubtful whether they aid in catching trout.

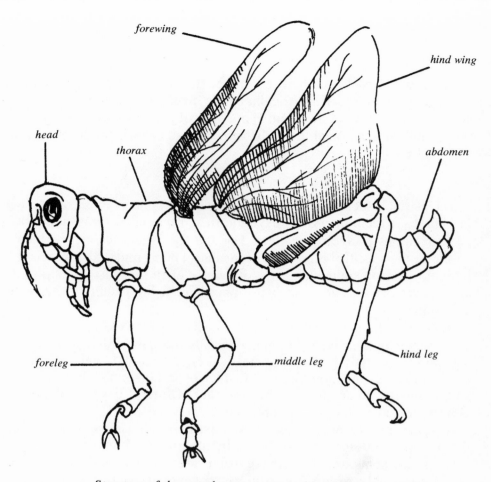

Structure of the grasshopper—a typical land insect.

Thorax

The thorax is the center of motion for insects. It is here that the wings and legs are connected to the body. The thorax consists of three segments, and the wings are attached to either the middle or rear sections. When not being employed in flight, wings are often folded flat over the back of the insect. In that position their visibility to the trout is often negligible, due to the opaqueness of the insect's body. Hence, though the great majority of terrestrial insects have wings, they seldom warrant imitation in the fly pattern: The trout simply cannot see them. Drowned flights of mating ants or termites are an exception.

One pair of legs are attached to each of the three segments of the thorax. The legs of terrestrial insects are modified according to the life style of the insect for such endeavors as digging, running, grasping, leaping, and carrying pollen. Legs can be distinctly visible from the vantage point of the trout, particularly when larger insects are involved, and they are often a vital element in the design of successful terrestrial imitations. Such materials as deer hair, quills, hackles, and feather segments are useful for fashioning artificial legs.

Abdomen

While the thorax is the center of motion for the terrestrial insect, the abdomen houses the reproductive and digestive organs. This body part varies in shape from angular to cylindrical to rotund. It is almost always a vital element in the image of a land insect the trout receives and imitating its precise form is important in gaining a high level of success in terrestrial patterns.

Terrestrials do not have bone structures, but possess an exterior skeleton or exoskeleton. This shell serves two vital functions: (1) It protects the soft inner organs of the insect, and (2) it provides a foundation for muscles to attach to. The cover is often called the cuticle and consists of various materials, predominantly chitin. Chitin is a tough, yet flexible, fibrous material. (One entomologist described it as a "tough dry kind of mucus.") It is not hard enough to protect the insects' internal organs, however. The coat of the insect must be stiffened with a material consisting of tanned protein called sclerotin. This substance is something like a plastic and when fully hardened is tougher than rock. The jaws of some beetles that contain sclerotin are capable of biting through metal. The protein represents a major attraction of terrestrial insects as food for trout.

In addition to sclerotin and chitin, insects of the earth also feature a thin layer of waxes spread like a film over their coat, with a light covering of varnish-like cement on top of that. The purpose of this layer is to keep the insects from dehydrating, but it also effectively keeps them from becoming saturated during rains. Because insects have such a large surface area compared to their volume, they would quickly evaporate if they didn't have this waxy "waterproofing" coat.

From the dry fly fisherman's point of view, the buoyancy this waterproofing provides insects with when they tumble into the stream is of major importance. The same waxy coating that protects the insects from dehydrating on land also makes them float like a cork when they enter the stream. Water cannot penetrate the varnished, waxy film, and terrestrials can float for remarkably long periods, dead or alive.

To see just how long it would take for a terrestrial to sink, I caught a number of ants and beetles and put them in a bowl of water. Several times I blew on and shook the water and even poked the insects to get them thoroughly covered with water. After several hours two of the ants sank. The rest were still floating *five days later* when I got tired of looking at a pan of dead bugs and tossed them out.

Yet though they float remarkably well, most land insects cannot remove themselves from the water's surface. The meniscus—the tension between water and air—is a virtual fly trap. Additionally, the surface area of a land insect is very great in relation to its weight. Increased surface area means more area for the surface tension of the water to exert its gripping force and a greater weight of water that must be lifted when attempting to leave the river. An angler walking out of a stream carries only about a pound or two of water on his body. Because its surface area is much greater in proportion to its weight, an ant must drag more than its own weight in water when struggling to free itself from the surface film.

For the ant, it is a bitter pill to swallow; for the trout, often a tasty treat.

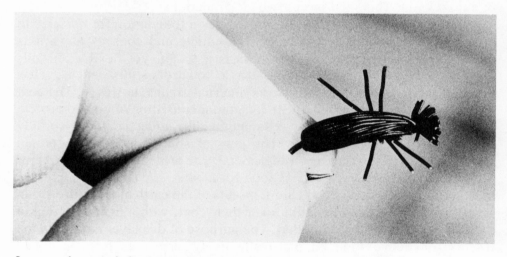

Legs can be a vital element in the design of certain terrestrial imitations.

The varnished waxy coating on insects virtually assures that they will float for extended periods in the water.

For the purpose of organization, the ties in Part III are divided into chapters corresponding to the major entomological orders. While entomology is a truly fascinating field of study, you do not have to know hundreds of Latin names or be able to identify insects on a species or genus level to enjoy terrestrial fishing. It *is* valuable to have a nodding acquaintance with the characteristics of the major land-insect orders, and the sketches and photos included in this book should help the reader in that basic task of identification. In some cases identification on a family level is also useful, since such a grouping frequently represents a species form that can be taken as a prototype and incorporated into a basic fly design. Patterns can then be varied with respect to color and size to suit different angling needs without burdening oneself with species identification.

Moreover, some working knowledge of the life cycle and habits of each order is a very practical thing. Knowing when to look for the mating flights of an ant colony can be every bit as important to a good day's fishing as knowing the emergence time of *Ephemerella subvaria*—and equally as interesting. The odd fact gleaned from an entomology book can be the spark of a new tie or the rationale for the standby we've carried for years. And because of the life styles of the various terrestrial groups, some are much more likely to end up on the trout's liquid dining table than others. For all these reasons, a profile of each order has been included with the ties. They belong together. And for orders where there are a significant number of different species that call for different imitations or presentations—or are simply unique—these have been added in a special section at the end of the ties.

As we've seen, the terrestrials are a big, diverse group of insects. But certain common characteristics in their life histories form the background for all the details that eventually bring them into contact with trout, and the fly tier.

A GENERAL ENTOMOLOGY

Growth of the Insect

Terrestrials start as eggs laid by adult females in such diverse places as stems of plants, undersides of leaves, rotten logs, animal dung, soil, leaf litter, or the bodies of other insects.

In most instances fertilization of the egg by sperm is necessary, but in some cases females can reproduce offspring without fertilization. Aphids, bees, and ants can display this form of reproduction. The season when eggs are laid varies as extensively as the shape and form of the eggs themselves. Some terrestrial insects lay their eggs in the spring after overwintering as adults. Others lay in the fall for hatching in spring. Many species lay eggs throughout the summer months. Terrestrial insects develop in a series of "molts" that occur when the insect outgrows its outer shell or exoskeleton. This cover (actually a skin and skeleton in one) splits down the back, and with the aid of a lubricating molting fluid secreted between the old "coat" and the new, the insect sloughs off his too-tight clothes for fresh ones. Immediately following the molt there is a brief resting period during which the new skin hardens. After this quiet period the insect is quite hungry and feeds heavily to fill out its new exoskeleton. The number of molts varies from species to species, and according to the weather and abundance of food. It can range from four to thirty.

The majority of terrestrial insects displays one of two forms of development: "complete" or "simple" metamorphosis. The latter is the more primitive method of growth and characterizes the grasshoppers, crickets, termites, leafhoppers, treehoppers, and true bugs.

In simple metamorphosis there are three stages of development: egg, nymph, and adult. Development consists of a series of molts that enable a progressive increase in size of the insects. The tiny newborn look like miniature adults when they emerge from eggs. The adult marks the final stage, after which no growth occurs.

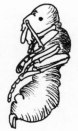

Complete metamorphosis characterizes the other orders—the beetles, ants, bees, wasps, moths, butterflies, and true flies as well as the small and relatively unimportant dobsonflies and alderflies (Neuroptera). This is the more advanced form of growth because it permits a greater specialization of life functions. There are four life stages: (1) egg, (2) larvae, (3) pupae, and (4) adult. The young (larvae) look distinctly different from the adults, and their only purpose in life is to feed and grow. Maggots (flies), grubs (beetles), and caterpillars (butterflies) are common examples of larvae of terrestrial insects. Though normally less important in the diet of trout than the adult stages of insects, larvae can become important fodder for trout when present in substantial numbers along streams. This applies primarily to the free-ranging, wormlike larvae of sawflies, butterflies, and moths.

The pupal stage is a quiet period of radical transformation. During this phase larvae metamorphose into adults. Structures of the larvae break down and adult forms develop (legs, antennae, wings, etc.). Pupation may occur in such structures as a chrysalis (butterflies), puparium (Diptera), or cocoon (moths). Since the pupal stage is one of quiescence, terrestrial insects in this form do not represent a source of food to trout.

The adult insect does not grow after it emerges from the pupa. This final form represents the most active period of the terrestrial insect's life. The vital chores of reproduction and dispersal take place during this stage, and only as an adult do insects develop wings which increase the likelihood that it may end up in the stream and ultimately in the trout's stomach.

The length of a complete life cycle for terrestrial insects varies enormously, from less than ten days to seventeen years or more. A great many insects have one complete life cycle per year. Aphids may produce thirty generations per summer. Others, such as the well-known cicada ("locust"), develop at the pace of a snail, going through one life cycle every seventeen years.

Rather than try to promote one style of tie, it is my intention to cover many of the approaches that have been taken in grappling with the problems and opportunities of imitating terrestrial insects as surface foods. The disposition of trout is so whimsical and unpredictable from day to day and stream to stream that no one style of beetle tie or one ant can be put forth as *the* answer to all such terrestrial fishing needs across the country. As such a diversified group, the land insects lend themselves well to creative and varied styles of tie. I hope the patterns described here will lead to further investigations, creations, and revisions in the terrestrials ties we now have.

All terrestrials are members of the class Hexapoda or Insecta. The insects are further subdivided into orders, suborders, families, genera, species, and in some cases, subspecies. Numbers vary, depending upon which entomologist you consult, but there are approximately twenty orders of insects. The major divisions are based on patterns of growth; body structure; form and function of legs, wings, and mouthparts; and other factors. Twelve of these orders can be considered "major" groups. These are tabulated below:

Odonata	(dragonflies, damselflies)
Ephemeroptera	(mayflies)
Trichoptera	(caddisflies)
Neuroptera	(dobsonflies, lacewings, alderflies)
Isoptera	(termites)
Orthoptera	(grasshoppers, crickets, roaches, mantids)
Homoptera	(aphids, cicadas, leafhoppers, treehoppers)
Hemiptera	(true bugs)
Diptera	(flies, gnats, midges, mosquitoes)
Lepidoptera	(butterflies, moths)
Hymenoptera	(ants, bees, wasps, sawflies)
Coleoptera	(beetles)

Coleoptera and the treehoppers are, incidentally, two of the oldest surviving living forms, going back in the fossil record to the time of the dinosaurs.

Certain terrestrial animals commonly spoken of as insects, such as the spiders, millipedes, and centipedes, do not actually belong in the Insecta class, entomologically speaking, since they have more than six legs. I have included ties in Part III, however, because from the angler's point of view, they often enter the water in the same way as land-based insects, and can have the same fishing value.

chapter four

ANTS

SAWFLIES • BEES • WASPS

(Hymenoptera)

It is fitting to begin our look at the major terrestrial orders with the ants, sawflies, bees, and wasps. For the fly fisher, the ants in particular stimulate some of the finest dry fly fishing of the season.

Small wonder! In point of sheer numbers ants surpass all other kinds of trout food. But the Hymenoptera order is not comprised solely of ants. It is, in fact, one of the most complex and highly evolved of all insect orders, divided into two major suborders encompassing fifteen thousand species found in North America.

In one suborder (Symphyta) are the sawflies and horntails. The abdomen of members of this suborder is attached over virtually the full width of the thorax, which means they lack the pinched-in "waist" common to most ants and wasps. Sawflies are full in body, while horntails are elongated and cylindrical in shape; there is little difference in the width of head, thorax, and abdomen. Sawflies draw their name from their well-developed ovipositor (egg-laying organ), which is shaped like a saw for making incisions in leaves or stems of plants, where eggs are deposited.

The larvae of most species in this suborder feed in the open on foliage; they look similar to caterpillars. Approximately one thousand species of Symphyta are found in North America. They destroy many plants and trees, primarily in their voracious larval form. As larvae, and to a lesser extent as adults, the Symphyta are occasionally consumed by trout.

The second suborder (Apocrita) is the larger and more highly developed

85

of the two, and the one of most interest to fly fishers and trout. Included in this group are the bees, wasps and, most important for the angler, the ants. This suborder is distinguished by the narrowing at the base of the abdomen that forms the easily recognizable "waist" or petiole. This constricted section is actually the front abdominal segment that fuses to the thorax.

The larvae of Apocrita are typically grublike. They rarely, if ever, figure in the diet of the trout and usually consist of helpless, immobile blobs. On the whole, Apocrita are considered beneficial insects. They figure highly in pollination of plants and prey upon many harmful insects, such as their relatives the sawflies.

LIFE CYCLE OF THE ANT

As the most advanced insect order, the Hymenoptera develop through complete metamorphosis. This form of growth affords the benefits of specialization in life functions. There are four distinct phases—egg, larva, pupa, and adult.

The birth of an ant community is often a dramatic and stirring event. The mating flight is the climax of the story and is itself a spectacular sight to witness, particularly on a trout stream. A fall of male ants onto a trout stream following the mating ritual stirs an orgy of feeding that often surpasses that induced by the heaviest of mayfly hatches. Gorging themselves on the winged adult "sexuals" (as they are called in entomological parlance), trout slash at the thousands of floundering insects whose life function has been fulfilled with this single nuptial flight.

Swarming, as the flight is sometimes called, is the climax of events that have been building up in the nest for many weeks, but it is only the beginning of the queen's arduous task of founding a community. Reacting to some little-understood time clock (that hinges on such variables as temperature and amount of daylight), the queen of an established nest begins releasing fertilized eggs a number of weeks before the flight is to occur. The eggs develop into sexually mature ants with enlarged thoraxes that house the flight muscles.

What determines the precise timing of the actual flight is not fully understood, though humidity, temperature, barometric pressure, and length of day are all believed to influence the moment of takeoff. The signal is received by worker ants in thousands of different communities in the same geographic area, often by several different species. Swarms that visibly pepper the sky are common. Cross-fertilization is clearly one of the major benefits of this mass participation by different ant colonies. Also, the basic task of finding another ant to mate with is enhanced when tens of thousands of such insects fill the air.

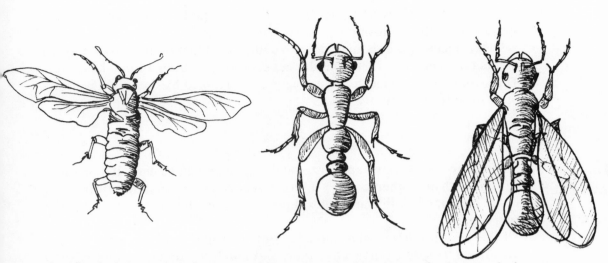

Saw flies lack the "waist" that is so evident in ants. At right is a winged male ant; only the sexuals among ants grow wings and these are used only once in their lifetime.

Mating typically takes place in the air, and sometimes on trees, bushes, or the ground. Soon after mating the males perish, their sole life purpose of fertilizing the queen accomplished. Many queens also succumb to the rigors of this single flight: Their wings malfunction; birds swoop them up crisply in flight; predators eat them on the ground or in the water.

The queens that survive the flight begin the arduous task of founding a community. The female typically chooses the ground to dig or find a hole that will form her cell. Some choose rotten logs in which to found their community.

Once fertilized the queen becomes a virtual egg-laying machine. She can produce non-sexual worker ants for her entire life, which may stretch for twelve to twenty years, as often as one worker every ten minutes. But the beginnings are perilous, and many queens die while attempting the arduous task. Indeed, the chore of founding a new colony in this manner is so difficult that many ant species do not even attempt it.

The queen of the common wood ant, *Formica rufa*, for example, whose nests of spruce and pine needles are a common sight in coniferous forests, cannot form a colony of her own. Some *rufa* queens return to their old nest after the flight. Here they take up quarters in some unused corner of the community and start laying eggs. As many as one thousand queens may lay eggs in various sections of a single wood ant nest. Other wood ant queens set up new satellite nests by taking a few workers from the old nest to help them break ground for a new community. Still others may invade the nest of smaller, weaker ants and either kill the resident queen themselves or encourage that nest's workers to do so. With the queen taken care of, it's a straight shot to the throne.

Other species of ants may never venture far from home. Some nuptial flights only get a few feet from the nest before consummation takes place. These ants return to earth and are eagerly welcomed by their own workers back into the community.

ANT LIFESTYLES

Of all the insects, ants appear to be the most similar to man. If you study the ants with more than cursory interest, it becomes exceedingly difficult to avoid anthropomorphic analogies, however misleading they may be in the long run.

Like us, ants are social animals. But also like humans, ants have a cantankerous side to their character, and much fighting goes on between rival colonies and factions. Ants are the only insects that deliberately use other insects as slaves. Ants even seem to be susceptible to "drug addictions" which take a heavy toll. Among all its food sources, the sweet fluid exuded by certain beetles is so favored that ants bring these Trojan horses into their nests to feed on their secretions. Meanwhile, the beetle is busy eating ant eggs and larvae!

The various ants in a typical community display different degrees of intelligence, and there are ambitious ants as well as sluggards. Ants, like humans, often seem to get bored with a particular task after a few days or weeks and change to another duty. Thus an ant may clean house for a while, then take care of the larvae, and the next week set out with a war party to pillage a neighboring ant colony or hunt caterpillars. One of the most sought-after duties is the cattle rancher's job. These dairymen take care of aphids, insects that secrete a sweet fluid known as honeydew. The aphids are groomed, moved from pasture to pasture as grazing conditions change, taken in out of the cold during the winter, and often treated more affectionately than fellow ants!

While there are some idlers in the ant communities, most of these insects are by nature energetic and active creatures. This incessant activity, of course, increases the likelihood that ants will wind up in the trout stream as misfortune befalls them on their travels.

One ant colony observed by the Swiss entomologist Auguste Forel collected twenty-eight dead insects per minute. In the course of one day up to one hundred thousand insect bodies were gathered. While insects make up a substantial part of the diet of many ants, few species are entirely carnivorous. As a general rule, the more meat in an ant's diet, the more primitive the ant species. Also, the larger the ant society, the less they depend on animal foods in their diet. The common wood ant is typical of the majority of ants in consuming both animal and plant matter.

Most ants build their nests underground. The moist soil along the riparian habitat of a stream is thus a particularly inviting locale. On certain stretches of the Gardiner River, a fine trout stream in Montana, "ant hill" nests are so common that one dare not stand still for long or ants will be crawling up your trousers or waders.

The ants are among the first insects to begin roaming about in the spring and last to hole up in winter. Ant imitations often produce good fishing during March, April, and May, when waters warm to a level where trout are encouraged to feed consistently on top. Ant flights are also common at this time of year on those warm, summerlike days that randomly crop up amidst the cold, wet progression of spring.

On spring creeks where water temperatures may remain in the fifties throughout the winter, warm, sunny days in December and January often see trout sipping in stray ants that have ventured out in the atypical weather. In the southern Appalachian states ant flies are particularly deadly patterns in winter.

Part of the explanation for this activity during cold weather stems from the fact that ants actually live in a different environment than ours. Insect weather is not the same as our weather. There is a thin layer of air just above the ground that is often warmer than the air surrounding us. Heat also soaks deep into rocks along streams and radiates slowly, warming ants nearby. It's not at all uncommon in winter and early spring to see ants sunning themselves on rocks like lazy lizards loafing about.

Prime ant fishing begins in April in the East, May in the West. Carpenter ants are bustling about in preparation for the spring mating. Aphids are emerging, luring the dairyman ants with their honeydew. Hunter ants are drawn out by the large numbers of insects roaming about. Activity will continue through summer months and slow only slightly on very hot days. In fall it will take many sharp frosts to put a complete halt to the travels of the ants.

From a daily standpoint, ant patterns have the same broad applicability. Depending upon weather conditions, ants may begin outside work at the crack of dawn and still be seen moving about at sunset. Ant activity usually goes on for twenty-four hours inside the nest; some ants rest while others work. Outside labor begins in the morning and heightens as the day progresses and temperatures mount, with more and more ants piling out in the afternoon. Toward evening most ants have slowly filtered back into the nest. But there are always stragglers wandering about even as dusk settles in a flush of orange on the river. If temperatures during the day are extremely hot, some ants may work at night.

Wingless ant patterns can thus be effective virtually any time of day. Those warm afternoons when most anglers are whiling away their time on shore waiting for the "evening rise" are among the best times to drop an ant imitation along a likely stretch of trout shoreline.

STRUCTURE AND FLY DESIGN

The larvae of ants are inaccessible to trout. The helpless, immature forms of Formicidae are carried like so much baggage around the ant nest and heaped in shifting piles while adults await their birth—very businesslike.

It's the adult ants that figure prominently in the diet of trout, and these mature insects have a peculiar shape which even school children have little difficulty in recognizing. The most distinctive feature of the typical adult ant is the thin constriction or "waist" known to entomologists as the petiole. It separates the thorax and the enlarged, round portion of the abdomen (known as the gaster). The waist, which is actually part of the abdomen, is the single most important aspect in all imitations tied to represent the ant.

The thin waist is the key in the memory of the trout: It tips the fish off to the edibility of the strange object passing overhead. Many early ant patterns of British and American origin failed to include this pronounced stricture in the middle of the fly, and it's doubtful that trout actually took such flies as ants, if they took them at all.

Most modern fly patterns call for the inclusion of a visible waist in the ant body. But in the actual dressing the typical ant fly often leaves much to be desired. All too often in their efforts to build large flies on small hooks, tiers virtually eliminate the crisp, thin waist of the ant, thereby sharply reducing the tie's effectiveness. The abdomen and head are built up so heavily that they obliterate the constriction between the two. If one is to err in this respect, it is far better to err on the opposite extreme by including a more dramatic and accentuated petiole than is actually present on the natural ant. Trout will strike such imitations far more readily than flies with indistinct waists. The waist is the key that excites trout and identifies the object to them as edible. Exaggerating this structural tag leaves no doubt in the trout's mind that the fly is an ant.

Like all insects, the ants have three distinct body parts: head, thorax, and abdomen. Most ant ties represent only two of these parts: the abdomen and either the head or thorax, or a combination of the two in the front hump on the hook. Such flies are usually effective, with the front knob suggesting the head of the fly more realistically than the thorax, which is usually smaller than the head and of a tapered, graduating nature. In many ants, in fact, these two knobs, the gaster and head, are the only prominent features present. The thorax is a mere wisp connecting the two. The small buildup of hackle or hair where legs are tied in the pattern is sufficient to represent the thin thorax of the natural. This two-hump strategy is a particularly good approach to imitating smaller ants on hooks sized #18 or less.

In certain other ant species, however, the thorax is a significant enough

Poor ant fly (left) has no noticeable waist. Good ant fly (right) emphasizes the waist.

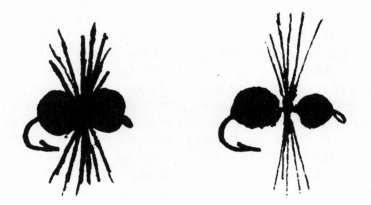

feature to warrant imitation. This is especially true where the larger ants are involved, such as the carpenter ants of the genus *Camponotus*. In tying flies of this sort care should be taken to keep the gaster round, the thorax slight and elongated, the head oval and very large.

Materials useful for representing the body parts of the ant are many and varied. Latex and lacquered thread are used for sinking patterns. But real ants float obstinately and buoyant materials are preferable for most situations: Cork is a good, durable material that never sinks, but deer hair and fur are perhaps the favorite body materials.

Legs of ants stand out prominently on medium to large specimens due in large part to the constriction of the petiole, which emphasizes the protruding limbs. Deer hair, hackle, and feather segments effectively imitate these features.

All ants have elbow-shaped antennae that they use for communicating and as olfactory organs. These features are generally too small for inclusion in fly patterns. The mouthparts of ants are represented by the three or four turns of thread used to whip-finish the fly, as well as by the eye of the hook itself.

Ant communities are comprised of several different sizes and shapes of animals. The ant that anglers imitate for day-in, day-out dry fly fishing is the worker—a non-sexual female ant. These are the smallest members of ant colonies and typically represent nine out of ten ants in an average community. They have smaller eyes and larger heads than queens and males and lack wings.

True sexuals represent only a small portion of the ant community and are readily distinguishable from their worker counterparts. The queens are much larger than the workers and sexual males. In rare instances they may actually be as much as one hundred times larger than the workers. Males are also larger than workers, but are much smaller than queens. The thorax of both males and queens is enlarged to house the extra muscles required for flight. The body silhouette seen by the trout when winged ants are on the water is thus somewhat different than the worker's. The waist between gaster and thorax is not quite as sharply defined in the sexual forms.

Wings of sexual ants are tough and glassy and may vary in color from smoky gray to hyaline. The wings actually consist of two pairs joined together by tiny hooks. When trout become selective to mating ants during a nuptial flight, wings can definitely increase the effectiveness of the fly. However, the wings can protrude from the ant's body in a number of different ways, from semi-erect, like a mayfly's, to flat and rooflike, in the manner of a caddis. The positioning of the wings and the angle at which they protrude varies from species to species and may range from virtually flat to a forty-five-degree angle—very close to the position in which a mayfly dun holds its wings. The wings may also be held flat over the back, both on one side of the insect's body, or protruding straight out from both sides in a spent position when the ants set down on the water. Fortunately for the angler, trout usually feed with such abandon during these falls of mating insects that a winged ant floating in any one of these positions will score.

Ant patterns are the nearest thing to universally productive flies anglers have. Over the time of day and the flow of seasons, in diverse regions of the country, there is rarely a situation where the right ant fly will not afford good to excellent dry fly fishing.

FISHING THE ANT

But there is a catch: Not just any ant will do. Even with over seven hundred ant species recorded in North America, trout can sometimes be quite discriminating as to the particular ant they want to eat. At other times they can be quite *un*selective, sipping in a little yellow ant one minute and a carpenter ant the next. Most often there is a particular size and color of ant that will produce better than others on any given day astream. Discovering *which* ant is a process of investigating the streamside habitat and trying different patterns until you hit paydirt. Trout can also show a definite preference as to the style of ant tie they want to attack. In my fly boxes at least three or four styles of tie for the Formicidae are present in two or more colors and sizes from #10 through #24.

Though some tiers question the importance of color in flies, where ants are involved it can be of major consequence because the flies often float partially submerged in the surface film. Here both color and form are distinctly visible to the trout.

Certain species of ants also have multicolored bodies, such as the Allegheny mound ant (*Formica exsectoides*). It has a reddish head and thorax and a gaster that is often dark brown, almost black. When naturals show such mixed coloration, it's wise to incorporate it into any patterns tied to imitate them.

Ant patterns can produce any time from the cessation of snows in spring through the graying of trees in November. Workhorse patterns will be wingless dry ants, and the most commonly used flies will run from size #14 through #20. If rises are sparse and you're trying to "pound up" fish, the larger patterns usually work better, such as the #12s through #16s. Trout sipping daintily in low water signal tiny patterns.

Ants must usually be cast in the traditional fashion above the trout and floated without drag over the lie. There are occasions when use of the

Some ant styles I carry regularly; at right are two winged ant ties.

"sound cast" with a fairly large ant or a cork fly can draw frenzied strikes, but these are the exception rather than the rule.

Any water that can hold trout is a choice place to toss your ant. Shoreline areas are naturally good. but ants can be found in every portion of a river, and trout in midstream seem quite as fond of them as shore-huggers. If you find mound-type ant nests along the shoreline, this is certainly a good place to fish the flies.

Fur Ant

PATTERNS   "Hmm!" Old Man Hartzog grunted, propping the Fenwick under his elbow as a plump, fourteen-inch rainbow, bucking like a wild steer in Black Hole on Falling Springs Run, strained the fragile tippet alarmingly tight. "This ain't no good. Those fish are so frenzied they hit that ant you just gave me in the middle of this Caenis hatch."

Hartzog is an institution on this gentle little limestone creek in south-central Pennsylvania. For years on end, until a stroke tragically cut back his streamside outings, he was a regular visitor to Falling Springs. Faded green trousers hanging from his lanky frame as he strode about, he always had a ready smile on his leather-skinned face as he watched other anglers, fished himself now and again, and studied the trout and their habits with an intensity few of us ever muster.

"You won't like this fishing today," he would warn sadly on an ill-timed weekend visit. "Just stocked it. Too many little fish and too many fishermen."

Hartzog is keenly aware of the Falling Springs trout's appetite for terrestrials. His fly boxes, treasured all the more dearly because waning eyesight has prohibited him from tying his own, are stuffed brimful of crickets and lacquered wet ants. Beetles are always there, and hoppers fished through the bristling meadow stretches draw heavy, boiling takes in summer from full-bodied browns and rainbows.

But most cherished of all by Mr. Hartzog are his tiny, fur-bodied cinnamon ants. "The smaller the better," he says, and it is gratifying to dress flies that meet his demanding standards. Though he does not fish this fly exclusively, the reaction of trout to these tiny brown ants is etched firmly in Hartzog's mind. Even when they are on the water during the prolific spinner fall of *Tricorythodes,* many trout will sip the ants in greedily. And when the hatch has diminished, the fur ant will produce throughout the most blistering of summer days.

Hartzog is not alone in his appreciation of the fur-bodied, hackled ant. It is a deadly pattern that has stood well the test of time. Many skilled fly fishermen, if forced to choose one pattern for day-in and day-out fishing, would point to the fur ant.

The fly is durable, the epitome of simplicity in construction, and productive over a broad range of waters. The basic design of the fur-bodied ant, like so many terrestrials, evolved in Pennsylvania. The fly, which Charlie Fox says "we were fishing a great deal by 1934," was originated by Bob McCafferty. The pattern was first tied as a wet fly, in large sizes. Eventually McCafferty tied the imitation with fur knobs and hackle in the midpart.

"Bob McCafferty died prematurely," Charlie adds. "Had he lived he would have been one of our recognized greats."

The basic fur ant is productive from sizes #10 through #28. Traditionally, the fly has been tied in two colors: brown or "cinnamon" and black. The brown ants are recommended in small sizes, probably to imitate the cornfield ant (*Lasius niger*) or perhaps the big-headed ant (*Pheidole bicarinata vinelandica*). The black ants are supposed to be tied in large sizes to mimic the carpenter ant.

However, even the most casual observer will quickly point out that there are some quite large brown ants, as well as some tiny black species (*Monomorium minimum,* for one). Moreover, there are some ants that are a deep mahogany brown, others that are bright orange. Still others are yellowish, and more than a few have a combination of colors, with dark gasters and lighter colored thoraxes and heads. Since ants float semi-awash in the surface film, often breaking partially through the meniscus, their colors become distinctly visible to trout. Ants tied in various shades from pale yellowish tan to jet black will all take trout on the right occasion. Ants dressed with the so-called hot orange dyed fur are extremely potent. There is something about this color that seems to excite trout and urge them to strike.

Dyed seal's fur is a very good material for tying ants with a semi-translucent appearance, particularly when the spin-dubbing method is used. This tying technique retains the translucency of the material and makes for a lifelike representation of glassy-toned ants. However, seal tends to tie on rather fuzzy and must be trimmed with scissors to give a clear silhouette of the ant shape.

The fur I usually employ for ants is rabbit. The virtues of this material far outweigh any disadvantages it may have. Dressed with a good flotant, rabbit fur ants float very well. Exceedingly pleasant to work with, the material has few bothersome guard hairs and dubs into neat, tight bodies. Even the normally troublesome #24's are a cinch with this fur. If you buy a white rabbit skin, you can cut it into pieces and dye the fur into a lifetime supply of four or five common ant shades.

For those partial to the modern synthetics, polypropylene can be substituted for the fur in these patterns.

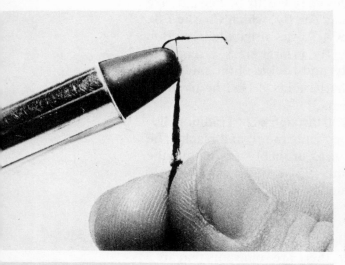

1 Attach a down-eye dry fly hook in the vise (Mustad No. 94833 or No. 94840) and bind 6/0 thread to the rear of the shank. Spin a small amount of rabbit or seal fur onto the thread. Wind the dubbed fur onto rear third of hook to form a neat, oval shape. This forms the prominent gaster of the ant.

2 Select a hackle with barbules slightly longer than the gap of the hook and attach firmly at middle of fly with thread. Wind the hackle two or three times around hook shank and tie it off in front of the wrappings.

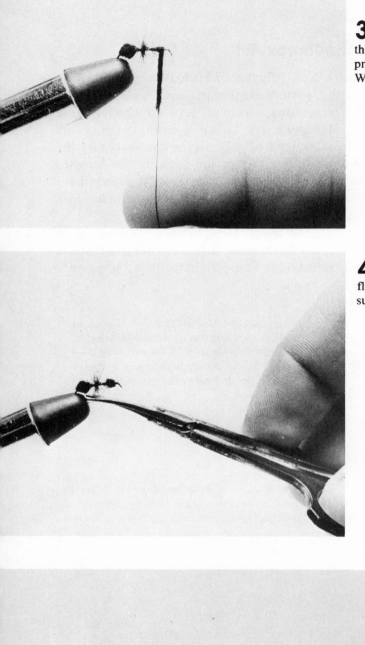

3 Dub on another patch of fur, about the same amount as was used to form the gaster. Wind this onto the forward third of the hook shank in a prominent oval hump to form the head of the ant. Whip finish.

4 This step is optional, but most tiers like to trim a V-wedge out of the bottom hackle of the fly, so that the imitation will float low and flush in the surface film. Apply a drop of lacquer to head.

5 Completed Fur Ant.

The Thorax Ant

The two-hump fur ant is such a deadly fly that one is loathe to attempt any changes or improvements in this pattern. One variation that has proven particularly effective with the larger ants, however, is to simulate all three body sections: head, thorax, and abdomen. This is a natural step in any attempt to mimic precisely the silhouette of ants. In the two-hump fly the abdomen is suggested by the rear hump of fur, the head by the forward knob. The thorax has scant representation in this pattern—the place where the wisp of hackle is tied on. In the larger flies, size #16 and up, including a thorax in the fly can be a valuable addition to the pattern.

Since this process takes up a slightly longer tying surface, 2X long shank hooks (Mustad No. 94831) can be used if desired. Be sure to keep the thorax in this design smaller and more elongate in shape than the head and gaster.

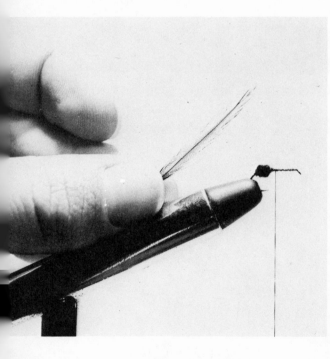

1 Fasten a Mustad No. 94833 or 94831 hook in vise. Bind the tying thread to hook and dub on fur. Wrap a tight oval shape with fur onto rear third of hook shank. Select dry fly hackle with barbules one and a half times as long as the gap of the hook.

2 Bind hackle in with thread immediately in front of fur knob. Dub in small amount of fur—about half as much as was used in rear knob.

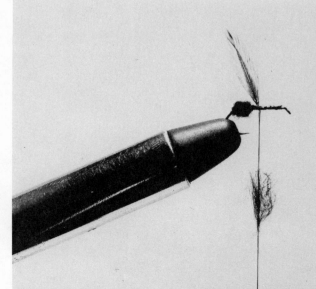

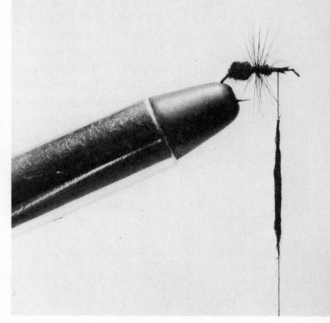

3 Wind the dubbing forward to form a thin thorax over the next third of hook shank.

4 Grasp tip of hackle in pliers and wind forward several turns over fur thorax. Clip off excess hackle. Dub on more fur for head of fly. This should be the same amount as was used in the rear section of the ant.

5 Wind the dubbed fur onto the front third of the hook to form a prominent oval knob. Whip finish ant at eye of hook. Apply a drop of cement and trim V from bottom hackle if desired.

No-Hackle Fur Ant

It was an early summer morning many years ago when Doug Jones and I pulled into the parking lot at Fisherman's Paradise for our first visit to this Pennsylvania limestone stream. A crashing rainstorm the night before had made for a fitful night's sleep in the tiny camper. At dawn a raucous pair of ducks began a jabbering conversation, eliminating the last chance of rest before our day's fishing.

Much to our amazement, the stream still flowed its standard milky shade of green. A quick trip into nearby Bellefonte for breakfast renewed our energy and we hit the water with a burst of red-eyed enthusiasm. I asked Doug what pattern he would try.

"Cinnamon ant," he replied.

It was exactly the fly I had in mind, but then I saw Doug's patterns.

"No hackle!" I exclaimed in a startled tone.

"I don't think you really need it on such small flies," he said.

It seemed a reasonable theory. Though trout have keen vision, few anglers would suggest the fish can see the miniscule legs on a #24 fly. But would the simple imitation of two fur humps float?

Indeed it would—and take trout too. The browns were lined up along the shore like cordwood. Each few feet upstream there was another trout hovering next to the grassy bank. With his delicate seven-foot Orvis, Doug laid the fly inches above the last fish. With but rare exceptions he was greeted with a hearty rise. The cinnamon fly proved a deadly pattern that day, all day long.

The No-hackle Ant .

The no-hackle ant is best reserved for hooks sized #24–28. This fly's supreme virtue is simplicity in tying, and even those of us who normally shudder at the prospect of tying #24s and #26s will find these imitations easy to work on small hooks. The fly is tied by simply winding an oval hump of fur for the gaster, wrapping the thread forward to leave a thin waist, and dubbing another hump for the head of the ant. This imitation provides a good, crisp silhouette of a tiny ant, which must appear to the trout as two tiny dots barely connected.

The fly should be dressed heavily with flotant and squeezed dry after taking a fish. Using this procedure, I've taken close to a dozen trout on a single fly of this type without sinking it.

The Deer Hair Ant

One of the greatest virtues a fly pattern can have is simplicity in construction and design. The deer hair ant draws kudos in this respect; it is easy to assemble and the materials list consists of one small bunch of deer hair.

Like many patterns whose time has come, this fly was apparently developed separately by two anglers several thousand miles apart. In the February/March, 1973 issue of *Fly Fisherman* magazine William N. Reinholdt, Jr. described this fly pattern as the Calcaterra ant. Ozark angler-tier Paul Calcaterra was given credit for the design of the fly.

Unknown to Mr. Calcaterra or Mr. Reinholdt, the renowned Pennsylvania tier Chauncy K. Lively had described a similar pattern—almost identical, really—in the December, 1962 issue of *Pennsylvania Angler* that he called the carpenter ant. Lively said, "I did (another) piece about it in the 1964 *Fisherman's Digest* and have since had correspondence with anglers from Maine to Oregon who swear by it." The only difference in the pattern Lively presented in the 1962 piece and the fly described as the Calcaterra ant is that the legs of the Pennsylvania-born ant emanated from the head of the fly, the Ozark's from the thorax.

As an interesting aside, Lively reports being accosted on the Letort by a fly tier who chided him for committing this faux pas, since the legs of ants obviously emerge from the thorax of the insect—not the head. Of course, as Lively pointed out later, the ant's legs actually float askew in random fashion when the insect is in the water, and the origin of the legs in the artificial does not prove of vital consequence. However, Lively in the November, 1974 issue of the *Pennsylvania Angler* submitted his revised version of the fly with legs protruding from the midriff of the insect.

The only other difference between the revised Lively version and the Calcaterra ant is that the Pennsylvania pattern includes two humps in the forward section of the fly to simulate the thorax and head. Calcaterra's version has only one knob of hair here. Both versions work splendidly, and the pattern is an exceptional fish-taker. The hollow deer hair and the bunching of the hair into air-catching knobs make for a very buoyant imitation. No flotant is necessary with this pattern, though you can dress it if you choose.

The major drawback of the deer hair ant is that it is not particularly durable. However, its ease of construction is a compensating factor, and a good supply can be dressed in just a few hours. The fly is tied primarily in black, but brown works well also. Sizes #14 through #20 are practical; if you try to tie smaller than this, it is hard to get a good, clean outline of the crisp ant form with this tying method.

1 Attach Mustad No. 94833 (or 94840) hook to vise. Wind 6/0 thread to rear third of hook shank. Select a small batch of deer hair (twenty to forty strands).

2 Bind the hair firmly to the rear third of hook.

3 Trim the butts of the hair at the middle of the hook.

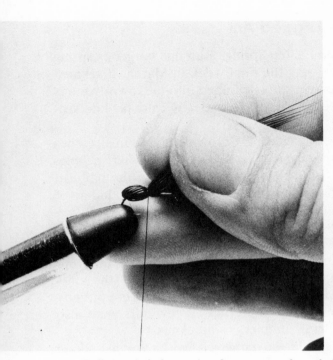

4 Pull deer hair forward to form a smooth oval hump that will represent the gaster of the ant. Attach with several wraps of thread.

5 Select eight strands of deer hair, four from each side, and pull back towards rear of hook. Make several wraps again in front of these eight sections of hair that are to form the legs. Next, lift the hair at front of hook and wrap the thread forward beneath hair to the eye of the hook.

6 Pull forward front bunch of hair (but not the eight sections reserved for the legs) and bind at eye of hook to form head of ant.

7 Clip the excess butts, whip finish, and apply drop of cement or acrylic to head and you have a finished Deer Hair ant, otherwise known as the Carpenter Ant or the Calcaterra Ant.

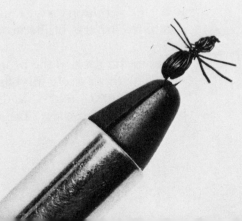

The Legged Ant

The sun bore down brightly on Falling Springs Run that gorgeous spring day. Though the calendar said it was the final week in March, it seemed more like a morning in May. Temperatures climbed into the low seventies by one o'clock and winds remained uncharacteristically calm for kite season.

The stream bed was barren of foliage—pale brown with silt in stretches where cattle and ducks had scoured the mud flats, honey-gray where pebbles lined the naked floor. Several fish were feeding robustly on the pinhead sized midges drifting in the surface film. Others, foraging with shudders of their long bodies against the bottom, rooted for nymphs and crustaceans. A few, inches from the shoreline, seemed to lie in wait for an early land morsel to drop into their channel.

It seemed too early for most terrestrials, but the limestone rock outcroppings in the greening fields were warm to the touch. They hoarded the sun's heat, and it was easy to see why several varieties of ants were already venturing out to embark on the first spring forage. A few ants were also rustling about on the tree bark with summerlike quickness.

Two anglers were working the glide above the road with nymphs, taking the odd trout. They ignored the rises peppering the surface, now with increasing frequency.

I climbed the fence and walked up to the next meadow. Large black-and-white Holsteins with bells around their necks were grazing slowly toward the stream. My casting muscles had atrophied during the quiet winter spent writing and shooting at grouse and woodcock. It would take a while to get back timing. Without much expectation, I cast at a fish lying motionless against a rock ledge. It inspected the fur-bodied, hackled ant apprehensively, then turned away disdainfully. Another trout rising to midges in the adjacent current was shown the fly. The fish finned back under it, but turned panic-stricken and shot back to its holding position.

"Interested anyway," I muttered to myself. But subsequent casts over two more trout proved fruitless. Pausing on a grassy stretch, I took out my fly box and eyeballed the ant imitations. Now seemed as good a time as any to try the variation on the ant theme I had dressed during the winter. The fly combined aspects of the normally deadly fur-hackle ant and the deer hair ant.

Rabbit fur formed the prominent head and the gaster hump of the abdomen. The thin petiole was suggested with several wraps of thread. The legs were deer hair—four strands tied flared and separated, protruding from both sides of the waist. The fur allowed a clean, accurate imitation of the distinctive ant body parts; the deer hair gave a realistic and prominent representation of the ant's legs.

The fly looked good. How it would fish I had no idea. Maybe it would sink. Maybe the trout would turn their noses up at it.

"One can only fail," I mumbled while knotting on the #18 imitation and dabbing milky Mucilin paste on the body parts of the fly.

Upstream, two mallards ignored a bitter rebuke from a hefty white duck as I stripped line from the Hardy Featherweight and delivered the fly above a shore-hugger. "Floats good," I noted.

As the fly neared, the fish worked his pectorals excitedly, rose, and swallowed the ant deep into its mouth. I tightened and the fish wallowed. When I extracted the fly from the trout's mouth a few minutes later, I expected it would be a gnarled mess. Surprisingly, not even a leg had broken off. I rinsed the fly briefly, squeezed it dry, and again it floated well as I placed it above a midstream rock. There a rainbow sucked it in while arching the leader taut.

By then one of the anglers fishing the glide below had worked up. "They've slowed down," he said pessimistically. "Haven't taken any in this last stretch."

"I've worked up a few on dries," I said.

"What pattern are you using?" he asked while climbing over a barbed wire fence.

"Black ant."

His eyebrows furrowed in a knot at the center of his forehead. "Ants in March?" he seemed to be thinking. "What kind of nut is this?"

"Well, as long as it works," he said after a long pause.

"The naturals are active already," I said.

He nodded with a halfhearted "Oh, yeah," before heading upstream.

Over the next stretch of water several fish working steadily on nymphs came up to the legged ant. One large trout struck the fly with such vengeance that it startled me, and I lifted hard and popped the one-pound Maxima tippet. By late afternoon the brief outing had produced eleven fish. The fur-hair ant had proved its worth admirably by scoring on difficult waters at an unpropitious time of year.

The fly has since shown itself to be a valuable imitation to have stashed in the vest. The deer hair legs float the fly far better than one might expect, provided the two fur bulges are treated with a good flotant. It is not a pattern recommended for extremely rough water, since the fly doesn't float quite as well in broken flow and is rather difficult to see. I reserve the legged ant for slow, slick waters where trout get a long, hard look at our offerings and the most realistic fly possible is desired. In larger sizes, such as #14's and #12's or 2X long #16's, the thorax of this ant can be represented with a small dubbing of fur. For smaller ants I prefer simply taking a few extra turns of thread. The ant is effective in various colors from yellowish tan to coal black. When choosing hair for the legs, try to pick pieces with a thickness that seems appropriate for the body size of the insect.

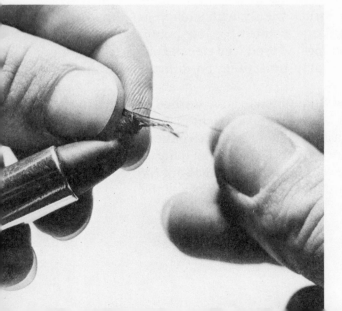

1 Secure a dry fly hook in vise and attach 6/0 tying thread. Pull off a small amount of fur to form the gaster of the ant.

2 Wind fur onto rear third of hook to form gaster.

3 Select four or five strands of deer hair for legs. Hold legs flat over middle of hook and attach firmly with thread.

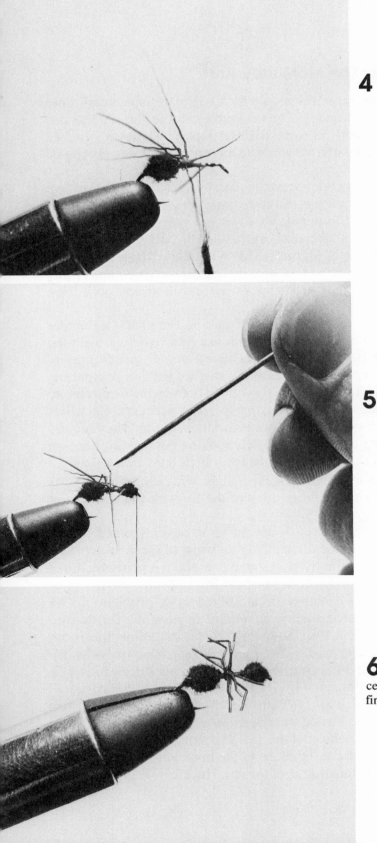

4 Figure eight thread around and between legs to secure and separate them.

5 Wind thread forward several turns and dub on more fur to form head of the fly.

6 Apply a drop of liquid acrylic to legs where they are bound to the hook. Whip finish, apply cement to head and trim legs to appropriate length: a finished Legged Ant.

The McMurray Ant

Cork has fallen in and out of favor as a fly tying material several times over the last three or four decades. The venerable George Harvey was one of the earliest tiers to use cork for terrestrials (though he has since switched to deer hair for most of his patterns) when he incorporated it into his classic inchworm pattern in 1934.

On the majority of waters cork terrestrials can be absolutely devastating: Forty to fifty fish a day is not out of the realm of possibility.

Cork flies have increased in popularity in recent years to the point that one commercial fly company specializes exclusively in cork flies. This is the Corkers outfit run by William S. McIntyre, 106 White Gate Road, Pittsburgh, Pennsylvania 15238. Since he first began marketing these flies commercially seven years ago, McIntyre has produced over forty thousand cork flies, most of which imitate terrestrial insects.

There are a number of reasons why cork has become such a popular material for terrestrials. For starters, cork flies are easy to deliver with the roll cast. Since traditional fur and feather flies have a greater specific gravity than water, they must depend entirely on the surface tension present between air and water to float. A saturated fly will not float on the meniscus; so fur flies are virtually useless when roll casting to surface-feeders. Cork flies overcome this deficiency because they are naturally buoyant. They require no false casting and can be rolled to all likely looking holding lies beneath shoreline brush and overhanging branches for a high float every time.

When roll cast in this manner, cork flies alight with a subtle splat. As we've seen, this often brings trout rushing to the fly with the pale fire of hunger burning in their eyes.

In spite of these advantages, cork ant patterns never seemed totally satisfactory, mainly because the distinctive thin waist of these insects was difficult to incorporate into the fly. Legs also presented a problem, since they were tough to attach to the cork in a realistic fashion.

Ed Sutryn of McMurray, Pennsylvania solved both problems in an ingenious manner and created such a novel and devastating fly that he patented the invention back in 1965. Says Ed, "As far as I know, this is the only patented fly on the market today. In fact, I only remember one other fly that had this distinction and that was the Palmer Grasshopper which was popular thirty or forty years ago."

The patented design, which Sutryn calls the "McMurray Ant," consists of two pieces of cork or balsa wood threaded onto a piece of monofilament to represent the abdomen and head of the ant. The mono between these two segments is used to fasten the assemblage to the hook and, when wrapped with thread, represents the thin thorax of the ant. Hackle is wrapped around the midsection to imitate the ant's legs. Much of the effectiveness of this pattern can be traced to its distinctly thin waist—the key trout seem to home in on in identifying ants as edible objects.

Sutryn's is a strikingly original approach to representing the ant form, but he modestly credits the trout for inspiring his fly:

> The ant in question came about as the result of a frustrating afternoon on Fishing Creek, near Lamar, Pennsylvania. This creek has a large native population of brook trout and this particular day I stood at the head of a riffle which was just boiling with rising trout. After throwing everything in my box at them I retired in defeat without having even one fish rise to my flies. On the long drive back to Pittsburgh I discussed the day with my fishing partner, but neither of us could come up with an idea of what the trout were feeding on.
>
> After I got home, I remembered something. I was standing under a large oak tree by this riffle and had to keep brushing large black ants off myself. This brought to mind a trout that I had observed some years back feeding on something invisible in a clear, spring-fed pond. When I caught this fish (on a live grasshopper) and examined the stomach contents, they consisted of about two tablespoons of large black ants. This pond was surrounded by large overhanging trees, and I just put two and two together.
>
> When it came to building the fly, I was ready for something different. I never cared for any of the conventional methods of tying ants, so I decided to use a cork body. I whittled two pieces of cork . . . tied them to the back of a hook and came up with a real good looking ant. However, as I looked at it, I knew it would never hold up under heavy use. Then I got the idea of stringing the cork on a piece of monofilament and tying the monofilament to the hook.
>
> When I tried the fly out on several streams I knew I had a winner. On limestone streams, where I had been habitually skunked, the trout took the ant so deliberately and innocently that my conscience even bothered me.

After developing his pattern, Sutryn next went through the lengthy procedure of obtaining a patent and developing a system of making the flies commercially—a process that took four to five years. They have been on the market via only a limited number of tackle houses, including the Angler's Roost in New York City, and by direct mail from Sutryn at Box 104, McMurray, Pennsylvania 15317.

Manufacturing the McMurray ant was a part-time operation for Ed until 1977, when he retired and began devoting more time to the ants. Sutryn says, "There is one thing about my mail-order sales that impressed me and that was that a large percentage of my customers took the time to write and comment on the effectiveness of the ant." And well they should: It is a convincing fly.

Sutryn ties the ants in sizes #12 through #22, in both black and cinnamon. Since creating the pattern, he has switched from cork to balsa for the body.

Though the process looks rather tedious, the McMurray ant is actually fairly simple to construct. Materials needed include the following:

Hackle	Pencil with needle imbedded in eraser (sharp end out)
Candle	Monofilament from 0.010 to 0.015 inches in diameter
Tweezers	Balsa cylinders (cork also works)
Tying thread	Razor blade
Dry fly hooks	Model airplane paint

1 Cut two pieces from balsa or cork cylinder with razor blade to form abdomen and head of ant fly. One-eighth or 3/16 inch is about right for flies in sizes #12 through #16. Abdomen segment should be one and one-half times the length of head.

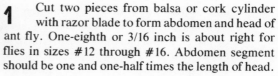

2 Ed Sutryn does not include this step in the McMurray Ant, but I like to round the corners of these two segments for a more realistic shape. Emery board works fine for this.

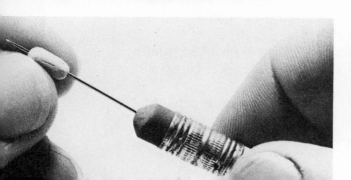

3 Rounded balsa pieces for a size #12 McMurray Ant.

4 Take a sewing needle and force the blunt end into the eraser of a pencil. This will make a tool required for the next step. Poke a hole lengthwise through each piece of balsa with the needle point. Twist the balsa gently on needle, but be careful not to make the hole too large.

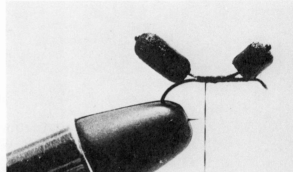

6 Dip the assemblage one end at a time in enamel paint, let dry, and repeat.

5 Position the head and abdomen segments at appropriate places on a short piece of mono (Sutryn uses mono ranging in thickness from .010 to .015 inches). There should be a wide gap between the head and abdomen. Distance between two segments should be just about equal to the length of the abdomen. Next, hold the end of the monofilament over the flame from a candle to melt it and create a bead which will keep the balsa segment from coming off the end. Repeat with other end and slide body segments tight against the beads.

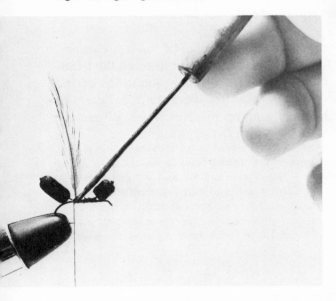

7 Place dry fly hook in vise and attach balsa and mono assemblage with ten to fifteen tight wraps of thread. The abdomen and head should jut upwards when mono is fastened tightly. Tie in a hackle of appropriate color hackle for legs. Sutryn prefers wet fly hackle for a more realistic appearance. An alternative for legs would be four or five barbules from grouse or crow feathers or several deer hairs. Apply drop of cement or acrylic over thread wrapping.

8 Wind hackle forward with two or three turns, tie off, clip excess hackle, and whip finish. Add drop of cement to the whip finish and clip V-wedge from bottom of hackle if desired.

McMurray Ant variations.

Winged Ants

Fishing to rising trout during a fall of mating ants is quite similar to fishing a heavy mayfly spinnerfall. While a flight of swarming ants can seldom be predicted, when it does occur and these insects fall spent on the water, fish go absolutely furious. The rising usually surpasses in intensity all but the rarest of mayfly feeding orgies.

The trout seem powerless to resist the taste appeal of these creatures. Hewitt thought it was the bitter taste of formic acid that attracted the trout. He may well have been right, since many ants contain quantities of the chemical. In *A Trout and Salmon Fisherman for Seventy-five Years* he describes encountering one such fall of ants on the Neversink River:

> One evening, on the Neversink, we noticed a great rise of trout in the large pool at the Big Bend. . . . There were large numbers of small black flies in the air. . . . and as I opened my mouth to speak one or two of them got in it, and to my surprise they tasted quite bitter. These were small flying ants, and were bitter with formic acid. The fish were evidently taking these small flies on account of this taste.
>
> I took some No. 18 flies and cut down the wings to make them about the size of the flying ants, and at once began to get fish. We took a dozen good-sized ones in a little while. [P. 195]

It's worth noting that Hewitt encountered this flight toward the end of May, since many sources suggest that swarming ants are a phenomenon of late summer and early fall only. It's true, August and September are common times for mating among ants, but flights can occur any time from early spring through November. I've discovered many varieties of flying ants on the water, from huge black carpenter ants to tiny brown specimens, as early as March.

But while they may occur at virtually any season, their appearance is never a totally predictable phenomenon. Mike Fong says that the appearance of flying ants is hard to pin down in western states: "I've encountered them from spring to late fall on streams and lakes throughout the West. Some of the best encounters were on the Truckee River in the Sierras of California in late June and the middle elevation lakes of southern Oregon at about the same time. For several years Lewiston Lake had good ant fishing, as did many lakes in northern California."

Rex Gerlach in his *Fly Fishing the Lakes* reports flights through late May and early June where he lives in northeast Washington. Charlie Fox says August 10 usually marks the appearance of flying ants on the Letort. Part of the reason why these mating flights are such unpredictable occurrences is that very precise weather conditions are required for the success of the undertaking.

Humid, calm, warm days are preferred for the mating ritual in most cases. It was just such a warm mid-September afternoon on the Beaverkill River recently when the flying ants salvaged in consummate style what was turning out to be an exasperating fishing day. Normally September is a lovely and productive time of year to fish this classic river. The dread rains and cloud cover of spring trips have vanished, and there is at least a glimmer of sunshine on most days. An invigorating crispness fills the air, and maples flaunt their sunburst hues with increasing vibrancy. There are often some late *Isonychia* popping up, coral-bodied mayflies in the evenings, and on dark days little olives float the smooth currents. Terrestrials have reached a peak of abundance, and they enter the water in myriad forms and sizes. It is a time of bounty, a season of harvest, and the trout, too, seek to reap the crop of land insects tumbling into the river.

But on this September trip it seemed as if someone had turned the calendar back to April. It rained and it rained and it rained. The river rose hard over night and in the morning was dark olive-brown, swollen, and raging so that Piano Rock in Hendrickson's Pool was nearly covered.

For five hours thick-headed dry fly fishermen pounded the waters. And we received scant reward for our efforts. A few fish came to streamers, but the trout absolutely refused to rise. Anglers would plug away for an hour or two, stop to commiserate over the weather, then renew their futile casting. Even the edge of Cairns Pool, which normally shows a few fish rising during the worst of conditions, was still.

And then, when frustration had nearly reached the rupture point, a glistening wing appeared on the slowly clearing currents. Quickly the insect was lifted clear of the water and examined. A winged ant crawled across a human palm in an excited state. The insect was brown, about size #18, with wings folded flat over the back.

But soon there were other forms visible in the flow as rises sprinkled the surface with increasing frequency. Smaller ants, #22s or #24s, with deep brownish black bodies were on the water in large numbers. And yet a third species appeared—black ants about size #20.

1 Secure a Mustad No. 94833 hook in vise and attach thread. Spin on fur and wrap around shank to form round abdomen section of insect, as in fur ant pattern. Next, select two hackle tips for wings. Bind to hook immediately in front of knob of fur, one on either side. Wings should angle slightly out to the sides and slant upwards at about a thirty degree angle for most ants.

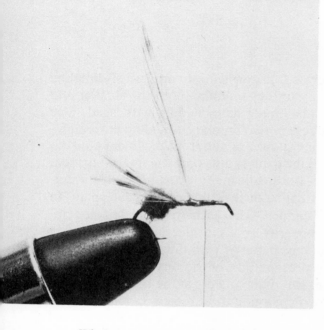

2 Select a hackle with barbules slightly longer than the gap of the hook and attach it in middle of hook.

3 Wind two or three turns with this hackle and tie off. Clip off the excess hackle tip, then dub more fur onto the thread.

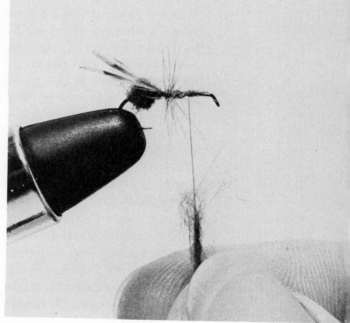

4 Wind fur onto forward third of hook to form head of winged ant fly, whip finish, apply drop of lacquer or acrylic to head and trim excess thread. Finished Winged Ant.

In an instant the dead stream was transformed into a maze of dimpling fish. The trout, responding heartily to flies imitating both the smaller and larger winged ants, fed with an abandon I have seldom witnessed. One trout, a fifteen-incher, took an ant every two seconds, timed by the watch.

Not long after the rise began, a fine shower of raindrops that blanketed the stream sent enormous quantities of the hapless ants onto the river's surface. They literally peppered the water, the smallest ant forms in greatest numbers. Many of the tiny ants were floating flush with wings spread spent, in the manner of a dying mayfly spinner. This circumstance led several anglers, perched like sentinels on gray rocks aside the mist-shrouded stream, to toss *Tricorythodes* spinner patterns with tails clipped off. The modified flies provided a good representation of the tiny ants, and those fishers' rods were seen bent deep. But other anglers at the head of the long gray pool who were frustrated by the gorging trout reeled up muttering as darkness enveloped the freestone river and turned their backs on trout porpoising wildly in the waning light.

Even a wingless ant in the proper size and color will usually take some trout during an intense fall such as this one on the Beaverkill. Winged patterns take more fish and are also easier to see. But ants may hold their wings in a variety of positions when riding the currents. Some hold them flat and rooflike, others erect like a mayfly dun, and still others out to the sides in a spent position. To be prepared for any eventuality, your box should be stocked with ants displaying all three extremes of wing position. For those who don't want to carry this many flies, ants with wings held semi-erect and angling rearward are the surest producers and offer a good compromise pattern. These wings may be fashioned of hackle tips, polypropylene, duck quill segments, or clumps of hen hackle. Mike Fong ties a productive pattern for western trout fishing that employs bucktail for the body, brown hackle to support the fly, and hackle tip wings. The illustrations below show tying steps for a hackle tip winged ant.

Flying ants come in a wide variety of sizes, from tiny ones too small to mimic with a hook, to large specimens measuring twelve mm in length. In the West ants imitated with hooks sized #10–16 are especially common. In the East smaller ants seem to predominate, with #18–24 being most common. Ties in brown and black will stand the angler in good stead for nuptial flights.

Sinking Ants

Just as wet flies as a group developed before dry flies, the wet ant pattern developed before the dry version. Just as there was scant logic for using wet imitations of mayfly duns, there is little rationale for tying wet ant patterns. Ants do not sink. Even after they have perished, the waxy, varnished covering on the outside of the insect prohibits moisture from penetrating and saturating the ant. Those who escape the jaws of trout long enough to drift through tumultuous rapids will bob up in the next pool, their backs still exposed above the surface of the water.

So why fish a wet ant? The only reason I can come up with is that they sometimes catch a lot of trout.

The classic wet ant pattern is constructed by simply wrapping two humps of thread with a waist of wet hackle between them. Lacquer or enamel is then applied to the body knobs to give a hard, shiny finish to the fly.

Another wet fly variation involves the use of thin strips of Mold-Tex to form the body. Bill Charles of Chicago developed this method of making ant bodies, and the procedure is described by him in detail in *The Fly-Tyer's Almanac*. While it's a rather involved operation, the end product is a very attractive wet ant. The soft body on this fly gives the angler a split second longer to set the hook before the trout ejects the fraud.

About the only time I use sinking ant imitations is when fishing freestone streams during the winter, when the water temperature is too cold for trout to come up topside. The sinking ants can be fished effectively in a number of ways, but the natural presentation dictates a dead drift float through productive-looking lies. The patterns are useful in reddish brown, dark brown, and black, with the latter the favorite color. Sizes #10 through #20 are best.

BEES, WASPS, AND SAWFLIES

Of the one hundred thousand-plus species in the order Hymenoptera, the only members whose larvae are consumed regularly by trout are the sawflies. These free-ranging immature forms feed avidly on both conifers and deciduous trees and can be locally important to the fisherman where sawfly infestations are heavy. Their preference for tree foliage makes them especially useful imitations on forested waters.

The larvae are dense and wormlike in form, closely resembling the caterpillar. Due to their heft, imitations of sawfly larvae should be built with a modicum of weight and fished with a sound cast where appropriate. There are several useful methods of obtaining the elongate form of the sawfly larvae. Thin cork cylinders can be used; spun deer hair works; wrapped deer hair is also effective. A single piece of turkey wing quill with a hook glued in also serves as an excellent imitation.

Long shank hooks are useful for mimicking the lanky form of these immature insects while maintaining a high-floating fly. For angling purposes, these imitations are virtually identical to inchworms and certain other caterpillar patterns. For step-by-step illustrations on tying these flies see chapter 7.

Adult sawflies, as well as bees, wasps, and yellow jackets, do occasionally figure in the diet of stream trout. Cutthroats seem particularly fond of these insects, and I have had luck with several imitations on the Yellowstone River. On forested streams in the East, bees, wasps, and yellow jackets can also produce. Fall is an especially propitious time for fishing these patterns, since early frosts often stun these insects and send them stumbling into the stream, especially if the hive happens to be close to the water's edge. Dave Whitlock notes that "wasp and yellow jacket patterns are among the best terrestrials on the White River in Arkansas after frosting begins in October."

It's worth noting, however, that some trout do not care for the taste of bees and wasps. Alfred Ronalds, who wrote in the nineteenth century, did some interesting studies on the feeding habits of trout on the midland streams of England. In a small hut that he built on a walkway over the river was a tube through which Ronalds would drop various land insects and watch the reaction of the trout. Interestingly enough, he found that the trout "does not feed upon the Honey Bee, or Wasp, or Bumble Bee." One trout he watched followed a bumble bee for three feet with its nose almost touching the bee before rejecting the insect. Another trout took the bumble bee after long inspection and then immediately spit it back out!

Charlie Fox has noted a similar reluctance in the browns of the Letort

Imitations of sawfly larvae are essentially the same as caterpillars.

Clipped Deer Hair Bee variations.

when it comes to bees. Says Charlie: "For about ten years I kept a dozen hives of honey bees at my home along the Letort. Some got into the water in one way or another, and the buzzing wings created an interesting disturbance, but I never saw one taken by a trout." Nonetheless, bee imitations have persisted and true to their unpredictable form, trout on other waters take these same insects readily. For imitations of the adults several standard materials prove effective. Bodies can be formed of fur, or deer hair wrapped or spun on the hook. Polypropylene, hackle tips, and deer hair tips form useful wings. Listed below are patterns for a bee and wasp that have proven productive at times. These can be altered with respect to size and color to match particular species prevalent along a stream. By varying the shape and color of the balsa segments, Ed Sutryn's McMurray ant can be fashioned into excellent wasp and bee flies as well.

Deer Hair Bee

Hook: Mustad 94833
Body: Deer hair spun on and clipped to shape of natural (Alternate yellow and black or white and black for yellow jackets and bumble bees.)
Wing: Natural deer hair tips or polypropylene tied in at thorax

Deer Hair Wasp

Wasps are fed upon by trout, especially in the fall when frosts stun the insects and send them tumbling into the river. This deer hair pattern relies on imitating the wasp's silhouette.

1 Attach a Mustad No. 94831 (2X long) dry fly hook in vise (Size #10 shown). Wrap 2/0 thread over last third of hook. Cut a fat bunch of deer hair and remove any loose fuzz or short stray hairs. Hair should measure two and a half times the length of the straight part of the hook shank for wings to turn out the proper length in this pattern.

2 Bind securely to rear third of hook with tight turns of thread. Wind thread forward just short of the mid-point of hook shank.

3 Grasp deer hair extending out from rear of hook and pull forward with right hand to form smooth, tapered knob of hair. This forms the abdomen of the wasp. Bind it down with thread to secure.

4 Continue wrapping thread forward over deer hair to eye of hook. Then wrap thread back to middle of hook.

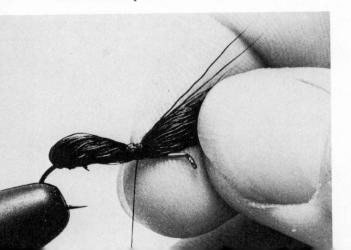

5 With left hand stroke deer hair tips towards rear of hook to form an oval head. Bind with tying thread by making several wraps. This head should be formed by pulling the hair back around the top, sides, and bottom of the hook—not just on top.

6 Divide remaining deer hair tips into two bunches to form wings. Wrap with figure-eight turns of thread to fasten wings flared out to the sides and just slightly rearward. Whip finish in front of wings and trim the excess thread. A light coating of acrylic over the midriff windings finishes the wasp fly.

The ant family, Formicidae, has been divided into as many as nine different subfamilies. Five of these form important groups: the Dorylinae, Ponerinae, Myrmicinae, Formicinae, and Dolichoderinae. The first two subfamilies are primitive ants. They include the infamous legionary carnivorous ants which may at times actually eat birds and small mammals.

The other three ant subfamilies—Myrmicinae, Formicinae, and Dolichoderinae—have evolved to a high level and include the most successful of the ants. The Myrmicinae encompasses many familiar ants, such as the harvesters and fungus-growers. This group includes over half of all ant species in America north of Mexico. The Formicinae are the most advanced of all ants and include the well-known carpenter and honey ants, as well as some slavemakers.

SOME COMMON ANTS

Listed below is a representative sampling of some common ant types that may be found along the trout stream:

LITTLE BLACK ANT (*Monomorium minimum*). This tiny ant is a common household pest, but its usual habitat is outdoors. It measures 1.5–2.0 mm and varies in color from black to dark brown. The ant is quite shiny in appearance and favors sweets and other insects for its food. It inhabits wood and soil, where it leaves small mounds of dirt.

ALLEGHENY MOUND ANT (*Formica exsectoides*). This ant measures 3–6 mm and favors insects and aphid honeydew in its diet. Its range extends throughout the eastern U.S. and Canada, where it is a serious pest of pines, cedars, and spruce. The insect has a fat head, dark brown legs, reddish or black abdomen, and reddish brown head and thorax. The ant makes its home in the ground, and nests may measure up to six feet in diameter and four feet in height. Nests are commonly found at openings in forests.

CORNFIELD ANT OR GARDEN BLACK ANT (*Lasius niger*). Found throughout North America, these brown ants measure 2.0–2.5 mm and eat insects and honeydew. Many aphids are dependent upon these ants to clean them and transport them to the locations where feeding is best. The ants, for their reward, lick secretions from the aphids. Their nests appear as small mounds, and mating flights occur primarily in August and September.

BIG-HEADED ANT (*Pheidole bicarinata vinelandica*). This ant usually runs 1.5–3 mm in length, varying in color from yellowish to dark brown. Its head is larger than both the abdomen and thorax. Its food consists of seeds, insects, honeydew, and picnic leftovers. It nests under stones or in rotting wood and is found as far west as Nebraska.

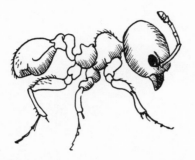

BLACK CARPENTER ANT (*Camponotus pennsylvanicus*). This is one of our largest (6–13 mm) and most common ants. It feeds on sap, other insects, fruit juices, and honeydew. It can be found on a wide range of trees including cherry, poplar, pine, fir, willow, elm, and oak. The ant does not eat the wood, but nests in it. Carpenter ants are found as far west as North Dakota and north into Quebec and Ontario. Mating flights typically occur from May through July. *Pennsylvanicus* is black, but the genus *Camponotus* has many brown species as well.

chapter
five

BEETLES

(Coleoptera)

Tanklike is perhaps the characterization that comes most readily to mind when describing the typical beetle—the order Coleoptera. Homely, slow and plodding; a bit clumsy, but tenacious and efficient over the long run. Durable to the utmost.

But as with any generalization, the analogy between tank and beetle breaks down quickly when one looks closely at the real insects. There are beetles as swift as greased lightning. There are beetles with rare and delicate beauty, such as the tangerine and black ladybugs. And there are beetles that are dexterous and agile, such as the ground beetles that climb sure-footedly up and down tree trunks in quest of succulent caterpillars. Indeed, if there is anything that can be said with sureness of the beetles, it is that they are a motley crew. Perhaps the only comparison with tanks that really holds is the quality of durability.

Not particularly intelligent insects, the beetles have survived in large part due to the tough armorlike plating of their outer wings and their ability to rapidly evolve variations in form and function to fit a changing environment. The Coleoptera have also adapted camouflaged coloration, a high fertility even for insects, and an opportunistic instinct that encourages them to seek out unused cracks and crevices and make them home.

Some 26,500 varieties of beetles are found in North America. Yet in spite of this staggering figure, the beetles are seldom noticed by the average citizen, due in large part to their reclusive life-styles and camouflaged coloration.

LIFE CYCLE

Beetles undergo complete metamorphosis (egg, larva, pupa, adult). Length of the complete life cycle varies immensely. There may be up to ten generations per year in some prolific species. Other beetles may take many years for a single generation to develop. The larvae are called grubs and range from short and pudgy to long and slender in shape. Some are rounded; others have a more flattened appearance. The head is usually well developed. The habits of the larvae vary considerably from family to family. Most often they develop from eggs laid in the ground, rotten logs, or forest debris.

On the whole, beetle larvae are inactive insect forms and spend much of their time under rotten trees and leaf litter or in the ground, and they don't figure as significant trout food very often. Some larvae, however, that are free-ranging and feed in the open on foliage may enter the trout stream. The larvae of the elm leaf beetle (*Phyrrhalta luteola*) is one example.

Seasonal life cycle of the Japanese beetle in the East (courtesy U.S. Dept of Agriculture).

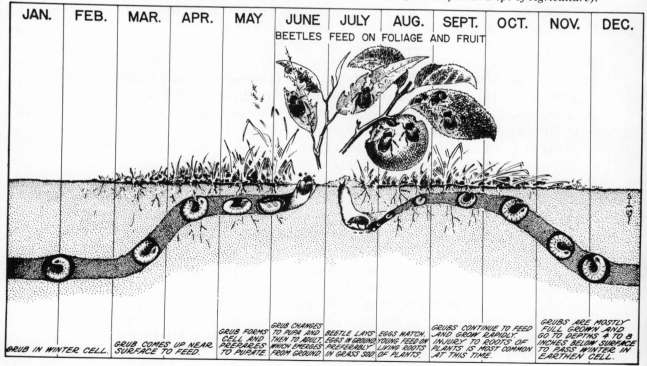

JAN.	FEB.	MAR.	APR.	MAY	JUNE	JULY	AUG.	SEPT.	OCT.	NOV.	DEC.

BEETLES FEED ON FOLIAGE AND FRUIT

GRUB IN WINTER CELL. — GRUB COMES UP NEAR SURFACE TO FEED. — GRUB FORMS CELL AND PREPARES TO PUPATE. — GRUB CHANGES TO PUPA AND THEN TO ADULT, WHICH EMERGES FROM GROUND. — BEETLE LAYS EGGS IN GROUND PREFERABLY IN GRASS SOD. — EGGS HATCH. YOUNG FEED ON LIVING ROOTS OF PLANTS. — GRUBS CONTINUE TO FEED AND GROW RAPIDLY. INJURY TO ROOTS OF PLANTS IS MOST COMMON AT THIS TIME. — GRUBS ARE MOSTLY FULL GROWN AND GO TO DEPTHS 4 TO 8 INCHES BELOW SURFACE TO PASS WINTER IN EARTHEN CELL.

Beetles feed on a wide variety of substances ranging from dung to aphid honeydew.

LIFE-STYLES

The carnivorous beetles are the primitive members of the Coleoptera order and number fewer than their plant-eating relatives. Favored fare includes ants, sucking insects, and larvae of many varieties, especially soft, vulnerable caterpillars. Some beetles are skilled hunters who stalk their prey actively. Others, the scavengers, gather the dead randomly. There are also parasitic species of beetles that live off of a single host insect.

The herbivorous beetles cover all bets. There's scarcely a plant in existence that does not have at least one beetle, and often dozens, that feed upon it. Shrubs, grasses, deciduous and coniferous trees, flowers, and weeds are all part of the beetles' grazing range. Some feed under the bark; others venture out boldly to chew on the tender leaves; some subterranean recluses munch on the roots; a few eat the wood of the tree trunk; still others consume the fruits and seeds. Needless to say, there are many beetles on the farmer's Most Wanted list—preferably dead.

Since most beetles do not travel large distances, the key to their habitat is the location of their food supplies. One species or another of beetle may be found just about anywhere along a trout stream. Streams with leaf litter, partially decayed logs, or brushy plant growth along shore are excellent locations to cast beetle imitations. Mature forests harbor many woodland species, and sandy soil areas along streams are particularly attractive to the tiger beetles.

Though some beetles that overwinter as adults may venture out boldly on bright, sunny days in December or January, fishing with beetle imitations generally begins in late March in southern streams; April and early May in the Northeast; late May or June in the West. During early spring days minute beetle forms are common on many trout streams. Peak beetle fishing extends from May through October in most areas, though some cold-resilient species will remain active into November and provide excellent fishing for bright-fleshed autumn trout.

Beetle species exhibit wide diversity in their daily activity schedules, as well. Temperatures and light are two vital factors influencing activity, though humidity, barometric pressure, and wind can also stimulate or inhibit movement. However, different species react in divergent ways to these environmental changes.

Japanese beetles, for instance, reach a peak of busyness in midafternoon. Tiger beetles are diurnal, and a tiny cloud blotting out the sun's rays can send them scurrying for cover. June bugs begin their food-gathering activities just before dusk. Most large ground beetles are active at night, and dispersal flights under the cover of darkness are common in this order. So it's apparent that there is no general rule as to when beetles may prove productive flies. Various imitations may be useful virtually any hour of the day or night.

In addition to being active over a broad time range, beetles show a number of other habits that almost seem designed to grow fat trout. Most blatant of these is the knack of purposefully dropping from their perch when something moves near them. This is a reflexive action also displayed by some of the true bugs (Hemiptera). Click and leaf beetles are the most notable members of the Coleoptera to display this behavior. And for beetles living along streams, it is often a fatal maneuver.

The inherent clumsiness that typifies most beetles also makes them likely candidates to fall into the trout stream. They often stumble like barroom drunks, tumbling about awkwardly over stones and twigs on the ground.

Flight is even more difficult. Aerial crashes are routine. The common June bugs which thump loudly into screen doors on warm spring evenings are familiar examples. (These heavy scarab beetles must literally pump air into internal sacs before they can even attempt to fly.) So difficult is the

The hard wingcovers of beetles (elytra) meet in a straight line down the back. They protect the thin hindwings of the insect, as well as the internal organs.

When tying imitations of thin beetles with prominent legs, such as this long-horned beetle (Cerambycidae), it's best to include these appendages in the fly pattern.

process of carrying their cumbersome bodies through the air that most beetles attempt flight only as a last resort. It may take a beetle several seconds to prepare for flight as it raises its elytra, slowly unravels his folded wings, and takes off. Once airborne, beetles nonchalantly bump into trees and bushes, stall in midflight, and often land short of their apparent destination. Frequently this means right in the middle of a trout stream. It's particularly common to see such crashes in the morning, when beetles attempt the first flight of the day. Apparently they are still stiff from their slumbers, and their metabolism has not risen sufficiently to carry them through the flight.

Suffice it to say that with their bulk, clumsiness, and abundance the beetles vie with the ants as the top terrestrial food items on the typical trout stream on a season-long basis. And so the beetle patterns account for at least as many fish taken as the famous ant dries. And in terms of size, beetles will draw even more large trout than the ubiquitous ant.

STRUCTURE AND FLY DESIGN

Beetles show remarkable variation in size, form, and color, the most common colors being black, brown, red, and yellow. Some species, however, feature bright metallic greens and blues. Others sport gaudy geometric patterns evolved to frighten or repel predators. Unfortunately for the fly fishers with poor eyesight among us, most beetles are dark in color, making them difficult to see on the water. (One trick that has proven valuable when fishing black beetles and other dark patterns is to position yourself so that you are looking *into* the brightest glare on the water. The black fly will stand out starkly against this shimmering background.)

In spite of the great variation in size, color, and form, most beetles are easily recognized by the amateur angler-entomologist. The distinguishing feature of beetle species is the structure of their wings, which are comprised of two separate pairs. The forewings (called elytra by entomologists) form tough, horny covers for the delicate, thin-membrane hindwings folded beneath them. The thin underwings perform the flying functions.

From the fly dresser's point of view, the beetle's body is the most important structural feature. It is this which determines more often than not the effectiveness of the imitation. The opaqueness of the beetle, its size, the shape of head, thorax, and abdomen, and the general color of the insect should be duplicated as precisely as possible when casting over discriminating trout. Since most beetles float low in the surface film, they provide trout with a clear view of their body shape and color.

But, since wings are folded flat over the back of the insect, they are rarely visible to trout. With few exceptions, the beetles do not spread either pair of wings prominently when they are on the water. Legs, on the other hand, do occasionally sprawl akimbo as the insect attempts to free itself from the stream, and when fishing in quiet water over fussy trout, these appendages can sometimes be important features in beetle imitations. At other times legless patterns seem to score just as well. Both size of beetle being imitated and the prominence of legs on the natural should be borne in mind when deciding whether to include these appendages in the artificial.

Often the noisy manner in which beetles enter the stream and the frenzy this appearance evokes in trout tends to override the fish's customary caution. Trout frequently charge beetles and seem to key more attention on general body shape and color than minute anatomical details.

FISHING THE BEETLES

"You're having entirely too much fun," the silver-haired angler on Barnhart's called out accusatively as I set the hook in what appeared to be yet another trout taken over a short period that morning.

"No, this one's just a chub," came my sheepish reply as I worked in the heavy-scaled fish.

It was a morning for beetles on the Beaverkill. Even the chubs were taking them in greedily. Wind whipped harshly out of the northwest, buffeting low-hanging cumulus clouds across the June skies. Casting was a chore, and many times it was necessary to stop fishing and wait for a lee in the gale to shoot the fly out.

Proof positive that trout like beetles—in a wide variety of size and shapes: These six beetles were extracted from the stomach of a small brown trout.

But the wind also carried a bounty from shore for the heavy browns residing at the tail of Barnhart's Pool—chunky scarab and leaf beetles, true bugs, and small ants were swept from the oak, maple, birch, and weeds edging the river. Even as I waded cautiously into the shallow tailwater, a small brown beetle (a chrysomelid) plopped clumsily onto the surface. It kicked vainly, struggling to open its wings. Then a sharp boil broke the surface and the beetle vanished.

A pair of canvasbacks soared with a swish of wings overhead and landed halfway up the long, fertile pool as I nervously tied a deer hair beetle to the thin tippet. A Beaverkill regular had regaled me the day before with tales of huge trout lurking in the final few hundred feet of this enormous pool, and now I finally found the attractive stretch of water vacant and beckoning.

A brief patch of sunlight streamed through the clouds. I scanned the water sharply and spied the trout that had made the rise moments earlier. It was a large brown finning quietly in water barely a foot deep. Hunchbacked, I cast low and sideways, punching the line through the breeze and dropping the fly with a hard splat next to the fish. Darting sideways, it grabbed the fly. I set the hook solidly, and the trout responded with a sullen, head-thrashing fight at close quarters. Seventeen inches and thick across the back, it was a handsome brownie.

Other bright brown trout came hard for the beetles dropped with a "plunk" to the side or slightly behind their holding lies. In the shallow, crystalline water their every movement was clear—making for a visually stimulating angling experience. The trout fought tight, bulldog battles, seemingly reluctant to leave their cherished positions at the tail of this classic pool. Only two of the fish, a pair of sixteen-inchers, ran hard against the drag. The others slugged it out close in, giving up every inch grudgingly.

The tails of pools such as Barnhart's can provide exceptional fishing with terrestrials, especially since they are often neglected by the average fisherman who thinks the only good places to fish are the riffles, heads of pools, and deep midsections. Others are intimidated by the difficulty of fishing shallow tailwater.

To be sure, the water in these locations often mingles conflicting crosscurrents, and the stepped-up tempo of the flow as it approaches rapids can present problems with drag. Water may be very shallow at the tails of pools, and the fish, which are usually wise and large, can be both skittish and finicky. But the dedicated angler sees this as an engaging challenge and resorts to such tactics as slack casts, across or downstream deliveries, and the sound cast to fool these oft-exceptional fish. And if he is smart, he'll have a beetle on the end of the leader.

Trout in these positions seem to harbor a special affection for beetles, especially when the fly is plopped down with a sound cast. If your first efforts do not succeed, try delivering the fly in various other positions near the trout—to the side, on his head, in back of him, etc.—and experiment with different beetle weights, sizes, and colors. These fish can be quite meticulous in their preferences.

Tails of pools are excellent places to cast beetles to, but they are by no means the only spots along the stream that will produce. Among the best locations are breaks in the flow: Eddies, logjams, rocks, backwaters, sloughs out of the main current, and slow-moving shoreline waters are particularly good choices. In short, relatively still water is a fine place to pitch larger flies. Here the trout is a hunter and often cruises for his meals like a bonefish on the flats. It will investigate any likely noise that may signal a floundering victim. For fishing these waters the dense beetle patterns are preferable because sound can function as your most important element of appeal to the fish.

There is another type of beetle fishing, however. It involves the use of the lighter, "quiet" beetle patterns—flies tied with clipped hackle and various styles of flat wings over the top. This sport more closely approaches mayfly fishing or fishing with the ants. The fly is cast well ahead of the quarry and floated quietly down over it. These flies are usually smaller than the dense patterns and are particularly deadly when fish are actively working the surface—whether they're feeding on beetles or not.

These silent beetle patterns are best where there is sufficient current to carry them down over the trout's position, since there is little sound involved when they touch the surface and fish cannot be "brought to the fly" as they can with heavier offerings. These flies are especially choice offerings on the difficult spring creeks such as Henry's Fork of the Snake, Silver Creek, and the Letort.

Beetles come in virtually every shade of the rainbow, and black, brown, gray, and green have proven useful over the course of a season. Black is generally considered tops by most experienced terrestrial fishermen, but if a specific beetle is prevalent in the shoreline habitat, it's best to match the natural as closely as possible in size, shape, and color.

Even if you do not see many naturals about, don't rule out beetle imitations. The majority of beetles are reclusive insects, and those that venture out in the open are often so well camouflaged that they are impossible to see. They do not force themselves to our attention. And even when the beetles do not seem particularly abundant, some still manage to find their way into the water. Those that do almost without exception are eaten by trout. The trout rarely are able to feed exclusively on beetles, but they must taste good as they sure get eaten when they're available.

The earliest beetle patterns devised by English anglers were fished as wet flies. Ronalds catalogs several such imitations in his *Fly-fisher's Entomology*, including the peacock fly, which he recommended for imitating a small beetle that was abundant on warm, sunny days in spring. The Marlow buzz (hazel fly, shorn fly) was another frequently used beetle imitation. This fly Ronalds used to ape a beetle that appeared on poplar leaves in June. The body of the fly was made of black ostrich herl twisted with peacock herl. Wings and legs were represented with a furnace cock's hackle. Also endorsed in *The Fly-fisher's Entomology* were red beetles and ladybird beetles. Of the ladybird, Ronalds remarks: "a famous fly for both Trout and Grayling, and may be used till the end of September."

PATTERNS

Modern attempts at imitating beetles have concentrated on the insect as a surface food. Like so many other pioneer developments in dry fly fishing, the wellspring for beetle patterns was the Letort and the creative efforts of Charlie Fox and Vince Marinaro. The ubiquitous Japanese beetle was the impetus for their first experiments, and first report of the beetle's potential as a dry fly was contained in a February 1944 article in the *Pennsylvania Angler* by Charlie Fox. Fox's first patterns consisted of coffee beans which were slit and attached to a used hook with part of the old fly body remaining. The fly took fish on many streams but proved too fragile for extended use.

The trout of the Letort were particularly finicky about their beetle feeding. Marinaro's eventual solution to the problem of providing a delicate fly that gave the image of a large, robust body was a stroke of genius. Instead of fashioning the fly from solid materials, he used a palmered hackle clipped flat with a junglecock eye tied flat over the top of the hook to give an illusion of depth and solidity. Marinaro theorized that a trout cannot judge the thickness or depth of a terrestrial insect but only its width and length; that is, its silhouette. The result was a large, opaque fly that remains light and easy to cast. The flat overwing gives a solid background to the palmered hackle, and thus the bulk of the insect is represented without any excess weight.

This basic design has proven highly effective over ensuing years and still serves well to imitate leafhoppers and small true bugs, as well as beetles. When the importation of junglecock was outlawed some years ago, fly tiers devised a number of acceptable and sometimes superior substitutes for the fragile eyes required in the original pattern. The basic design of the fly, however, has remained the same.

While the bulk and opaqueness of beetles is well represented in this approach to beetle fly designs, there is one aspect of the natural it does not account for: the heft and density of beetles, particularly the larger specimens. This, as we've seen, can prove of major importance in the feeding of trout. Indeed, the heft which Marinaro attempted to circumvent has been emphasized in some patterns for use with the sound cast. Being able to slap a beetle loudly to the surface can be an important tactical advantage, and flies tied specifically for this type of fishing represent a quite different solution to the beetle pattern dilemma. Bulk and density have been purposefully incorporated into the patterns to appeal to the trout's sense of hearing. Solid materials such as cork, spun deer hair, and wrapped deer hair have been utilized in creating these "heavy" flies. These flies also float low and flush in the surface film, exactly as the natural insects do: The bellies ride below the surface, the back of the pattern above the water.

With some exceptions this second approach to beetle fly designs has proven preferable for imitating the big Coleoptera—sizes #18 and larger. The clipped-hackle, flat-wing method is best suited to the smaller flies—#16 and down. Both solutions are valid, and both styles are well worth carrying in the fly box. My experience includes many situations where one weight of beetle fly and fishing method drew a complete blank while the other made the day's fishing. And often it is the exact opposite combination of beetle pattern and fishing method that one would expect. Eighteen- and twenty-inch rainbows have ignored big beetles plopped enticingly next to them only to sip in a #22 palmered-hackle beetle moments later. And I have seen tiny mountain brook trout ignore seemingly appropriate #18s and #20s and then slam into #10 Crowe beetles.

Even during low, transparent water conditions big beetles slapped onto the surface may draw charging strikes, while the tiny Coleoptera fail to produce. Tom Baltz and I ran into just such a situation on Clark's Creek north of Harrisburg several summers ago.

The stream was virtually dried up that August day, and trout darted nervously through the thin pools as we approached the stream. The situation dictated light lines and fine leaders. Both of us agreed that tiny flies were the order of the day as we slipped along the stream and separated for the morning. I dutifully offered pinhead cinnamon ants, tiny deer hair beetles, flat-wing beetles, and jassids to the fish: None produced. Tom was having the same luck. When we met and compared notes, the only fly that had taken trout consistently turned out to be a #12 deer hair beetle dropped to the surface with an audible splat—precisely the opposite of what we thought should have turned the trick.

Crowe Beetle

John Crowe's simple tie, the Crowe Beetle, has proven one of the most potent terrestrial patterns in existence, particularly for large eastern browns. Described in his book, *The Modern ABC's of Freshwater Fishing*, Crowe's pattern is a classic example of the dense terrestrial imitation that allows an audible presentation to draw trout to the fly. However, it is a quite flexible tie, and many fly dressers produce these imitations in sizes #20 and smaller for a quiet, traditional presentation. They work this way too.

The method Crowe uses to tie these flies is also rather flexible. By varying the amount of deer hair used in tying the fly, the hook size, the position at which the hair is attached to the hook, and the final trimming of the excess hair, a wide variety of beetle forms can be represented to match the family most prevalent along a given stretch of water.

For instance, when Japanese beetles or other large, rotund insects are on the water, I tie this fly with a large amount of deer hair fastened farther up toward the eye of the hook than normal. This gives a very fat beetle form. No legs are included, since the broad shape of the naturals generally obscures the trout's view of these appendages. The head is clipped short and results in a squat, heavy scarab beetle. For longhorn or rove beetles, the fly can be constructed with a smaller amount of deer hair and a 2X long shank hook to give a more elongate beetle form. The legs, which stand out so prominently on these lean beetles, can also be included.

The major drawback of this fly is its fragility. Depending on how the trout take the beetles, anywhere from one to six fish might be taken on a single fly before it loses shape. However, the ease of constructing the Crowe Beetle largely overrides this drawback. Even an average tier can dress a dozen of these beetles in an hour.

Thread and deer hair are the only materials needed. It's best to use a fairly heavy thread when tying this fly (say 2/0) for a tight, compact assembly and increased durability. Black is the overwhelming favorite color, but brown, green, gray, and rust also produce at times. Sizes #8 through #22 are practical; #10 through #16s are utilized most often.

1 Attach a dry fly hook in vise and spiral on tying thread to the mid-shank; use 2/0 thread for this fly. Cut a bunch of deer hair to form the fly. For a chunky fly of size #10 or #12, this should be a bunch close to the thickness of a pencil. Pull out any excess fuzz or short hairs.

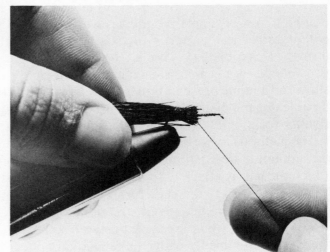

2 Bind the hair tightly on the hook. You can attach the hair further up towards the eye of the hook and sort out three or four strands on each side of hook. Wrap thread so that these flare out to the sides.

3 Here is the hair bound to the rear of the hook; now wrap the thread forward almost to the eye.

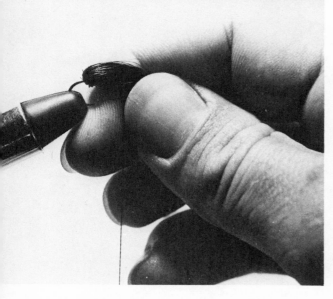

4 With your left hand, grasp the hair and pull it forward, making sure a smooth, even body is formed.

5 Make two wraps of thread loosely around the hair, just behind the eye. Slowly pull it tight, flaring the hair in front of the eye. Take several more tight turns of the thread.

6 Whip finish and trim head of fly to form oval knob. Apply head cement or liquid acrylic to thread wrappings and beetle is complete.

Crowe Beetle variations.

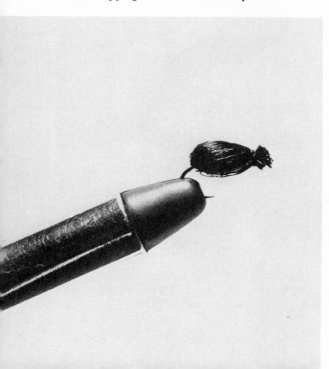

Cork Beetle

The benefits of cork as a tying material were treated in the chapter on ants (see page 108). For tying beetles, cork can be especially useful because it lends to even the smaller patterns a density and heft that can draw the attention of recalcitrant trout to the fly. Cork makes a durable imitation that roll casts well and floats precisely like most beetles do—breaking through the surface film on the bottom, protruding out of the water on the top. Cork can also be carved to represent any of the many variations in beetle form and painted to match exactly the markings of the naturals.

I especially favor cork where shoreline trees prohibit backcasting to dry the fly in the traditional manner. It is also a good material where trout are shy and want small beetles, yet show an inkling for a fly that makes a tiny splat when it enters the water. Here #16, #18, and #20 Cork Beetles shine.

Usually the sharp, clear silhouette of the beetle body carved out of cork is enough to fool trout. However, legs can be installed in these flies by using a needle to thread either rubber hackle, feather barbules, or actual thread through the cork. Limbs should be kept short.

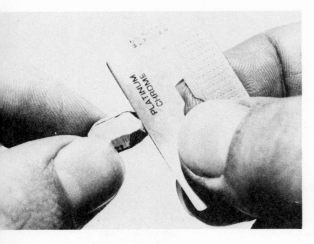

1 Cut a piece of cork to the approximate size and shape desired for a natural beetle. The bottom of the beetle should be flat.

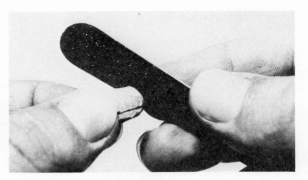

2 Sand the cork body to smooth, final shape with an emery board.

3 Cut a slit or a very thin wedge down length of the bottom; do not cut further than halfway through the body with the razor blade.

4 Apply epoxy in the groove and force an appropriate-size dry fly hook tightly into the slit; if necessary, apply more epoxy to give a smooth bottom finish. At this stage the fly can be placed in vise and thread wrapped around body for extra durability, if you choose. Paint the beetle body.

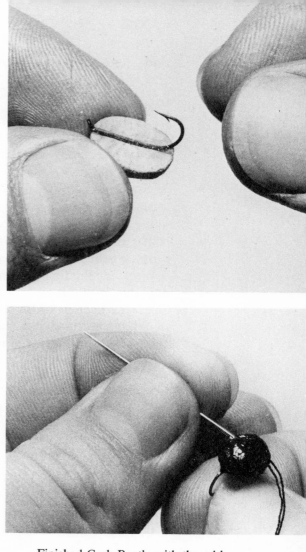

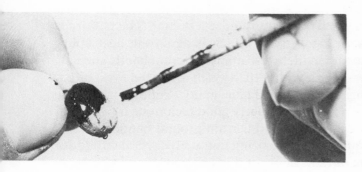

5 If legs are desired, take needle and appropriate sized thread and insert through body, just above hook shank. Repeat and trim legs to desired length. These legs can be lacquered, if you prefer.

6 Finished Cork Beetle with thread legs.

Some Cork Beetle variations.

Clipped Hair Beetle

This pattern deserves a position midway between the dense, heavy beetles and the light, clipped-hackle beetles, for it is neither light nor heavy and can be effective when floated daintily over rising fish, as well as delivered with a light plop onto the surface.

Some very choosy fish have fallen for this fly, and it is a particular favorite because it floats high and dry and does not require a flotant. The pattern is quite durable, lasting through many trout. Black is again the best color, since this shade matches the undersides of so many different beetle species. Sizes #6 through #20 are practical, with #10 through #16 used most often. By varying the final trimming of the clipped hair, many beetle forms can be imitated with this style of tie. It is a particularly good technique for simulating large beetles such as the June bug and certain ground beetles.

When naturals with prominent legs are being imitated, several strands of deer hair can be left sticking out the sides, or duck or goose quill fibers can be tied in to represent these appendages.

1 Attach 2/0 thread to rear of dry fly hook. Select small bunch of deer hair. (Optionally, you can trim the tips of this hair.)

2 Hold hair over top of hook shank and wrap thread over middle of hair with two loose turns. Slowly tighten thread and release left hand at same time. Hair should flare and spin partially around the hook. Work thread through spun hair and take two turns in front of hair.

3 Fly should now appear like this. Select another batch of hair and repeat operation immediately in front of hair already spun on hook.

4 As you continue to spin on bunches of hair, push them tightly together with fingernail and thumbnail of each hand.

5 Work up to eye of hook, hold hair out of way with left hand and whip finish.

6 Remove fly from vise and trim with scissors. Trim a flat bottom first and be sure to leave enough bite to hook trout surely. Trim the sides, top, rear, and front to natural beetle shape. Optionally, you may sort out three or four strands of hair on each side of hook to form legs.

7 Apply drop of cement or acrylic to head wrappings and the Clipped Deer Hair Beetle is complete.

Wonderwing Beetle

Clear skies and a bright June sun had lured me from the cabin near Woodstock; but as I rolled north on U.S. 522 through West Virginia and Maryland to the Pennsylvania state line, clouds were gathering conspiratorially over the mountains.

The hills rise sharply above Everett, Pennsylvania. Black and white cattle graze precariously on the steep slopes. There are ruffed grouse in the woods, and English setters loafing outside their houses is a common sight along Route 26. Yellow Creek flows through the region, and it is a rich, alkaline stream. The headwaters are narrow and flat and bordered with meadows; two dams trap loose, drifting sediment. In the fly area below, the gradient picks up and the stream shoots through rocky, forested terrain. Natural reproduction is limited, and large holdover trout are taken each year from the Yellow.

As I climbed from the truck, raindrops began speckling the asphalt road. Swallows swooped over the streamside meadows, snatching up the terrestrial insects flitting about. As I rigged my tackle, I noticed a brownish green leaf beetle with orange head crawling across the edge of an elm leaf nearby. Taking the hint, I tied a clipped-hackle beetle to the tippet.

"You got a camera?" a local angler queried as we met on the narrow trail through the woods. "Watch out for turkeys. There's a bunch of 'em in here."

"And the trout?" I countered.

"Not much," he complained. "I got two little ones in five hours.

"There's big ones in here, though," he added, parting on an optimistic note.

A rise dimpled the water midway across a small pool upstream. I flicked the beetle out gently, and it floated softly over the trout's lie. He took swift and clean and cut tight circles through the milky green water before succumbing to the pressure of the rod. The fish was a hefty twelve-inch brown, and I sacrificed it to provide dinner and to examine his stomach. I rapped the trout on the head and slit his belly; pulling the V-tab beneath his jaw, the entrails and gill structure came out complete. I dissected the bulging stomach and there was one recognizable mayfly in him—*Ephemerella dorothea*, the delicate sulphur. There was one stonefly nymph, one black ant, and there were *six* varieties of beetles! Green, brown, and black; rotund, angular, and cylindrical forms were represented. Most were of the family Chrysomelidae, the leaf beetles, though scarabs were also there. The naturals could be imitated with hooks from #14 through #22, but most were small, averaging 5 or 6 mm.

I stuck with the #18 brown beetle and took two more stocked trout in the next pool. But later I switched to a black imitation, and the action seemed to quicken. A bright native with red adipose fins was among the trout that took this fly. Fighting strongly in the glide, it leaped clear of the surface the instant I struck. For several more hours the trout continued to sip in the quiet beetle imitations as I worked up the stream—brightening the sullen mood of a cloud-dampened day. The pattern that scored on those Yellow Creek trout was one of several successful alternatives to the junglecock that was originally employed in the clipped-hackle beetle fly tiers have devised. This particular imitation used the so-called "Wonderwing" tied in over a clipped-hackle body. This wing is formed by stroking the barbules of a feather in reverse direction and then attaching it to the hook backwards.

This novel wing was discovered by a Mr. Golden over two and a half decades ago. Golden prescribed them for use as the upwings of mayflies. However, they are especially useful in tying the flat wings of terrestrial patterns such as true bugs, leafhoppers, and beetles. Several types of feathers can be used for this purpose, including large webby rooster hackles, duck breast feathers, and the small feathers present at the base of a duck's flight feathers. These beetle patterns are easy to tie, and the finished wing has an attractive, veined appearance.

1 Attach dry fly hook in vise and wrap on tying thread. Select a hackle with barbules one and a half times the length of hook gap and attach at rear of shank. Dub on rabbit fur for the body.

2 Wrap fur forward to form a plump, oval body. Stop far enough back from eye of hook to leave room for wing.

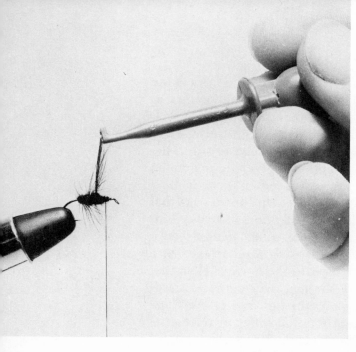

3 Wrap hackle forward over fur body and tie off.

4 Clip away hackle on top of fly to make room for wing. Select a feather for the wing. A large webby rooster hackle is shown, though duck breast feathers and other types can also be used.

5 Grasp tip of feather with left hand and stroke barbules in opposite direction with right hand. Photo shows how the wing should look when you're ready to tie it in.

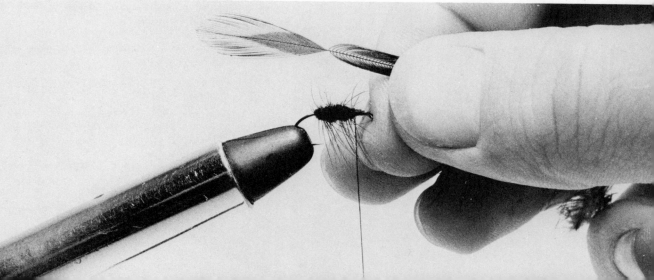

6 Hold wing flat over beetle body with right hand and take several turns of thread over the wonderwing, just behind eye of hook.

7 Clip excess hackle in front of eye of hook. Also trim hackle tip extending beyond the end of the wonderwing, being careful not to cut into the wing fibers.

8 Take several more turns of thread at eye of hook and whip finish. Trim a V-wedge from the bottom hackle so fly floats low and flush in the surface film. A touch of cement on the head completes the Wonderwing Beetle.

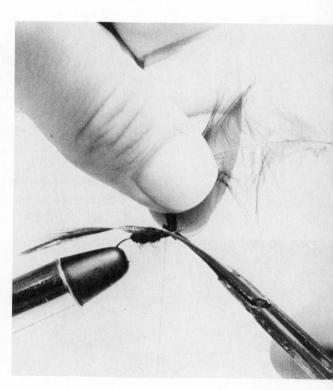

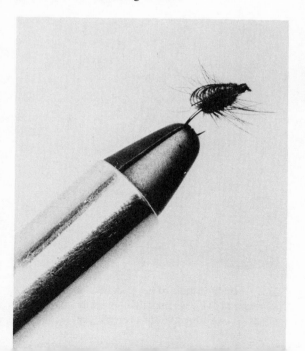

Feather-Wing Beetle

The same feathers used for the wonderwing can be employed in a more traditional fashion by lacquering two of them together, trimming, and tying in flat over the palmered hackle as a single wing. Mallard feathers work well for this type of beetle pattern, but so do certain wing and body feathers from the ruffed grouse. The dark greenish throat feathers from a ringneck pheasant that Ernie Schwiebert recommended in his *Remembrances of Rivers Past* are also very good.

My Beetle

Dave Engerbretson, Rocky Mountain Field Editor for *Fly Fisherman* magazine, developed some ten years ago an original variation of the clipped-hackle beetle tie that he calls simply "My Beetle." The pattern employs either duck or goose quill segments tied in at the rear of the hook and drawn forward over trimmed hackle to represent the wing and body of the beetle.

Dave says, "Whenever I find that I can't match the hatch, I don't know what the trout are taking, or they're not taking what I think they should, my 'Ace-in-the Hole' fly is a black beetle on a #16–24 hook. It's amazing how often the fly brings results. I guess I've probably caught more big fish on the Henry's Fork on my beetle than on everything else combined! And I've used the same pattern other places here in the West, in the East, and the mid-West. It's super!"

Dave adds that this pattern is "also good in brown, using a mottled turkey quill. I've even made some cute little lady bugs with an orange quill and a couple of black paint spots."

1 Attach dry fly hook in vise and bind on tying thread. Select a section of black wing quill (dyed goose or duck). This will form the overwing.

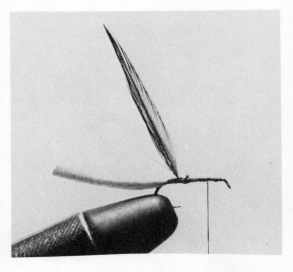

2 Attach to rear of hook shank, just forward of bend in hook; then tie in black hackle one and a half to two times width of hook gap.

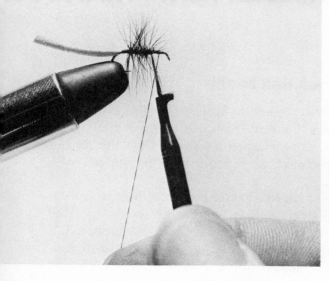

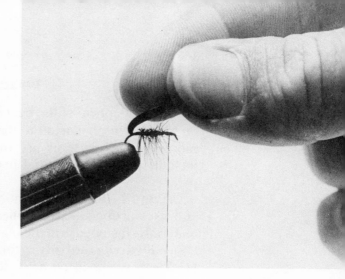

3 Wind hackle forward palmer-style, tie off small distance back from eye of hook and trim away excess hackle tip.

4 Clip hackle short on top and slightly longer on bottom. Sides should be left long to represent the legs. Pull quill section forward.

5 Lash quill section down behind eye of hook with thread. Take several turns to secure tightly and trim excess quill. Next, whip finish fly and clip away excess thread. Add drop of cement or acrylic to windings.

6 Clip away all but two of the projecting quill fibers. These two will form the antennae.

7 Finished version of Dave Engerbretson's "My Beetle".

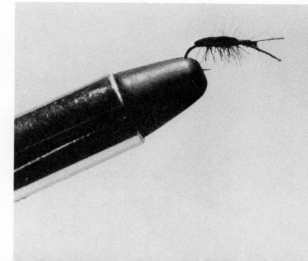

Peacock Herl Beetle

The great appeal of the beetles described so far is their lightness and the fact they rely on illusion to make the trout think it is taking a thick, juicy morsel. Other patterns use the same clipped hackle to float the fly but include a more substantial body, such as peacock herl, fur, or polypropylene.

Clayton L. Peters of Pennsylvania ties beetle bodies of polypropylene and uses artificial raffia pulled over the top to form an overwing. This material is fastened in at the rear of the hook before the body is wrapped. It's then pulled over the body to form an overwing and lashed down with thread. Hackle is wrapped on next, then clipped top and bottom. The synthetic raffia is next pulled forward again to form the thorax.

One variation on this theme uses peacock herl to form a body, with either a duck quill or artificial raffia tied in at the rear of the fly and pulled over the body to form the wings. Flies tied in this manner are offered by several mail-order fly tackle houses.

1 Attach a dry fly hook in the vise and wind on tying thread. Cut a section of artificial raffia to form the overwing; avoid trying to use too wide of a piece. (A section of mallard wing quill can be substituted for the artificial raffia in this pattern.)

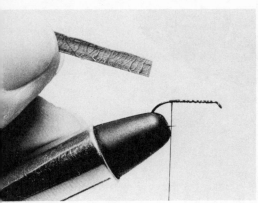

2 Bind a piece of raffia to the rear of the hook. Select two or three strands of peacock herl to form the body of the fly and bind on with thread immediately in front of raffia.

3 Attach a dry fly quality hackle in front of herl. Barbules should be one and a half to two times as long as gap of hook.

4 Grasp ends of peacock herl and wind forward to a point slightly behind the eye of the hook. Tie off tightly here.

5 Next wind hackle forward and tie off at same place.

6 Clip excess hackle tip and trim hackle on top of fly flat, and pull the raffia forward to form overwing of beetle pattern. Bind tightly with thread and trim away the excess.

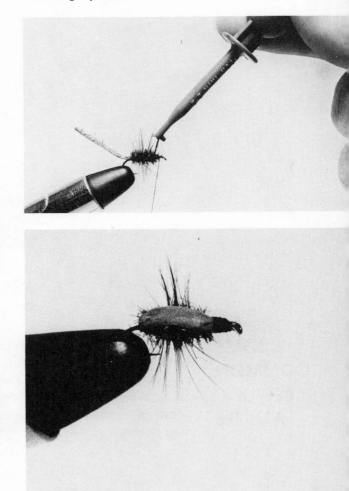

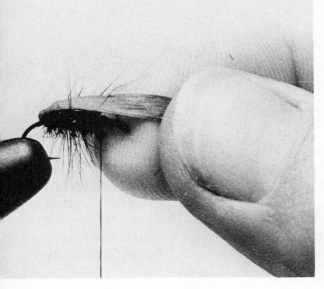

7 Whip finish, apply drop of cement and trim hackle flat on bottom of fly. Completed Peacock Herl Beetle.

The Fur Beetle

For some small beetles I occasionally use a simple pattern of fur and hackle. To construct this fly, tie in a hackle at the rear of a small dry fly hook. Next spin fur on the thread and wrap on an oval body. Palmer the hackle over the body and tie it off at the front of the hook. Trim the hackle on the sides so that it equals the width of the body. Then clip it flat on top and bottom to make a compact, flush-floating beetle that works especially well in #24 and #26.

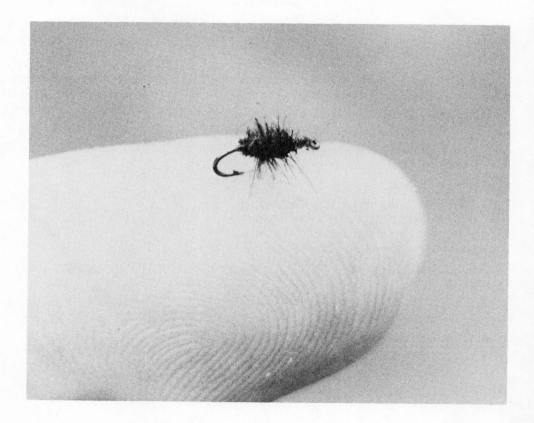

SOME COMMON BEETLE FAMILIES

The Coleoptera order is divided into two major suborders: Adephaga and Polyphaga. The Adephaga are carnivorous as a general rule and contain only two families of interest to the trout fisherman. These are the ground and tiger beetles. The Polyphaga suborder encompasses eight families of special concern to the fly angler. Brief descriptions of these ten families are listed below.

GROUND BEETLES (Carabidae). The ground beetles constitute a large, well-distributed family with over two thousand five hundred species occurring in North America and twenty thousand worldwide. Mostly night-roamers, some are fierce warriors, consuming many caterpillars, slugs, snails, and harmful insects. Their habitat includes fields, pastures, and forests, and they can be found under leaves and stones as well as out in the open. Adult ground beetles may live over three years and vary widely in size, from 3–34 mm. Most are dark and shiny; some are iridescent shades of blue, green, or brown.

TIGER BEETLES (Cicindelidae). As their name implies, these are hunting beetles. They feed heavily on insects of all sorts. They are diurnal and prefer bright, sunlit days. Clouds will immediately slow down their activity. Some are gregarious, others solitary. Adults live two or three years. They are graceful-looking beetles and often feature beautiful colors. Tiger beetles measure 11–18 mm. Favored habitat includes sandy areas, woodland trails, shores of lakes and streams, rotten logs and trees.

ROVE BEETLES (Staphylinidae). This is another large family containing some twenty-six thousand species worldwide, three thousand eight hundred in North America. They can be identified by their short wing covers (elytra), which only partially cover the abdomen, and by their elongate shape. They range in size from 10 to 21 mm and black, yellow, and brown are common colors. The beetles are widely distributed, and many are active predators that can run quite fast. They are found near decaying animal and plant matter and under stones and logs.

DARKLING BEETLES (Tenebrionidae). This family includes over 1,300 species throughout the U.S., though they are found mainly in the West. They vary widely in size, from 2.5 to 22 mm, and are generally slow in motion and a bit clumsy. Brown, gray, and black are typical colors. Mainly nocturnal, they prefer dry, warm areas and are found in fields and forests.

SCARABS (Scarabaeidae). The scarabs constitute a very important beetle group from the fly fisher's standpoint. Over thirty thousand species have been described worldwide, one thousand four hundred in the U.S. Many of these insects are good fliers and often sport bright colors.

Included in this family is the very common May beetle genus (*Phyllophaga*), with over one hundred species in North America alone. The adults feed on leaves of trees such as elm, hickory, oak, beech, maple, birch, poplar, willow, walnut, pine, and locust. They are common from April through July, especially in the north-central states.

The June bug (*Phyllophaga drakei*) is properly included in the May beetle genus, strangely enough. This common brown beetle is fed on heavily by trout wherever it is found. On tiny native brook trout streams in the

Shenandoah National Park I've found eight- and nine-inch brookies gorging on these huge beetles; and thousands of miles west Dave Whitlock reports that "rainbow trout on the White River system in Arkansas feed heavily at night from May through July on several large species of beetles such as June bugs."

The well-known Japanese beetle (*Popillia japonica*) is also included in this family. This copper and green beetle causes serious agricultural damage but is a very important source of food for trout on many eastern streams during summer months. In the summer of 1977 the Associated Press reported that state inspectors in California had captured three hundred fifty Japanese beetles that rode on the outside of airplanes traveling from the East. Damaging infestations are expected in years to come since all the stowaways were not apprehended.

LONG-HORNED BEETLES (Cerambycidae). This is another very large family with one thousand four hundred species in North America, twenty thousand worldwide. On the whole they are large beetles, some measuring up to 50 mm. They have a distinctive oblong, nearly cylindrical form, and the antennae are sometimes longer than the bodies. Adults feed on pollen, flowers, bark, leaves, and wood. They are swift runners and good fliers. Larvae, which develop from eggs laid in the solid parts of wood or beneath bark, are destructive, feeding on live and dead trees, as well as shrubs. Brown is the most common color, though patterns of stripes and blotches are often present.

WEEVILS (Curculionidae). Weevils constitute the single largest family of insects in the animal kingdom with some forty thousand described species, two thousand in America north of Mexico. The adults and larvae vary widely in shape, often featuring a dense covering of scales. The weevils receive their common name "snout beetles" from a prolonged head that forms a snout. Many species actually live inside plant tissues. The weevils measure 2–12 mm and are often black or brown in color.

LEAF BEETLES (Chrysomelidae). The leaf beetles represent another prominent family. Over twenty thousand species are known, one thousand four hundred occurring in North America. Leaf beetles are frequently consumed by trout from spring through fall. They are slow moving, active in the day, and leave holes bitten all the way through leaves they feed on. Some larvae are free-ranging and also feed on leaves. Adults come in many colors, including yellow, green, brown, and black. They can be found virtually anywhere plants grow. Typically they are oval and squat in form and measure from 1.5 to 12 mm.

CLICK BEETLES (Elateridae). Click beetles are represented by some eight hundred species in North America. The larvae, called wireworms, are generally subterranean. These beetles have a peculiar ability to right themselves with a loud click as they flip themselves several inches into the air. They instinctively drop off their perch when approached. Size varies from 2.5 to 44 mm, and black, gray, and especially brown are typical colors. Habitat includes soil, shrubs, flowers, and decayed wood.

BARK BEETLES (Scolytidae). This is a good-sized family of beetles that can be quite injurious to trees, particularly conifers, which they infest as both dead and living trees. Short and stocky in appearance, the Scolytidae are often called engraver beetles because of the patterns they cut into sapwood. Though these insects spend much of their lives inside trees, they do travel about quite a bit in search of new host trees, at which time they become available to trout. Size is 2–10 mm, and black and brown are the most frequent natural colors.

FIREFLIES (Lampyridae). The fireflies are a fairly small beetle family in point of numbers; only fifty species are known in the U.S. However, they are often very common along trout streams in the evenings. The most common species is *Photuris pennsylvanicus*, which emerges during July and August. It is predaceous and has a life cycle of two years.

The luminosity of the rear abdomen of these beetles is thought to be connected with mating. However, it is present even in the grub (larva), and adults continue to shine after death. Charlie Fox attaches considerable significance to artificials imitating this insect for summer fishing in the meadows.

LADYBIRD BEETLES (Coccinellidae). Ladybirds comprise a moderate-sized family with four hundred species in North America, two thousand worldwide. They are beneficial insects and are used by gardeners to control aphids and other harmful insects. The grublike larvae have been known to eat up to forty aphids in an hour and have justly gained the name "aphids-wolf." Colors vary widely among ladybugs, with two to fifteen spots present among the various species. Size ranges from less than a millimeter to seven mm. In the West these beetles migrate in large swarms high into the mountains, where they hibernate as adults in enormous piles buried beneath a covering of leaves and snow.

Ladybirds have long been admired by people of various cultures—one of the few insects held in this respect—and they are often thought to bring good weather and bountiful crops. The trout too are fond of these bright-colored Coleoptera.

chapter
six

GRASSHOPPERS . CRICKETS
ROACHES

(Orthoptera)

Grasshoppers, crickets, and roaches are large and chunky, and capable of drawing surface rises from some of the heaviest trout in a river. The grasshopper is the most important Orthopteran from the fly fisher's vantage point.

But the order is not comprised solely of hoppers. The Orthoptera (formed from the Greek words for "straight" and "wing") include the crickets, shorthorn grasshoppers, longhorn grasshoppers and katydids, mantids, walkingsticks, and cockroaches, among others.

The major families of interest to the fly fisherman are the shorthorn hoppers, crickets, and cockroaches. Mantids, walkingsticks, and such other Orthopterans as katydids and mormon crickets are no doubt occasionally eaten by trout, but they seldom are common enough to warrant attention from the fly dresser.

The name "grasshopper" as commonly used applies to the shorthorn hoppers, the antennae of which are briefer than their bodies. (The term "locust" is reserved for shorthorn grasshoppers that group together in swarms and actively migrate when they outgrow the available food supply.)

The Orthoptera are comparatively primitive insects. They lack the high degree of specialization that characterizes the ants, for instance, and the cryptic habits of the beetles. Size has no doubt been a hindrance to the group as well, since it is primarily the larger insects that have fallen by the wayside as evolution has progressed.

155

LIFE CYCLES   All members of the order Orthoptera develop gradually by simple metamorphosis: egg, nymph, and adult. The common number of molts is five, though crickets may have up to a dozen nymphal stages.

Eggs are deposited in the ground in pods during the fall, with eight to twenty-four eggs per mass normal. Many hoppers lay close to two hundred eggs. The cricket may lay up to 300 banana-shaped eggs about 2 mm long. Roadsides and fence rows are favored locations for ovipositing, and eggs are usually laid at depths of one to three inches.

Eggs hatch from early to late spring, depending on the species involved. Some hoppers hatch in the fall, however, and overwinter as partially developed nymphs. The young hoppers lack wings, and immature females lack ovipositors. They are still quite active, and many immature hoppers and crickets enter the trout stream and are taken by fish.

Except for the absence of wings and size difference, nymphs look quite similar to adults at every stage; from five to a dozen molts take place through spring and summer as the insect grows. Each time the nymph splits its old skin down the back and crawls out. The young hopper or cricket enters a quiet resting stage before and after the molt—the former to prepare itself for the change; the latter to allow the new, soft body parts to harden by exposure to the air. It may take anywhere from forty to eighty days for the insect to fully mature. Crickets are particularly slow growing, and it's usually autumn when full-grown specimens of this insect appear in numbers. Hopper populations fluctuate directly according to the weather. Cold, wet conditions mean increased mortality of nymphs and eggs; dry, hot weather promises enormous quantities of hoppers.

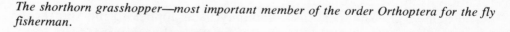

The shorthorn grasshopper—most important member of the order Orthoptera for the fly fisherman.

The structure of crickets, hoppers, and roaches varies considerably, but all have straight, thick, leathery forewings that act primarily as wingcovers for the thinner, membranous hindwings. The hindwings—net-like and often brightly colored—are the principal flight organs. They are folded like a fan when not in use and are almost semicircular in shape. A very small percentage of the insect's body weight is typically devoted to wing muscles, and they are not great fliers. (Some of the species in this order lack wings entirely.) Most crickets don't even try to fly, and the aerial travels of cockroaches are largely confined to gliding leaps from high perches.

But both crickets and grasshoppers have large thighs for jumping and can leap large distances—an ability which frequently sends them plummeting into trout streams as they miscalculate their destination. Roaches are primarily running insects, rather than leapers, and have six equally developed legs.

The males are the notorious music makers of the order, by the way. This "stridulation" is created among crickets by stroking a file on the lower side of a front wing against a rough spot on the top side of the opposite wing, to attract female crickets.

FISHING THE HOPPERS

A katydid.

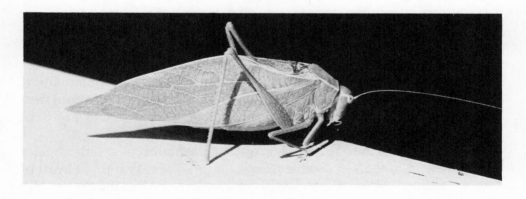

Female cricket uses long ovipositor to deposit up to three hundred pale, banana-shaped eggs in the ground.

From the fly tier's viewpoint, the major features of hoppers, crickets, and roaches is body shape. Legs can also be important, particularly in hopper and cricket patterns. Legs often play second fiddle to wings in some traditional hopper patterns, and this may be a mistake. Often the wings are invisible or barely visible to the trout. They are folded over the body, and only the tip is visible in certain mature grasshoppers. Legs, on the other hand, figure prominently in the impression a trout gets of the typical cricket or hopper on the water. The insect often kicks forcibly as it struggles to escape the surface film.

Color of crickets is usually black, brown, or a mixture of the two. Grasshoppers come in a wide variety of hues, with yellow, green, and brown predominating. Cockroaches may be any shade from black to pale reddish brown.

There has been a proliferation of hopper patterns in recent years (more so than for any other terrestrial). Since the trout often get reckless in a real hopper frenzy, almost any pattern that provides the bulky body silhouette and size will deliver under these circumstances. Many anglers find that a Muddler Minnow fished dry will do the job quite admirably when the fish are looking for hoppers.

Casting hopper imitations to trout that are actively feeding on the naturals is one of the sweetest of angling pleasures. Fish often get carried away when hoppers are available and strike with the abandon one would expect from a naive fingerling. The appetite trout of all sizes and species display for these large terrestrial entrees is sometimes phenomenal. Wisconsin angler Tom Wendelburg told me he did an autopsy on a ten-inch trout that had "twenty hoppers (by count!) to one-inch in its stomach, but took my dry fly." This kind of grasshopper gluttony is actually quite common.

While active hopper-feeding trout present rich angling opportunities, these flies are also good searching patterns. Their bulk and the impact they make on the water are often enough to bring trout up even though they were not pursuing naturals.

Hoppers are also the one type of terrestrial that has become truly popular in the West. And there's a sound reason for this—the West is the heart of hopper country. Most of the classic trout waters in Montana, Wyoming, Colorado, and Idaho flow through grasslands that become literally infested with hoppers by late summer. A walk along a western stream on a sunny day in August will create a grating symphony of buzzing and crackling as thousands of hoppers bristle and leap in the meadow grasses. Though there is certainly excellent hopper fishing on Eastern waters, it is in the "hopper belt" of the West and Midwest that fishing of this type reaches its prime.

Hopper fishing can begin much earlier in the year than many anglers

Immature shorthorn grasshopper; note the absence of wings and the prominence of legs on the nymph.

suspect. Quite a few hoppers overwinter in the nymphal stage, half-grown, in regions with mild climates. These insects may be fully mature by May in eastern areas. John Crowe in his *Modern ABC's of Freshwater Fishing* describes a woodland grasshopper that appears during the first week in May and is fully grown and active by the end of the month. In western Virginia hoppers appear early in April, with specimens from 8 to 30 mm present. Most are nymphs that have overwintered in the immature form, though some winged adults are also seen.

Even when hoppers do not overwinter in the nymphal stage, eggs normally hatch during April, May, and June. The immature forms that emerge from these eggs are not as big as they'll be in August or September, and they lack wings, but trout have the chance to eat large quantities of them. The nymphs do have strong legs and seem to leap rather indiscriminately in their youthful abandon.

Sometimes grasshopper nymphs of one specific size will abound in a streamside meadow. Here it's clearly best to match the immature hoppers as closely as possible in form and size. This may mean going down to #16 or #18 but even these miniatures are relished by the trout.

Once they do make their initial appearance in spring, hoppers increase in numbers and sizes through summer and early fall. Only repeated sharp frosts in autumn will still them.

Hopper activity during the day varies greatly with the weather. As dawn cracks, hoppers turn their bodies at right angles to the sun to soak in its radiant warmth and build up their body heat. By nine or ten o'clock they are usually foraging about under full steam. When the sun sinks behind trees in late afternoon, they quickly abort their activities. The best days for fishing the imitations are hot, dry ones with lots of sun; if there is a wind blowing across the stream, chances are even better that many naturals will be blown into the water. Cloud cover slows hopper activity, and hard rain can just about bring it to a halt.

Fortunately for the angler, just about the time the hoppers are turning in for the day the crickets are tuning up, filling the air with their steely chirping. Crickets will be active during the day as well, especially in the fall, but I've found the best fishing with these imitations occurs right at dusk. Crickets are more sluggish than grasshoppers, and they seem to have an innate fear of water that hoppers lack. They become available to trout less frequently than hoppers, but must have the same strong taste appeal to the fish.

Crickets and hoppers are large enough to make a significant splat when they fall into the stream, and the sound cast can be very useful when fishing these imitations. Most of the time I prefer to cast the flies above the trout and drift them quietly over the fish. If the trout fails to strike, a gentle twitch may do the trick.

Hoppers and crickets are especially deadly on shore-hugging trout. Some anglers like to cast their imitations purposely up on the shoreline grass and gently twitch them loose into the water. This makes for a highly realistic presentation and often results in a slamming strike.

Both for ease of delivery and manipulation of the fly, a fairly long rod is best for hopper fishing. Something in the 8–9 foot range taking a 5–7 weight line is not out of place for tossing Orthoptera patterns.

Virtually any grassy stretch of water can offer good hopper fishing. On freestone streams there really doesn't have to be any evidence of feeding fish to draw strikes, either. I've found "blind" fishing with hopper patterns a very productive way to spend hot summer afternoons plying the riffles, pocket water, and undercut banks of such big eastern and western streams as the Lackawaxen, Beaverkill, Au Sable, and Yellowstone.

PATTERNS

Letort Hopper

Of all terrestrial insects, the hopper has probably been the stimulus for more novel fly dressings than any other. It seems everyone who casts a fly line has his favorite version of the grasshopper, and the preferences of trout vary widely from stream to stream.

The Letort, as in so many cases, was the initial proving ground for Ernie Schwiebert's excellent hopper pattern. The creation of the imitation is described in his usual consummate style in the story "Grasshopper Wind" in *Remembrances of Rivers Past*. During their early testings, Schwiebert and Ross Trimmer came up with the close-to-final version of the hopper:

> The silhouette of the wings and the trailing deer hair proved important. The absence of hackle permitted the bulk of the fly and its yellow-dubbed body to float flush in the surface film. The light pattern created by the dressing in the surface film looked hopper-like and promising.
>
> *Looks good,* observed Ross Trimmer. *Maybe we'll name it the Letort Hopper.*
>
> The trout liked it fine. We used it with good success on the Letort and pulled up trout that were not feeding on many occasions. [P. 108-9]

With one final alteration in the pattern—the substitution of a bulky, clipped-hair head for the small, silk-wrapped one—the final Letort Hopper was born. Says Schwiebert, "We tried the following pattern the next morning on the Letort and it worked wonders on demanding fish" (p. 109):

Hook: Sizes six thru sixteen 2X long down-eye
Silk: 00 yellow
Tails: None
Body: Yellow nylon wool dubbed on yellow silk
Wings: Brown-mottled turkey glazed with lacquer
Legs: Brown deer body hair
Head: Trimmed deer body hair butts

1 Secure a 2X long dry fly hook in vise and wind on tying thread. Dub on a body of yellow rabbit fur.

2 Cut a section of mottled turkey wing slightly longer than the hook shank and spray it with acrylic. Bind the turkey wing segment over top of the fur body with thread.

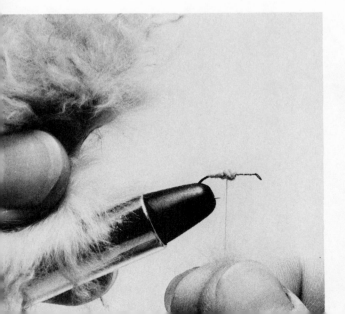

3 Cut a bunch of natural deer hair and even the tips in a hair stacker.

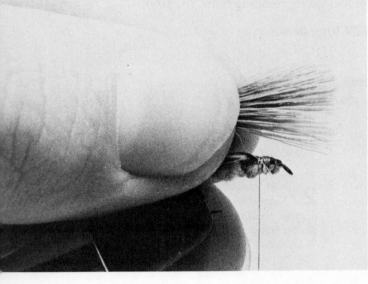

4 Hold the hair over the turkey wing so that tips extend just slightly past the end of the turkey segment; then take two loose turns around the hair. Slowly pull it tight, causing hair to flare in front of the thread. Take several more turns through hair and whip finish head. Trim the butts of hair to form a fat, angular head.

5 Finished Letort Hopper.

The only alteration I like in this pattern is the substitution of rabbit fur for the nylon wool. Another variation that some tiers prefer is using two rather than one piece of turkey quill for the "wings" and tying them slightly down along the sides instead of as a single overwing on top of the back. Tied in this manner, the turkey segments actually represent the legs of the hopper.

Green or tannish colored fur can also be substituted for the yellow body to match different species of hoppers. Yellow undersides predominate in many of our most common grasshoppers, and trout seem particularly susceptible to patterns tied with this color. But when greenish hoppers abound in streamside meadows, I've had excellent results with like-colored patterns. Tied with a very pale, almost milky green body, the Letort hopper also imitates the snowy tree cricket that is sometimes encountered along the water. However, for this fly it's best to clip the head very small to match the naturals.

The virtues of the Letort hopper are readily apparent. It is easy to tie, floats low in the surface film like the naturals, and is a durable pattern. On eastern waters it is probably the most popular of the hopper ties.

Joe's Hopper

Joe's hopper is a favorite pattern in many areas, particularly in the Midwest and West. The fly does not present quite as realistic a silhouette as some other hopper patterns, but it nevertheless has an uncanny ability to catch trout. Fishing the South Branch of the Au Sable in Michigan one afternoon, I managed to drum up a meager number of small browns and brookies on sundry land flies. A conversation with two Ann Arbor anglers at day's end revealed that they had absolutely devastated the trout with Joe's Hoppers. Ever since that day I've kept a few of these traditional hopper patterns stashed in my vest.

Hook: Sizes #6 through #18; regular or 2X long
Thread: Black or brown
Tail: Thin strip of red goose quill or red deer hair
Body: Yellow yarn or wool with loop formed at bend of hook
Rib: Brown or ginger hackle tied in by tip at bend of hook
Wing: Turkey wing quill sections sprayed with acrylic
Hackle: Grizzly and ginger or brown

Dave's Hopper

Dave's hopper is the creation of fly tier extraordinaire Dave Whitlock of Cotter, Arkansas. The fly arose from Whitlock's dissatisfaction with traditional hopper ties, and it gives a highly accurate impression of the hopper image to the trout. As Whitlock says in *Art Flick's Master Fly Tying Guide* (where complete tying instructions for this pattern can be found), "It casts well, floats in all types of water when dressed with a flotant, and has wonderful fish appeal" (p. 115).

Hook:	2X long; sizes #6 through #14
Thread:	Brown
Tail:	Natural deer hair dyed red
Body:	Yellow orlon wool
Rib:	Brown hackle
Underwing:	Pale yellow deer hair
Wing:	Cut section from turkey wing quill
Collar:	Natural brown deer hair
Head:	Deer hair

Harvey's Deer Hopper

Spun and clipped deer hair makes excellent bodies for many types of terrestrials, and for hoppers it is no less useful. Buoyancy and durability are two of the major virtues of this type of hopper fly, though exact duplication of the hopper form can also be achieved by trimming the spun hair.

Pennsylvanian George Harvey has tied a pattern of this type that is effective over a wide range of waters throughout the country. The fly uses

yellow deer hair clipped to form the body, a tuft of natural brown deer hair on top for wings, and red duck or goose quill fibers tied in along the sides for legs.

Al's Hair Hopper

"The problem of who originates a pattern," Al Troth wrote in his letter, "is a tough one." Indeed it is. In 1962 Troth was tying the pattern illustrated below commercially, with the exception of red goose quill legs. In 1968 Chauncy K. Lively had an article in the *Pennsylvania Angler* which described a virtually identical fly, except that the pattern was constructed of deer instead of elk hair and had red goose quill fibers extending out the sides for legs. Liking the addition of the legs, Troth included these in his patterns. As Troth says, "I saw Lively's and liked the addition and so added them on."

In any case, Al's Hair Hopper is an exceptional grasshopper pattern for many reasons. Troth describes some of the influences in his growth as a topnotch fly dresser:

> While living in the East, I fished every summer in the West . . . 1950, I believe, was the first year. . . . Fly construction in western patterns is sometimes not as fussy as eastern flies. I started using a lot of new materials that were not used too extensively in the East, many times combining the best of both. My tying is practical and for the fish; I prefer tough flies and use materials that aid in the floating or sinking of the specific pattern being tied.

Of Al's Hair Hopper he says:

> I recommend deer in my instructions, but this was only because I felt many people could not get good elk hair to do the job. Elk wasn't too readily available about 10 years ago in most fly tying supply houses.

The late Jack Hoerner from California was a personal friend of mine and was tying the Hoerner hair dry fly. In 1962 I started using the technique for the hair bodies used in the hopper and cricket.

The 'plop' the fly makes as it hits the water surface must sound much like that of the natural and I'm sure the trout are tuned in to this feeding call.

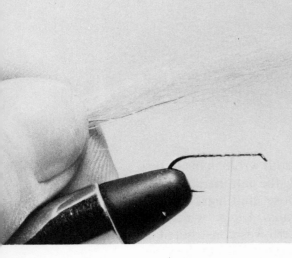

1 Attach regular or 2X long dry fly hook in vise and bind on tying thread. Select a bunch of dyed yellow bucktail or elk rump hair dyed yellow. For a #12 fly a bunch approximately the same diameter as a wooden match is appropriate.

2 Approximately one-third the length of hook shank back from eye, bind down the hair at the butts and spiral thread tightly to bend of hook, forming segments as you go. Take several extra turns at the end of the body.

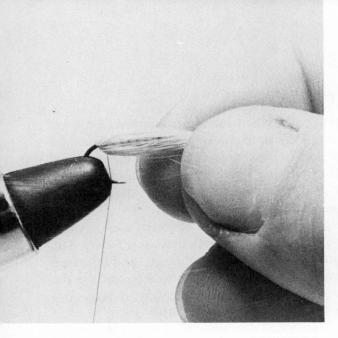

3 Grasp the hair and pull it forward so that it is distributed evenly around the hook. Hold the hair with your right hand and wrap the thread forward, again forming segments in the body. Tie the hair down just in front of first tie-in point, and trim away any excess hair.

4 Tie in two red goose quill fibers with natural curve away from body. These should be selected from the short side of the goose feather. Several sprayed fibers of turkey wing can also be substituted for the legs (shown).

5 For wings, select a bunch of natural deer hair, even the tips in hair stacker, and tie it in on top of yellow body hair, where the legs are attached.

6 Trim the deer hair butts to a squarish shape, and wind the thread through the hair to the eye. Whip finish, apply a drop of lacquer, and Al's Hair Hopper is complete.

Nymph Hopper

I use the nymph hopper frequently when immature hopper forms are present in meadow grasses. It is a very simple design consisting of a rabbit fur body with small bunches of deer hair extending from the sides for legs. The pattern is best reserved for imitating small hoppers; otherwise it becomes difficult to wrap the fur on thickly enough to simulate the dominant head and prothorax of the naturals.

The hoppers prevalent along the lovely Gibbon River in Yellowstone Park on one of my summer trips were just such small, immature forms. The prominent legs were the outstanding features on the naturals, and I dressed several of the simple ties in olive and yellow to match those bustling in the meadow grasses. The wind was strong and the sun bright; it seemed a perfect day for hoppers, even though it was early in July.

I approached the stream cautiously and dropped the simple nymph hopper gently along the opposite bank. A sharp strike came on the third cast, but I missed the fish cleanly and he wouldn't repeat his error.

Upstream twenty yards the Gibbon spread smoothly over lime green weed beds, where three fine browns jockeyed for position. They grabbed the stray crustacean and occasionally jerked up to the surface to inhale a small hopper. The wind whipped briskly across the sedge grass and the size 16 hopper came down hard on the glassy water. The largest trout bobbed his head up and had the fly firmly in his jaw. After releasing this fish, I rose the second and missed him, but could not interest the third beyond drawing a slight shudder of his body as the fly floated past him. But the nymph hopper had proven its worth by drawing strikes from three out of four wild brown trout on these difficult spring creek waters.

1 Attach a #14 to #18 dry fly hook in vise and wind on thread. Dub on a thick body of rabbit fur halfway up straight part of hook shank; the body should be thicker towards the mid-point of the hook. Then select a small bunch of natural deer body hair and even the tips in a hair stacker.

2 Hold the hair by the tips over top of hook so that they extend slightly beyond the bend of hook. Take several turns of thread over hair and tighten. Hair should flare to the sides and slightly up.

3 Trim excess deer hair butts in front of thread.

4 With tying thread, separate deer hair into two bunches that flare out to the sides and slightly up. Use figure-eight turns to secure the hair legs in this position.

5 Dub on more fur and wind thread and fur towards the eye of the hook to form a thick thorax and head. Whip finish head, apply drop of lacquer, and your Nymph Hopper is complete.

Cork Hopper

Cork's advantage is that it can be carved to match the hopper silhouette precisely. The material is also durable and makes a heavy pattern that can be slapped to the water when called for. However, it is not a satisfactory material in large sizes because of this same weight. Casting becomes too much of a chore with cork hoppers above size #8 unless you use a big, powerful rod.

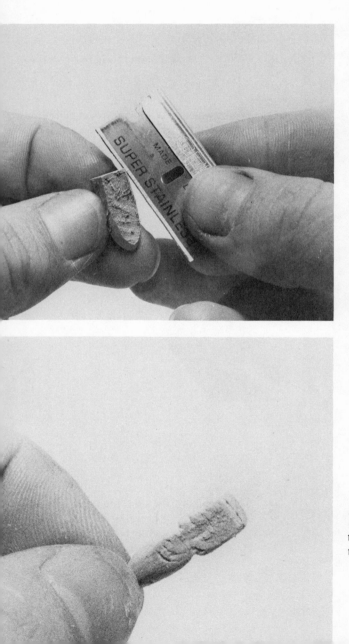

1   Take a piece of cork and with razor blade trim to approximate hopper shape.

2   Use emery board for final shaping of the hopper body. At approximately the mid-point of the body, make two indentations in the sides where the legs are to be attached.

3 Cut a slit or very thin wedge along the bottom of the cork body for the hook. Apply epoxy and insert hook. Allow glue to dry, making sure hook is straight.

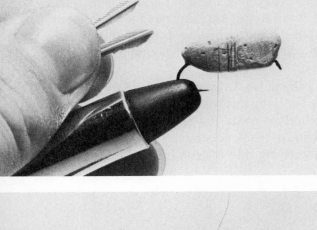

4 For legs, select two quills and cut out appropriate-sized segments, leaving a bit of the feather on the quill. Mallard wing feathers are shown here, though other types will work.

5 Trimmed quill legs should look like this and when tied in place they should extend slightly beyond the body. Attach hopper body in vise and wrap on thread where legs are to be attached. With thread fasten on legs so they slant slightly upwards and out from body. Wrap thread forward and attach two moose mane fibers on top of head to form antennae.

6 Whip finish thread, apply lacquer, and trim antennae to correct length, and paint the desired color: Finished Cork Hopper.

Letort Cricket

The Letort Cricket pattern was created by limestone creek fisherman Ed Shenk late in the summer of 1959. The Letort hopper had been a very popular fly that year in the meadow stream waters of the Cumberland Valley, and Shenk found that some fish were becoming immune to the lure of the oft-presented fly. In *Night Fishing for Trout* Jim Bashline quotes Ed Shenk on the origin of the Letort Cricket: ''One fish in particular would inspect the hopper but just wouldn't inhale it. I sat and pondered the situation and idly watched a big cricket hopping about at my feet. 'Why not a Letort Cricket?' I reasoned. I used the same tying style as for the hopper, except all ingredients were black. Next morning I took the above-mentioned fish on the first cast—a three-and-a-half-pound hook-jawed brown'' (p. 126).

Shenk uses either 2X or 3X long shank hooks in sizes #12–18 for daytime fishing, #6 and #8 for night. Steps for tying this fly are the same as those for the Letort hopper except that the body is made of black fur, the underwing of black goose quill, and the overwing of black deer hair. The head is formed by trimming the butts from the overwing into a cylindrical shape.

Hair Cricket

Another of Al Troth's patterns, the hair cricket is constructed similarly to Al's hair hopper. Troth says ''the cricket pattern I have never seen in print; it is basically the same as the hopper, except that I added a wing for a better silhouette.'' This is not only a durable cricket pattern, but it also floats extremely well and is an excellent choice for fishing heavy waters.

Hook: Regular dry fly in #10–16; 2X long in #6 and #8
Thread: Black 2/0
Body: Elk hair (flank) dyed black
Underwing: Black-dyed goose sprayed for durability
Overwing: Black-dyed deer flank hair in small sizes, elk in larger sizes
Legs: Black-dyed turkey or goose pointer quills (use short side)

Harvey's Clipped-hair Cricket

Some tiers favor clipped hair for their cricket bodies. Since the insects are rather plump, this method is excellent for obtaining the desired bulk while keeping the fly light. George Harvey ties the body of his cricket pattern by spinning black deer hair on the hook and trimming to shape. The wing is a small clump of deer hair tied on top, and legs are represented with two goose quill fibers, one tied on each side.

Deer Hair Roach

Deer hair clipped to a flattish, oblong shape makes a fine pattern for imitating night-roaming roaches. Rust-colored hair is best, and several long strands of hair can be left extending from each side for legs in this pattern.

Turkey Quill Roach

A large number of terrestrial insects can be imitated by trimming a turkey wing feather to shape and gluing a hook in the tough quill section. It makes an excellent roach fly because the flatness of the insect and its low-floating profile are duplicated precisely with the material. This method of tie is not as durable as some, and the protruding legs are vulnerable to breakage. In spite of this, the turkey quill roach has duped some fine fish over the seasons.

COCKROACHES (Blattidae). These are the oldest members of the Orthoptera, and one of the oldest surviving insect forms. Most people think of cockroaches as indoor pests. Actually, only about ten percent of the fifty-five species of cockroaches found in this country ever find their way into houses. The other species commonly roam in woods habitat and occasion-

SOME COMMON ORTHOPTERA

ally slip into the realm of the trout during their night food gathering. Since the insects are distinctly flat in form and float low in the surface film, they present an elongated, oval shape to the fish. Roaches commonly venture out just as dusk is falling to feed on animal and vegetable refuse, and roach imitations are best in the last half hour of daylight and the next few hours. I've found roaches in the stomachs of woodland stream rainbows up to twenty-two inches. Big browns that hide out during the day also seem to have a penchant for these flat brown insects.

SHORTHORN GRASSHOPPERS (Acrididae). Though six hundred species of grasshoppers have been identified in North America, five of them are particularly common and account for over ninety percent of the damage done to crops each year. They are described below.

MIGRATORY GRASSHOPPER (*Melanoplus sanguinipes*). Range of the migratory grasshopper encompasses most of the western U.S. The color is reddish brown or yellow with red on legs and a black patch on the neck. Length is 24 to 30 mm. This grasshopper prefers well-drained, light soil and open areas with sparse vegetation. It is the most destructive grasshopper in the country, migrates in massive swarms, and is widely distributed throughout the West.

TWO-STRIPED GRASSHOPPER (*Melanoplus bivittatus*). The two-striped grasshopper is found throughout North America. Color varies from greenish yellow to brownish, with yellow stripes and red on the upper legs. Length is 24–34 mm.

This hopper favors lush vegetation and moist, heavy soil. It eats such foods as clover, grasses, alfalfa, corn, wheat, and fruit trees.

DIFFERENTIAL GRASSHOPPER (*Melanoplus differentialis*). The differential hopper's range extends throughout North America. The color is yellowish brown with black markings; legs are yellow. Length is 36–46 mm. Like the two-striped grasshopper, the differential favors lush vegetation and moist, heavy soil. It eats fruits, grain, and forage crops as well as weeds and grasses.

RED-LEGGED GRASSHOPPER (*Melanoplus femurrubrum*). Heaviest concentrations of this hopper occur in the Northern Great Plains. The color is brown or gray or green with a yellow belly and red on the hind legs. Size is 18–24 mm. This hopper prefers moist soil with thick vegetation.

CLEAR-WINGED GRASSHOPPER (*Camnula pellucida*). The range of this grasshopper includes all of North America, though it is particularly common in the West. Color is pale brown or yellow with brown spots on the front wings. Size is 12–24 mm. This hopper feeds on grains, crops, and range grasses. It is most frequently encountered in mountain meadows, grass-covered openings in forests, and grazed plains land, though it can adapt to many habitats.

CRICKETS (Gryllidae). Several types of crickets may be encountered along trout streams. The house cricket (*Acheta domestica*), field cricket (*Acheta assimilis*), and snowy tree cricket (*Oecanthus fultoni*) are three familiar ones. The common field cricket and house cricket both measure 12–24 mm and appear quite similar to the untrained eye. The house cricket is black, while the field cricket may be black or brownish black. Though both have country-wide distribution, the field cricket may well be the single most abundant member of this order in terms of numbers.

The snowy tree cricket is pale green and measures about 14 mm in its adult form. The insects prefer trees and shrubs growing in semi-open areas, where they feed on treehoppers, aphids, leaves, and flowers.

chapter seven

CATERPILLARS BUTTERFLIES • MOTHS

(Lepidoptera)

Moths and butterflies comprise the second largest insect order, with 120,000 described species. It is well known due to the graceful, brightly colored adult butterflies, skippers, and moths, which intrigue amateur entomologists with a bent for collecting.

The name Lepidoptera comes from the Greek words meaning "scale" and "wing." A literal interpretation thus reads "scaly wings" and describes well this order's adults, which are covered with tiny scales layered like shingles on a roof. To the casual touch this covering first appears as a powdery dust, but close examination reveals minute, flat scales.

The Lepidoptera are commonly divided into two suborders—the moths (Heterocera) and butterflies (Rhopalocera). Though they are quite similar in form, there are several ways to differentiate between the two suborders. The most reliable distinguishing points are the antennae. Butterflies typically have club-shaped antennae, and they are never feathered. (The name Rhopalocera means, in fact, "clubbed horns.") The antennae of moths are more tapered and are generally feathered or covered with hair.

A less reliable method of distinguishing butterflies from moths is the way the insects hold their wings while resting. Moths usually hold their wings spread flat across the back or angling slightly out to the sides. Butterflies typically rest with their wings upright. Moths are also generally nocturnal insects, while butterflies are active during the day.

A final difference is in the apparatus the insects use during metamorphosis. The pupae of butterflies (chrysalids) lack any outer covering and

typically hang from a tree branch. Moths pupate in a silken cocoon, often in the ground or in holes dug in plants by the larvae.

Adult butterflies, as well as certain moths, are among the most exquisite creatures on earth. Coloration is often brilliant, forming striking patterns intended to frighten off predators. Many display cryptic hues that allow them to blend in with the leaves, trees, or flowers they commonly land on.

The diet of moths and butterflies consists principally of nectar from flowers, though the juices of decaying fruit and honeydew from aphids and leafhoppers are sometimes consumed. Mouthparts are designed for sucking, though in some families no food is taken by the adults.

Adult Lepidoptera pollinate many plants and are considered beneficial insects. The larvae, on the other hand, are among the most destructive of insects and feed almost exclusively on plants. Each year they do millions of dollars worth of damage to crops and forest trees.

LIFE CYCLES

With the moths and butterflies we also come to a startling shift in the life stage most important for the angler. Whereas immature larval stages of most terrestrial insects with complete metamorphosis, such as the ants and beetles, are relatively unimportant from the fisherman's viewpoint, the exact opposite is true of the Lepidoptera. It is the adults that are of comparatively minor importance, while the larvae can be extremely productive flies over a broad range of waters and for a substantial segment of the angling year.

Adults

LIFE-STYLES

This is not to say that adult butterflies and moths do not pose some angling possibilities. Most anglers have seen trout leaping out of the water to catch a cabbage or sulphur butterfly fluttering low over the water. Many have no doubt toyed with the idea of creating a butterfly imitation.

Edward Hewitt came closer to succeeding at this task than anyone when he devised his classic Neversink skater. This fly, tied with two large hackles wound concave sides inward on a #16 light Model Perfect hook, was skipped with a lively motion over the surface to mimic natural butterflies flirting with death. Hewitt first wrote about this fly in the August, 1937 issue of *The Sportsman* magazine and synopsized the material later in *A Trout and Salmon Fisherman for 75 Years:* "The butterflies did not rest on the water; they sometimes touched it but were always moving. When they did touch the water they did so very lightly and were away again. . . . How was

I to do this? I went back to my camp and tied several flies, finally making what is known now as the Neversink Skater. . . .

"[It] could be made to alight on the water like a feather and be jumped and dragged over the surface without getting wet or going under. It ought, therefore, to make an impression on the fish similar to a butterfly" (p. 132).

The Neversink skater has proven to be a fine fly. Hewitt even tossed the big flies onto the hallowed waters of the Test, where he took fish against the protests of old Lunn, the riverkeeper: "He was most astonished at seeing trout caught in this way."

Moths also elicit rises from fish, and over the long run they are probably more important in the diet of trout than butterflies. They are heavier built insects and doubtless offer more of a meal to a feeding fish. Moths are also nocturnal, making them active in the final twilight hours and the black of night when big browns are often cruising on the lookout for chunky morsels.

Another time when adult moths may be taken in numbers by trout is during their final moments of life, after eggs have been laid and the insects' only remaining task is to die gracefully. At this time great numbers of moths may fall helplessly to the stream as their flight muscles atrophy.

Moth patterns have never really been popular among fly fishermen, probably because few anglers like to fish in darkness when these imitations are most effective. And few dry fly purists have the gumption to draw out these "bass bugs" in broad daylight. In the smaller sizes (#12 through #20), caddis-type patterns such as the flat wing, or a simple fly with a rabbit fur body and deer hair wing serve well.

For larger moths, whose purpose is to drum up big trout in the twilight and dark hours, several varieties of patterns have proven productive. Clipped deer hair is especially useful for representing the thick, chunky moth bodies. Several wing materials work. Dave Whitlock uses marabou for its fluttering action in the water when twitched, polypropylene makes quality wings, and hen hackle feathers are also good.

Moths might well draw strikes during the day, but it's from twilight to midnight that they really do their work. The flies can be fished dead drift through riffles, but in slow-moving pools an occasional subtle twitch may be necessary. Strikes on the drop are common.

Larvae

It is the varied larvae of the Lepidoptera order that deserve the closest attention of the terrestrial fisherman. Included in this aggregation are such diversely named insects as cutworms, loopers, oakworms, woollybears, armyworms, measuring worms, bagworms, leaf rollers, and the well-known inchworms. All of them are caterpillars, and all display the familiar fat, wormlike shape which trout learn to recognize early in their lives as an easy, satisfying meal.

Caterpillars have thirteen segments—ten in the abdomen, three in the thorax. The three thoracic segments each bear a pair of legs; the abdominal segments have four to ten prolegs—unjointed, fleshy appendages. Many of the larvae are covered with fine hairs (setae), a characteristic that has given rise to the common nickname "woollybears." The majority of caterpillars, such as the common inchworm, lack such readily visible setae and are sometimes referred to as "naked" larvae by entomologists.

From the fly dresser's vantage point, the structure of caterpillars is a joy to behold. They represent a simple form that can be embodied successfully with any number of materials, including cork, balsa, wrapped or spun deer hair, turkey quills, hen pheasant quills, and other more traditional materials.

The habits of the larvae make them particularly vulnerable to trout. Virtually all of them are plant-eaters that feed openly on many varieties of trees and shrubs found along trout water. Furthermore, most caterpillars are not very agile, and in their greed to reach for the next mouthful of leaf many tumble into the trout stream. Others may be blown from their streamside perches by strong gusts, and still others are washed in by rains.

Many caterpillars use silken threads to lower themselves to the ground for feeding or to drop out of sight when escaping predators. They then try to climb back up the silken thread to their perch in the tree, but it doesn't always work out this way. Sometimes the thread breaks or the caterpillar unknowingly lowers himself into a trout stream—into the waiting jaws of a fish.

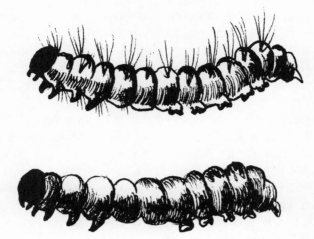

Caterpillar with prominent setae (top); "naked" caterpillar (bottom).

Caterpillars of different species may be found on shoreline vegetation virtually anytime from April through October in the East. In the West caterpillars are active from late May through September. The majority of Lepidoptera larvae emerge late in spring, and caterpillars are usually thickest from May through July. Many moth and butterfly species are apparently cyclic in their appearance. Several lean years can be followed by heavy infestations. Tom Wendelburg says there is a green larva that emerges in great numbers on Michigan's Au Sable every seventh year—at which time exceptional fishing may occur to these patterns.

FISHING THE CATERPILLARS

Rolling north along Interstate 81, the Cumberland Valley's pastoral landscape merges gently into mountainous terrain near Harrisburg. Sprawling farms and tall-stalked corn fade as blue mountains angle inwards towards the highway. The limestone farmhouses, aluminum silos, and bright red barns of the valley give way to sharply rolling hills tamed only with the odd wooden house and small garden plot. The densely forested Appalachians rise abruptly at Harrisburg, where the broad Susquehanna flows temptingly along the highway.

It is the trout of tributary Clarks Creek that beckon this spring day. The stream has recently been classified as "fish-for-fun" water by the Pennsylvania Fish Commission, and the trout have responded well to the protective regulations that allow only one fish over twenty inches to be creeled each day.

Clarks is a classic freestone stream flowing in a broken procession of pools and short riffles through dark stands of fir, elm, birch, and maple. There are ruffed grouse that swoop down from their conifer roosts with a thunderous flush of wings, and turkeys thrive in the mature forest habitat. The creek has excellent aquatic hatches in the spring, but it is as terrestrial water that Clarks stands out in my mind.

In the summer beetles and treehoppers take difficult fish during low water periods, and crickets fool trout at dawn and dusk. Numerous species of Diptera buzz through the dense shoreline shrubbery, and ants of varied form and color regularly roam the rich streamside habitat.

The air is sharp and bracing even now at noon as I hike down to the water. It comes as a welcome relief from the abnormally hot, dry spring we have experienced. A sharp breeze rushing in from the northwest buffets richly textured clouds across the blue sky.

The stream runs slow, and its flow has shrunk noticeably from the dearth of spring rains. Trout are plentiful, and I spy several browns and a brookie with bright, white-edged pectorals waiting at the pool. The brook trout darts with nervous swiftness to the surface and strikes with a loud splash—beating out a small brown for a chance meal.

Caterpillars. The larvae of the gypsy moth are everywhere, as I see now with eyes freshly awakened by the striking trout. Many of them are large, approaching two inches in length; others in earlier stages of growth measure slightly more than an inch.

They are dark gray with brown hairs bristling from their plump bodies. Bright red and blue tubercles mark their backs. The caterpillars are on maples, elms, even on the dark green firs lining the stream banks. But the birch trees with their tender oval leaves and sinewy gray trunks are most heavily infested. The insects feed in packs, ravaging the tender fare in systematic fashion.

But beneath them lurks a hunter. A sharp gust blowing down from the mountain ridge ripples the stream and shakes the shoreline vegetation. Two larvae drop from their perches and in quick succession a pair of rises break the water's surface. The caterpillars are gone.

Hurriedly I search the fly boxes for a replica of the caterpillar. A clipped deer hair worm on a long shank #8 hook is close, and I clinch it to the 6X tippet.

"This will be fine fishing!" I mumble nervously as the slender Leonard works out the fly line. With a sharp splat the deer hair larva drops behind a brown hovering in shallow water. The trout turns and swirls, hesitates skeptically with nose nearly touching the fly, and takes hard. With a quick side motion I set the barbless hook in the jaw of the fish, and a thrashing fight shatters the stillness of the clear pool. Next come two brookies. Already fat from the morning's feeding, they climb onto the hair imitation—still enthusiastic. There are two refusals and one more brown before I work up from the small pool to the next swift glide.

The fish are skittish in the low water, and much of the day is spent on my knees. Casts must be delivered with precision. Flies dropped on the head of the fish send a frightened trout fleeing for cover; those placed gently in front of the fish draw interested looks and in a few cases strikes. Casts dropped more than eighteen inches behind the trout are ignored entirely or inspected and refused. It is the fly plopped six to twelve inches behind and to the side of expectant trout that draws a sure take. Casting the bulky larva imitation with this accuracy is difficult and puts some challenge into fishing that would otherwise be too easy to hold an angler's interest for long.

The fish feed frantically the afternoon long. Even as I depart, bulging rises are apparent as the trout feed on the big, succulent insects tumbling in from

Clarks Creek: Small, heavily-wooded streams such as this offer excellent opportunities for caterpillar fishing.

land. From noon until 5 P.M. forty-four trout were fought and released in the sparkling currents of Clarks Creek. The majority were browns—some spring stockies, some wild fish. A surprising number of brookies fell for the gray caterpillar, and five rainbows joined in the feeding frenzy.

Since caterpillars are rather densely constructed insects, they make a significant splash when they fall into the stream. Sound is often the key trout use. If the fish are at all hesitant about feeding, it is the larvae floating quietly in the current that will likely be ignored.

The angler can often take his cue here and deliver the fly with a modest splat to simulate the entrance of the naturals. Since most larva patterns are heavy, the sound cast is easy to execute. There are some occasions when fish prefer caterpillars floated quietly over them, however, and here the fly must be set down gently. Lighter patterns, such as a dry version of the woolly worm, are best for this situation.

It's important to represent the general size and thickness of the naturals most prevalent along the water, but I've found trout less "color-conscious" when feeding on these larvae than on many other terrestrials—ants, for example. Perhaps the sudden appearance of such large morsels excites the fish so much that they momentarily abandon their usual discretion. Often several different sizes of larvae will be present also, even though they may be the same species. In this case size isn't a critical factor either, so long as the artificials match some of the naturals active along shore. The fish may be taking several different "sizes" of natural anyway.

As a general rule, forested waters are the prime places to fish caterpillar imitations, though some varieties do feed heavily on shrubs and weeds. Small streams often provide exceptional caterpillar fishing because the overhanging branches deposit the larvae far out into the flow, and so every trout in the creek will be on the lookout for them. When working larger waters, it's best to concentrate on the shoreline holding lies, where spots directly beneath larvae-infested trees are prime casting targets.

Dapping is a delivery technique that has proven particularly effective with these terrestrials. Since many caterpillars weave silken "life lines" which they scurry up and down, the angler can actually use both leader and fly to mimic this rather tantalizing setup by simply dangling the fly off the end of the leader—in which case the rod is imitating a branch, of course.

At times this fishing can become downright hilarious. While working a forested edge of Yellow Breeches Creek some time ago I came upon an eighteen-inch rainbow holding motionless in a snag near shore. An experimental caterpillar tie made of a single piece of turkey quill was attached to the tippet, and I was within "pole's reach" of the trout. Dapping seemed the logical strategy. Circumspectly I raised the rod above the rainbow and prepared to drop the offering over the fish.

But before I could lower the fly, the fish suddenly grew excited and began rotating its pectorals in a rapid motion as it eyeballed the strange object dangling above its head. In a flash the trout lept three inches clear of the water and tried to nab the fly dangling in the air! I was stunned and must have pulled the fly away, because the fish missed its mark. While I attempted to get the rainbow to leap again, a smaller brown from upstream saw the fly, swam down, jumped at it himself, but also missed. The rainbow now chased out the brown and after a minute or two hurled himself clear of the water again and stabbed at the fly.

Again he missed.

After resting the fish momentarily—and my nerves, which were nearly shot by now—I started the teasing again by dangling the fly inches above the water is if it were a caterpillar hanging tenuously on a weak silken thread.

This proved to be too tempting for the trout. He struck a third time. Dropping the fly as the fish cleared the surface, I hesitated, then struck, and the rainbow was finally hooked. As you can imagine, the fight was anti-climactic after this performance.

This kind of fishing probably has too many subliminal links with making Fido leap for a stick to be a satisfying angling method over the long haul. It's also quite nerve-racking to try to fish at such close quarters without bungling the hooking. But it's an interesting fishing experience to try. Believe me.

PATTERNS   Caterpillars have inspired several varieties of patterns, beginning with the classic palmered wet flies used for centuries. Ronalds suggested a palmered fly for use in early spring, especially after a flood or on windy days. The large red palmer was recommended for imitating a caterpillar found ''on nettles and on rank grass.''

The palmer's descendant, the woolly worm, is a close representation of many caterpillar species. It is a favorite wet fly among western fishermen, even though the Lepidoptera larvae actually float remarkably well.

Modern dry fly patterns have focused by and large on imitating a single family—the geometrid moths, which include the famous inchworms. With slight alterations in size, shape, and color, the same approaches to fly design embodied in these patterns can be used for representing the full spectrum of Lepidoptera larvae found adjacent to trout streams.

Cork or Balsa Caterpillars

George Harvey, dean of Pennsylvania fly tiers, probably had as much to do with the modern upsurge of interest in terrestrial fishing as any other person. ''I first started tying terrestrials back in the thirties,'' Harvey says. ''The one that received the most publicity was the green inchworm. The first was tied using cork.'' The green worm proved to be such a deadly fly, in fact, that it was outlawed at the Fisherman's Paradise on Spring Creek by fish commissioner Charles French soon after its creation. (The fly has since become legal, however.)

Cork caterpillars are extremely simple to construct. Just take a cork cylinder of the proper size, cut a slit or very thin wedge for the hook, and epoxy a dry fly hook in place. Paint the fly and you're ready to catch fish. For a more durable fly, thread can be wrapped around the body to bind it to the hook more firmly.

Bill McIntyre, who markets cork inchworms and other terrestrials under the tradename Corkers, described to me the method he uses to construct his flies: ''I wrap each cork body with silk thread, providing not only durability but also a more natural appearance by giving body indentations duplicating the insect's segmentation. Before painting I also prime each fly and this not only prepares the cork for a better finish, it also soaks into both the silk and the cork, thus binding them into a solid piece. This prevents most of the unraveling common to fur and feather flies due to sharp teeth. In this respect, silk is better than nylon thread as nylon will not absorb the primer.''

Balsa can be substituted for the cork to make an equally effective inchworm imitation. Segmentation can be emphasized with both of these materials by sanding evenly spaced grooves across the flanks with an emery board. Cork and balsa are especially useful for imitating the Geometrid larvae and other smooth caterpillars that lack prominent setae.

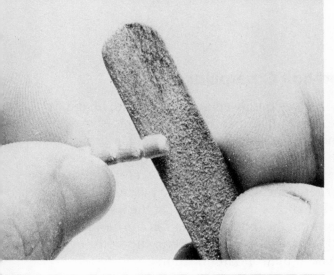

1 Take a one-eighth to one-fourth inch diameter piece of cork or balsa and round the edges at front and back. With an emery board file evenly-spaced indentations to give the fly segmented appearance. Cut a slit or a very thin wedge for long shank dry fly hook (Mustad No. 94831) of appropriate size.

2 Force a liberal amount of epoxy into the groove with a needle or bodkin.

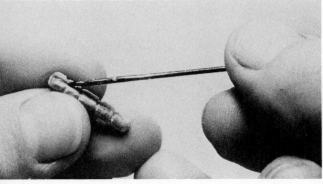

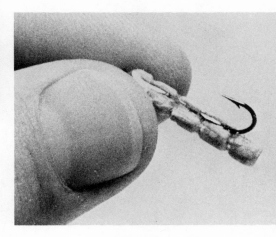

3 Insert a 2X long dry fly hook, smooth cement over the top of the hook and allow to dry. Apply two coats of model airplane paint. The fly can also be wrapped with thread before painting for increased durability.

4 Finished Cork or Balsa Caterpillar.

Clipped-hair Caterpillar

When Harvey's cork inchworm was outlawed at the Paradise, he didn't sulk over the apparent injustice. Instead, he created what he feels is an even better fly—the clipped-hair inchworm. This pattern is a bit more time-consuming to construct than the cork imitation, but it is also lighter, easier to cast, and every bit as durable as the cork fly. I've taken over forty trout on a single fly of this design before it came apart. The deer hair also has the added advantage of a soft feel that allows more time to set the hook before the trout detects the ruse and spits out the fly. Segmentation can be added to this pattern by wrapping tying thread at intervals along the body or by trimming indentations in the hair at appropriate locations.

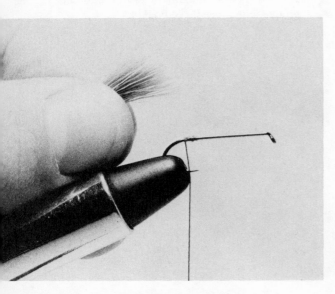

1 Attach a 2X long hook in vise and bind tying thread in just in front of bend in hook (use size 2/0 thread or larger for this fly). Cut a small bunch of deer hair and trim away the uneven tips.

2 Wind the thread twice over the hair on top of the hook shank, and slowly pull it tight, causing hair to flare and spin partially around the hook. Repeat process with additional bunches, working your way up the shank.

3 With thumb and forefinger of each hand, push the bunches tightly together as you work up for a firm, dense fly.

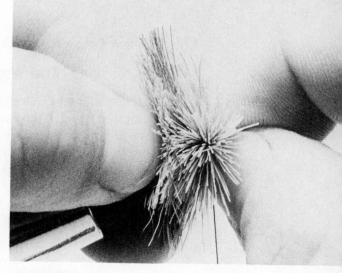

4 Continue to eye of hook, whip finish and trim excess thread. Take the fly out of vise and trim to proper elongated, cylindrical shape with scissors.

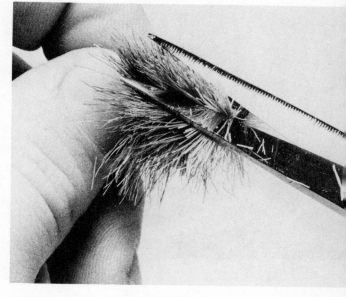

5 Finished Clipped Hair Caterpillar.

The Wrapped-hair Larva

This version of the Lepidoptera larvae has two major virtues: It's quick to tie and emphasizes strongly the segmented appearance that characterizes many caterpillars. Its major drawback is fragility. The imitations are simple to tie, and you can replace the tie on the same hook easily.

I generally reserve this style of tie for smaller larvae, especially the thinner caterpillars where spinning and trimming deer hair is impractical. These flies can be tied on long shank hooks or wrapped on regular hooks with the body extended beyond the end of the hook.

1 Attach a 2X long dry fly hook in vise and bind 2/0 thread to hook. Select a bunch of deer hair slightly thicker than you desire for the final body width of the fly.

2 Hold the hair over hook shank so the butts extend slightly beyond the eye of the hook and wrap thread loosely around hair just in front of the finger and thumb of your left hand.

3 Tighten the thread and wrap it towards the eye of the hook in evenly spaced turns, compressing the hair tightly for a segmented effect.

4 Whip finish just behind eye of hook and trim head and rear of fly to short knobs. A finished Wrapped Hair Larva.

The Chenille Inchworm

Mathew Vinciguerra is the resident angling historian of southern New York. He has spent his life in the area and knows as well as anyone the vagaries of nearby waters. He rates the terrestrial fishing on the Catskill and other nearby streams as excellent and the inchworm fishing on the Amawalk as some of the best anywhere.

"Since hatches are very limited on this stream," Vinciguerra says, "the inchworm becomes a major food supply in late June and July. When this stream was at its peak a few years back, you could watch the trout jump clear of the water to catch the inchworms as they hung above the water. All this also holds true for another stream in this area called the West Branch of the Croton, another brown trout fishery.

"The inchworm pattern that worked best," continued Vinciguerra, "was also the simplest, consisting of a piece of fluorescent chenille (green) tied at the front part of a #16 or #18 dry fly hook. These patterns could be fished wet or dry, but I felt they fished better dry. Of course, they were first dressed with flotant and fished in the normal dry fly manner."

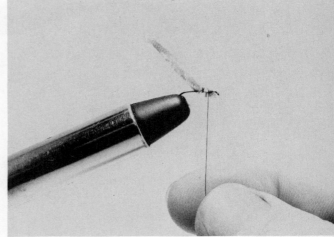

1 Clamp a #16 or #18 dry fly hook in vise and bind tying thread to front third of hook shank. The body will be formed with a piece of fluorescent green chenille.

2 Bind a section of chenille of appropriate length to front third of hook shank with thread.

3 Wrap the thread tightly to form an oval head for the inchworm. Whip finish, clip off excess thread, and apply drop of lacquer to wrappings, and your fly is complete.

Fox's Inchworm

Charlie Fox is not exclusively a meadow stream fisherman. He has devised a fine inchworm pattern along the lines of the pontoon hopper for use on forest-bordered waters in spring and early summer. Fox describes the construction of this pattern: "The tip quill part of a ringneck hen wingfeather is dyed inside and out, then the open mouth is plugged with cork. This is then tied to a long-shank hook." Lacquer, and the fly is complete.

The Turkey Quill Caterpillar

This is another larva pattern that is durable and easy to construct. Use a single piece of hard quill from a turkey wing feather for this tie; select a segment of the proper thickness by cutting higher or lower on the wing feather. The pattern can be constructed solely of the hard quill segment, or in trimming off the feather you can leave short protrusions to represent either legs or setae. The natural groove on the bottom of the turkey feather provides a perfect slot for inserting the hook when it is slit with a razor blade. Be sure not to cut the slit all the way to the ends of the quill segment, however, since this weakens the fly.

This pattern is appealing because it is light enough to be cast easily, yet dense enough to come down with a very subtle splat if you so desire. Color can be added to these flies with dye or model airplane paint. The paint tends to wear off after a few fish, however, and is not as satisfactory as dye.

1 Select a segment of turkey wing quill of appropriate thickness, and with a razor blade cut a length slightly longer than a 2X long hook.

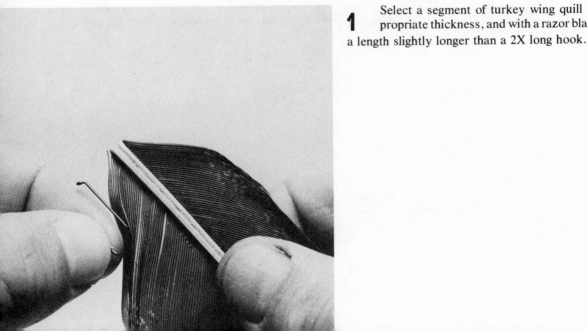

2 Trim the feather close to the quill, leaving small feather stubs to represent legs.

3 Trimmed quill should look something like this. You can dye it now, if desired, or wait and paint it later.

4 Cut thin slit down center of turkey quill, but be careful not to cut all the way to the ends.

5 Widen the slit slightly if necessary, then apply epoxy, and insert 2X long hook, allow glue to dry, and paint if quill was not dyed. Complete Turkey Quill Caterpillar.

The Dry Woolly Worm

The woolly worm is a very good caterpillar representation, particularly when tied on a long shank hook. The only trouble is that the fly sinks. Real caterpillars float like a chunk of balsa.

By substituting fur or polypropylene for the body, using a light wire hook, and dressing the fly with a flotant, a good topwater caterpillar pattern of the standard woolly worm design can be made. Dry fly quality hackle should be used, and it should be shorter than on the traditional wet pattern. Trimming a V-wedge from the bottom of the fly allows the imitation larva's belly to float partially penetrating the surface film like the naturals. This fly is especially effective when trout are spooky and want their meals floated quietly over them. By varying the color of dubbing and hackle and thickness of the body, you can imitate many species of caterpillars with this pattern.

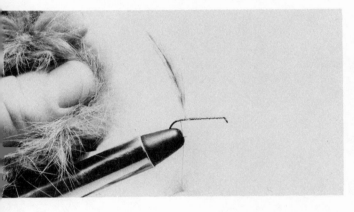

1 Attach a 2X long dry fly hook in vise and spiral thread over the shank. Attach a dry fly-quality hackle just forward of bend in hook; two hackles can be used if desired.

2 Dub on rabbit fur for body, and wind fur and thread forward to form a thick, cylindrical body.

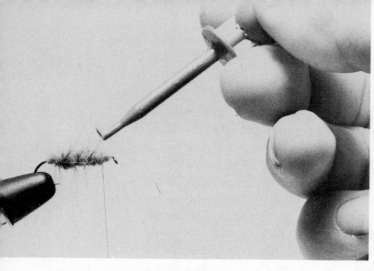
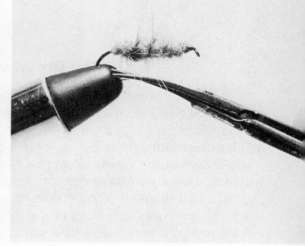

3 Wrap hackle forward over body palmer-style and tie off just behind eye of hook. Whip finish, trim excess thread, and apply drop of lacquer to head. Trim a V-wedge from bottom of fly for a flush float, and you have a dry Woolly Worm.

4 Woolly Worm variations: at bottom, the traditional wet fly, and two dry versions at top.

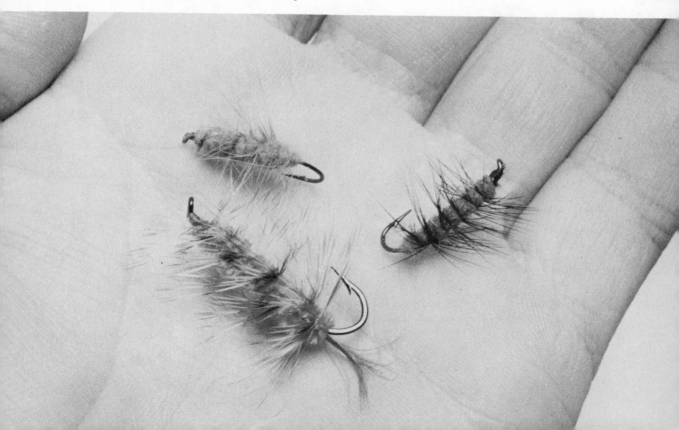

Neversink Skater

While the larvae are the most important trout food in this order, a few of Hewitt's famous impressionistic butterfly pattern should be stashed in every angler's vest especially for fishing quiet water. The Neversink Skater is a pattern that has taxed the analytical talents of countless fly dressers over the years. The master angler told few, if any, fellow fishermen of his special method for dressing these big imitations of adult butterflies. Vince Marinaro was the man who ultimately discovered the novel tying method, and he too kept the details largely secret for a number of years before describing his technique for dressing the fly in "Secret of the Neversink Skater," in a 1977 issue of *Outdoor Life*.

The fly ties best with large spade hackles—the few short feathers with long barbules found along the edge of rooster necks. Brown, black, and various shades of dun are useful, but the barbules should measure close to one inch, in order to form a fly with a two-inch diameter. The concave (dull) sides of the hackles are wound together around the middle of a small, light hook to form a sharp, knife-like edge of hackle barbules. This constitutes the entire fly. There is no body, no wings, no tail. Fished dead-drift, or with twitches and jerks across a calm surface, the skater is a deadly imitation. The two edges of hackle barbules from both feathers support each other. When the fly alights on the water, it rides on this sharp edge as it's skittered and fluttered in "butterfly fashion" over the trout. If the skater lands flat on its back, it can be gently inched up onto its hackle tips—at which time charging strikes are not uncommon.

1 Attach a #16 dry fly hook in vise and select two spade hackles from the edge of a neck with barbules at least one inch long. Hackles are fastened in as they are shown in this photo: *with concave sides forward.*

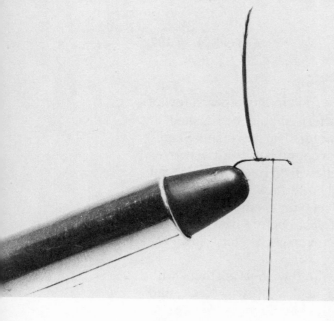

2 Bind unwaxed nylon thread to the hook; fasten one of the hackles in just behind the midpoint of the hook shank with the concave side facing forward. Bend the hackle stem up and take several turns of thread behind it. Trim the excess hackle tip.

3 Wind the hackle towards the eye of the hook. Fasten the hackle tip with thread and trim any excess.

4 With thumb and fingernails, push the wound hackle back towards rear of the hook to compact it.

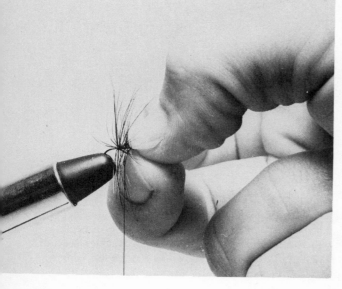

5 Fasten second hackle—concave side facing *rearward*—in front of the first one. Bend it upward and wrap the thread to point just behind the eye.

6 Wrap the second hackle forward, catch it with the thread, and trim the excess hackle tip.

7 With thumb and fingernails of both hands, push hackles tightly together. Whip finish, apply a drop of lacquer to windings, and Neversink Skater is complete.

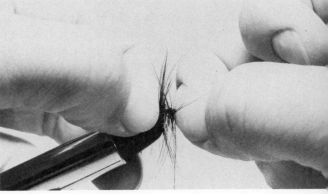

8 A finished Neversink Skater.

SOME COMMON CATERPILLARS

The larvae of most common Lepidoptera vary so little from species to species that precise identification of naturals is beyond the ability of all but highly trained entomologists. And from the fly fisherman's viewpoint, it becomes rather academic. Varying patterns with respect to length, thickness, and color are generally the only requirements necessary to match different varieties found along the stream. However, a brief look at a few typical Lepidoptera larvae will shed some light on the nature of these insects neglected by so many anglers.

GEOMETRID MOTHS (Geometridae). These common insects represent a very large family found worldwide. The adults—poor fliers as a rule—are sometimes eaten by trout. The larvae, however, are most important, and many anglers lump these caterpillars together under the name "inchworm." The larvae gained their common name "measuring worms" from the manner in which they hump virtually their entire bodies in the air as they move forward in a "looping" motion, as if they were measuring the earth by lengths of their body.

The caterpillars of this family are generally naked (setae or hairs are inconspicuous) and slender. There are over one thousand two hundred species of Geometridae in the U.S. and Canada alone; to give some idea of the complexity involved in precise identification of the Lepidoptera larvae, this one family contains a *small* subfamily, Hemitheinae (the green geometrids), that includes seventeen genera and sixty-four species.

All members of the Geometridae are foliage-feeders, and forests are their primary habitat. Several important geometrids include the fall cankerworm (*Alsophila pometaria*), the spring cankerworm (*Paleacrita vernata*), and the linden looper (*Erannis tilaria*). Clearly, with a family of this size there is much variation in color, but shades of green occur most often. Size also varies widely, but a great many of the larvae measure between 20 and 30 mm—roughly one inch.

GYPSY MOTH (*Porthetria dispar*). From a purely aesthetic viewpoint, the larva of this moth has a rather pleasing appearance when looked at singly. But to see them ravaging the plantlife in a forest and crawling over every tree in the woods is a heartbreaking sight.

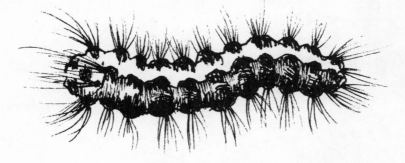

The gypsy moth was introduced into this country in 1869 by a French scientist who brought a number of egg clusters from his native country to Medford, Massachusetts in hopes of crossing the species with the silkworm. Eggs were accidentally spilled and larvae escaped. During the next twenty-five years the insect spread rapidly, stripping the foliage from millions of acres of trees. Their diffusion has abated in recent years, but infestations remain heavy in many areas stretching as far west as Minnesota, south to Texas, and along the Appalachian range.

The insects can devastate a forest, and a single female moth can lay up to four hundred eggs—usually on the trunks or limbs of trees. Eggs hatch in May and caterpillars feed for about six weeks on plants. Adults emerge after pupation during July and August. The larvae will attack virtually any tree, though oak, birch, and poplar are favored. Only the larger caterpillars, those measuring close to their full-grown length of two inches, feed extensively on conifers.

The larva of the gypsy moth is sooty gray and hairy, with yellow markings at the head. There are double rows of blue dots and red dots (tubercles) along the back of the larva.

Dave Johnson, who hails from the rich trout country of central Pennsylvania, says that "for the last couple of years our area has been plagued by an invasion of gypsy moths. The larvae this past summer had to be in many spots the most abundant terrestrial I've ever witnessed. From late May into July they're really sickening and are certainly taken by the trout."

NOTODONTID MOTHS (Notodontidae). Over one hundred species of this family have been recorded in the U.S. and Canada, and the larvae can be found on a wide variety of shrubs and deciduous trees. Colors range from brownish gray (poplar tent maker, *Ichthyura inclusa*) to black with yellow stripes (walnut caterpillar, *Datana integerrima*) to yellowish green (variable oak leaf caterpillar, *Heterocampa manteo*). The majority of these caterpillars occur in the eastern half of the country, but some, such as the red-humped caterpillar, occur throughout the U.S. and most of Canada. Size varies from 25 to 50 mm.

chapter
eight

LEAFHOPPERS . TREEHOPPERS
CICADAS

(HOMOPTERA)

With thirty thousand species, the leafhoppers and treehoppers are not only a large insect order, but also one of the most widely varied, in size and shape. They range from the wildly leaping treehoppers to scale bugs that look like inanimate fungus rather than living animals. They vary in size from the huge cicadas that may measure over two inches long to tiny aphids smaller than a pinhead. The length of a complete life cycle among the Homoptera is equally diverse, from those who spawn an entire generation in a matter of weeks to the slow-growing periodical cicada that takes seventeen years to mature.

The major insects included in the order Homoptera include the cicadas, froghoppers (spittlebugs), leafhoppers, treehoppers, planthoppers, aphids, whiteflies, scale insects, and mealybugs. All told, there are close to twenty families in this order. Only three of these insects warrant detailed scrutiny from the fly fisher—the leafhoppers, treehoppers, and cicadas. Occasionally froghoppers are eaten by trout, but they are so similar to leafhoppers in appearance that they can be lumped together for our purposes.

It's difficult to make sweeping generalizations about "Homoptera fishing" because of the great variety in life styles and size among these insects. But clearly, from a standpoint of day-to-day fishing, leafhoppers are the most important members of this order. They appear early in the spring and

LEAFHOPPER LIFE CYCLE

203

Cork Treehopper imitation.

can be found on the water throughout the entire fishing season. Some species even over-winter as adults and venture out on warm, sunny days in winter to feed actively.

Another common name for these insects is "dodger," referring to the nymph's habit of darting sideways to the opposite side of a plant when approached. Since they suck the juices of plants, leafhoppers cause much damage to all types of vegetation, from trees to grasses.

The insects range in size from 2.5 to 15 mm and come in a wide variety of colors, with yellow and pale green particularly common. The structure of most leafhopper species is quite similar, so from the fly fisherman's viewpoint this family can be represented with a single style of tie and varied in color and size when a particular species is present in numbers along the stream.

The leafhoppers develop by simple metamorphosis; five molts occur before the winged adult emerges. From egg to adult requires about two months, and for some species, as each generation matures, the insects migrate, travelling as far as three hundred miles.

Many leafhoppers winter as adults and feed whenever weather permits. By the late winter, the female develops eggs, three to four hundred of which are laid about the time the first spring growth begins. In five to forty days these eggs will hatch into young nymphs, which begin feeding on plant juices.

TREEHOPPER LIFE CYCLE

Treehoppers have received scant mention in the fishing literature, yet they are a common insect family and often end up in trout streams and the stomachs of fish. Treehoppers seem to be a particularly important food for trout in the late fall. I've taken numerous fish from freestone streams in October and November that had quantities of these insects in their gullets.

Treehoppers are odd-looking insects with high, humped backs (prothorax) that give them the appearance of thorns or buds on trees. This shape, coupled with green or brown coloration, camouflages the insects and helps to protect them from predators. Treehoppers also have well-developed hind legs and can jump enormous distances for their size.

The insects suck the juice from leaves, clover, wild plants, fruits, and crops. They are often found in grasses and shrubs, as well as in trees. Many species are, in fact, more commonly encountered on succulent clover and weeds than in trees. The exception would be in the fall, when many species fly to trees to mate.

The buffalo treehopper (*Stictocephala bubalus*) is a common species throughout the country. It is light green in color and about 9 mm long. Eggs are laid in young trees in the fall and hatch in the spring. The young go through five molts and feed on weeds and clover. After six weeks the adult emerges and spends some time feeding on weeds before returning to a tree to mate.

Treehoppers are relished by freestone stream trout.

CICADA LIFE CYCLE

The insects of the family Cicadidae, commonly mislabeled "locusts," are recognized as much by their song as by their appearance. The familiar steely drone of the cicada is a frequent accompaniment to a hot summer's evening. As with most insects, the song is only sung by the male cicadas, primarily to attract a mate. The high-pitched buzzing noise is created by vibrating membranes.

There are many species of cicadas besides the familiar seventeen-year periodical variety (*Magicicada septendecim*); in the U.S. alone over seventy-four species have been identified. *Tibicen dorsata*, which measures 54 mm, appears every year in the Midwest, sporting brown and black colorations. The dogday cicada (*Tibicen linnei*) is larger than the periodical cicada and has greenish edgings on its wings and lighter body markings. This cicada has a life cycle ranging from two to five years, but different broods appear each summer. The orchard cicada (*Platypedia areolata*), a common western species, measures only 18 mm and is bronze with greenish yellow markings.

From the fisherman's viewpoint *Magicicada septendecim* is the most important species. This seventeen-year cicada, the range of which includes roughly the eastern half of the U.S., lays its eggs in slits in trees and twigs from late May to early July. More than seventy species of trees are utilized for the egg-laying, though some of the most common ones are oaks, dogwood, apple, honey locust, and hickory. The young emerge six weeks later and drop to the earth. Here the antlike nymphs dig into the soil to find and suck the juices of roots. The cicada, growing at the pace of a snail, remains in this subterranean habitat for many years. Because of this slow growth rate a single tree can support an incredible number of cicada nymphs on its roots without perishing. Up to forty thousand cicadas may live off of a single tree.

When the time is ripe—late April through May—the cicadas emerge all at once during the night. They dig out of the soil and climb into trees where they undergo one final molt. The skin splits down the back and out comes the adult. Hundreds of thousands of adults emerge simultaneously. By coming out in such numbers, it is easier for the insects to find members of the opposite sex for mating. The vast quantities also ensure that a certain minimal number will escape the many predators waiting to snatch them up.

Adults live four to six weeks. The song of the seventeen-year cicada is somewhat somber, and the insect itself is slightly more slender than the dogday cicada. The eyes, wing veins, and legs are rust-colored; the body is brownish black. Adults measure about 40 mm.

If all cicadas across the country emerged at the same time—once every seventeen years—it would indeed be ridiculous to include these insects in a fishing book. However, there are actually many different overlapping broods of the periodical cicada that appear in different years. At least twenty distinct broods have been traced, and there is scarcely a year that the seventeen-year cicada doesn't appear somewhere. A lucky angler might be able to hit an emergence of cicadas several years running if he fished streams where the insects were ready to hatch at the proper times. In some localities up to seven separate broods may exist; the odds of hitting an emergence of cicadas here would be nearly fifty-fifty.

Charles Meck of Pennsylvania reports fishing the Little Juniata during the summer of 1973 when "thousands of cicadas fell to the water" and the trout gorged themselves on the sudden appearance of food. Yet Dave Johnson, who fishes Penn's Creek and other waters very close to the Juniata, writes that "the seven-year locust were *extremely* abundant" along the trout streams he frequents in 1974. Here is a case in point of overlapping broods of cicadas providing good sport for two years running in the same general area.

Cicadas differ in this short-lived appearance from most other terrestrials which are present for many months each year. However, due to their size and abundance during emergence periods, a few imitations of these insects should be stashed in every angler's box. It is a rare form of fishing you won't want to miss.

FISHING HOMOPTERA PATTERNS

The pace and duration of fishing treehopper and leafhopper patterns are virtually the opposite of cicada fishing. Where cicadas call for powerful rods and casts, leafhoppers require delicate tackle and a thistledown delivery. Cicadas are big, bulky bugs that incite slashing strikes from trout; leafhoppers are small, sometimes minute creatures that ride high on the surface film and the fish take them with gentle, sipping rises.

Leafhopper patterns will rarely bring up the old hookjaws that feed during cicada emergences, but due to their abundance over long periods of the season along virtually all trout streams, they must rank as the most important family in this order for the angler.

STRUCTURE AND FLY DESIGN

Leafhoppers

The jassid is the classic leafhopper pattern. It was created July, 1949. In *This Wonderful World of Trout* Charlie Fox describes Vince Marinaro's ebullience after originating the fly and its initial test on the Letort.

"About the fifth evening I was greeted by an enthusiastic and effervescing companion, 'I have the fly. Show me a jassid-eater and I think I can hook him.'

"There were two outcomes. First, I pointed out an incessant surface-feeder with which I had a nodding acquaintance and which, as far as I was concerned, was an untouchable fish. The trout was taken by the new fly on the first perfect float. Second, Vince handed me three of his beautiful little imitations which he called 'Jassids' '' (p. 23).

Over the ensuing three decades this clipped-hackle fly has proven its worth across the entire globe wherever trout fishing is done. But junglecock stocks have dwindled, and the flat wing has been replaced by any number of feathered and synthetic alternatives. Wing and body feathers from such birds as grouse, quail, mallard, and starling can be used; webby hackles from roosters are good substitutes when lacquered and cut to shape.

Leafhoppers can also be imitated with the wonderwing style of beetle pattern, and Dave Engerbretson's beetle tie also makes an exceptional leafhopper fly in smaller sizes. In short, virtually any of the clipped-hackle beetle patterns, when tied in small sizes, can represent leafhoppers as well. Which insect the trout takes the fly for, we'll never know. But the fact that the patterns represent two major orders (three really, when the true bugs are taken into account) can only work in their favor.

The clipped, palmered hackle tie with a flat overwing is far and away the best tying method for these light-bodied insects since many of them float high on the surface film. Some leafhoppers can, in fact, skitter across the surface and return to land when brushed or blown into the water. Most are not so lucky.

One example of a leafhopper tie is shown here. For others, consult Chapter 7 and tie the palmered hackle versions in small sizes (#18–24) and appropriate colors.

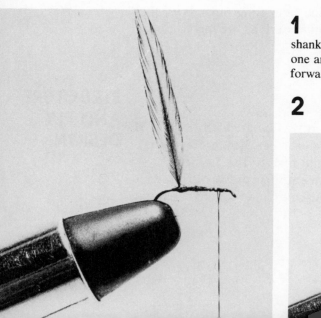

1 Attach a 3X fine wire dry fly hook (Mustad No. 94833) in vise and wind thread over hook shank. Attach dry fly-quality hackle with barbules one and one-half hook gaps long. Wind the thread forward to a point slightly behind eye of hook.

2 Palmer the hackle over the hook shank up to point where the thread is hanging.

3 Trim the hackle on top of the hook shank flat for placement of the overwing. Many gamebird feathers can be used for the overwing; this is a small feather found at the base of a mallard's primary flight feathers. Trim the stem to form a wing that will extend just slightly beyond the end of the hook. Spray it with acrylic.

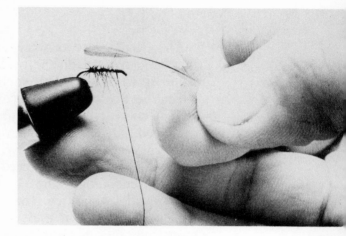

4 Attach wing flat over top of hook shank with several turns of thread. Trim excess feather stem.

5 Whip finish, trim a V-wedge from the hackle below the hook shank and apply a drop of lacquer or acrylic to head.

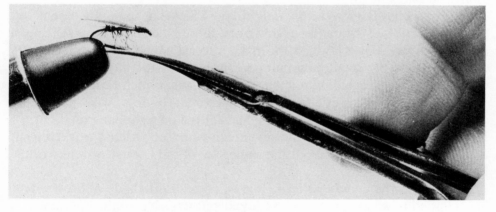

6 Completed Leafhopper.

Treehoppers

Treehoppers are somewhat denser than leafhoppers and often float lower in the surface film. For imitating their triangular forms three materials are particularly useful: cork, balsa, and clipped deer hair. You can't go larger than a size #16 hook for these insects, and #18s and #20s are usually more appropriate. Green and brown are the most common colors.

Cicadas

These bulky insects present a distinct challenge to the fly dresser due to their large size and distinctive behavior on the water. No one seems to have come up with the perfect solution to date.

Charlie Fox says he's taken some trout in wooded areas when the seventeen-year "locust" is thick on big brown Hewitt skater flies.

I faced the cicada dilemma one day on a small rainbow trout stream in western Virginia several years back. The insects were thick on shoreline foliage and enough had entered the stream to put the trout on the lookout for them. To encourage things, I tossed a few more in from my position behind a shoreline dogwood tree. They were devoured greedily, though some of the fish were so small it took repeated stabs before they could wrestle the monstrous flies down their tiny gullets.

Deer hair bass bugs were the only things I had that remotely resembled the big insects, so I trimmed one down and tossed it out to a trout shifting in a broken flow, and I hooked the fish. Several more trout attacked the outsized fly on the small mountain stream before "the day of the locust" came to a close—including one handsome fourteen-inch rainbow.

I asked George Harvey, dean of Pennsylvania fly tiers, what pattern he uses for the cicada and found that he had settled on a similar expedient. "I have tied deer flies to imitate the seventeen-year 'locust' that worked well. But I think any bass bug about the same size of the 'locust' would work," Harvey commented.

For his specific cicada pattern Harvey uses an off shade of brown deer hair clipped to shape on a size #4 hook, but adds "I don't think color is really important." Four blue dun hackles are tied in by the butts at the thorax to form the wings of the insect. The wings are an important part of Harvey's pattern, and he works this fly with a twitching motion to mimic the behavior of the naturals.

"When the live 'locust' is blown or lands on the water the wings actually buzz with the fluttering. I cast and retrieve with short, sharp jerks," says Harvey. "The first time I ever used the imitation—on the first cast—I caught an eighteen-inch brown!"

APPLE LEAFHOPPER (*Empoasca maligna*). The common name for this leafhopper is a bit misleading since the insect also eats many cultivated and wild plants besides apples, including grasses, tree leaves, and weeds. Adults are yellowish green with six or eight white spots and measure about 3 mm.

WHITE-BANDED ELM LEAFHOPPER (*Scaphoideus luteolus*). This leafhopper carries elm phloem necrosis, a virus of the American elm, and is perhaps the most destructive of all leafhoppers where forests are concerned. Nymphs are brown with a distinct white bar across the back, adults are more speckled in appearance. There is one generation per year, and the insect overwinters in the egg stage. The white-banded elm leafhopper is found as far west as Nebraska and south to Georgia.

BEET LEAFHOPPER (*Circulifer tenellus*). This species is common throughout much of the western part of the country. It measures 3.5-4 mm and varies in color from greenish yellow to brown to gray, often with darker markings. The insect is believed to be the only carrier of the virus curly top, which injures crops, flowering plants, and weeds. It's at home in dry regions and favors sunny weather. The beet leafhopper is common on non-agricultural lands and actually only attacks the crops in its path.

These insects overwinter as adults and feed whenever weather permits.

SOME COMMON LEAFHOPPERS

chapter
nine

MINOR TERRESTRIALS

TRUE BUGS (Hemiptera)

At dawn the first hint of color comes from the orange and yellow leaves, remnants of autumn on the foothills of the Massanutten Mountain Range. Fall is slipping away in the Shenandoah Valley, and the grays of winter will soon replace the bright green grass and yellowing trees.

But there is another bit of color apparent as I gaze from the cabin window—the brilliant halloween hues of the boxelder bugs perched by the dozens on the screened window. The orange and black half-inch "true bugs" hover by the hundreds around dwellings and decaying logs seeking a crevice in which to hide for the winter.

These common true bugs (Hemiptera) are often plentiful along trout streams in the fall, and they are well taken by the fish when they stumble into the stream. Charlie Fox and his cohorts call the little fellows "Joe bugs," and many others no doubt lump them incorrectly with the beetles. They actually come closer in appearance to leafhoppers—but even here there are significant differences.

Whereas leafhopper wings are generally similar in structure, true bugs have two strikingly different pairs of wings. It is from the front wings that the order derives its name. The forward half of this pair is thickened and leathery, resembling the elytra of beetles. The rear half of the forewings is membranous. Hence the name, "half winged."

213

Both of the hind wings of the true bugs, on the other hand, are membranous throughout. They are held folded beneath the front wings when not in use. The overlapping tips of the forewings form a characteristic X mark that is often used to identify the true bugs.

LIFE CYCLE

The majority of the twenty-three thousand species in the order Hemiptera are terrestrial insects, and most feed on plants. Some, such as the assassin bugs, damsel bugs, and ambush bugs, are predacious, but these are generally of less importance to the fisherman than the plant-eaters. Many herbivorous true bugs feed on the underside of leaves, a habit which makes them go unnoticed by all but the most observant anglers.

True bug metamorphosis is incomplete; young nymphs develop gradually through a series of molts. Only the adults bear wings, and the young are often brilliantly colored.

Many true bugs winter over as adults and are quite active late into the fall; some even venture out during the winter on warm, sunny days. The bugs typically hide under rubbish, grass clumps, leaves, bark, or in buildings as winter approaches. When they first appear in spring and again when they seek locations to hide in during the fall, they're likely to enter the trout streams in substantial quantities. Dribs of true bugs will fall from their perches on grass, brush, and trees throughout the summer months, however, and patterns imitating them can be effective at virtually any time of year.

TRUE BUG STRUCTURE AND FLY DESIGN

The forms of true bugs vary rather widely, though many species have structural similarities with the beetles. The same imitations and methods of tying for beetles can, in fact, be used to create excellent true bug patterns. The most common true bugs, such as the boxelder, are somewhat elongate and rounded in shape—about like a watermelon seed. Such squatter specimens as the stink bugs call for fuller-bodied imitations. True bugs run the gamut from 3 to 26 mm, though most are in the 4 to 14 mm range. Hook sizes #8 through #22 are usually appropriate. Color patterns can be quite distinctive in the true bugs, and it's wise to match as closely as possible the appearance of the underside of the naturals. Bright green, orange, black, and white are common hues, though many stink bugs, in particular, sport dull shades of gray and brown.

Three boxelder bug adults and a nymph (lower right); note characteristic X lines formed by the positioning of the wings on the back of the insects.

Fishing the true bugs is usually a straightforward affair of drifting the imitation gently over feeding fish or likely looking holding lies along shore. When the bugs are numerous, fish in midstream will also take imitations well. The heavier patterns, such as cork or deer hair imitations of stink bugs, can occasionally be fished with the sound cast.

TARNISHED PLANT BUG (*Lygus lineolaris*). This is a very common member of Miridae, the largest family in the order (one thousand six hundred species in the U.S. and Canada). The bug measures 5 mm and varies in color from dark brown to green with yellow, brownish red, and black markings. It feeds on crops as well as weeds such as mustard, goldenrod, and aster. The tarnished plant bug is found throughout North America and overwinters in the adult stage. Size #18–20 hooks and any of the clipped-hackle beetle patterns can be used to imitate this common bug.

BOXELDER BUG (*Leptocoris trivittatus*). This 12–14 mm true bug is common throughout North America. During autumn they become particularly noticeable as they try to get into houses for the winter. Remaining active late in the year, they crawl and fly about through November in many areas.

The wings of the boxelder bug are black on top with reddish orange line markings and orange underneath. The underside of the body is orange in the middle circled by black. Food includes boxelder, maple, ash, and fruit trees. They actually do very little damage, however, and one can't help but feel a vague affection for these handsome, big-eyed bugs.

Several patterns have proven effective for imitating the boxelder bug. Perhaps the best is a modified version of Dave Engerbretson's My Beetle. Use a section of dyed, bright orange goose quill for the overwing and black hackle wrapped on a size #12 or #14 2X long hook (Mustad No. 94831) for legs. (See pages 146–47 for tying instructions.)

STINK BUGS (Pentatomidae). This family contains many similar-shaped insects ranging from 8 to 15 mm in length. They are typically brown or green in color and are for the most part plant-feeders. They get their name from a fetid fluid they exude through two openings on their sides when aggravated. Stink bugs are squat and broad in appearance and often feature a triangle where head and thorax meet. Cork and clipped deer hair patterns imitate these dense insects well. Another option is to use a single piece of turkey quill cut to the shape of the bugs and epoxied to a hook.

Turkey-quill stink bug. Tying method is same as that for turkey quill caterpillar.

TRUE FLIES (Diptera)

For anglers the name Diptera immediately conjures up images of tiny midges of the Chironomidae family. While it's true that this predominantly aquatic family represents an important source of food for trout, other flies in this order, many of them terrestrial, are consumed by trout over the course of a season.

Diptera is a vast order encompassing 16,500 species in North America. Though they lack the structural diversity of other orders, true flies do vary considerably in configuration and size. The largest member of this order has a three-inch body and similar wingspan. The smallest true fly is only one-fiftieth as long.

Almost all true flies can be identified readily by their possession of a single pair of membranous wings—the forewings. The hindwings are reduced to knobbed, threadlike structures called *halteres*, which act as balancers during flight. The name Diptera, in fact, translates as "two winged" and applies to this distinctive single set of wings.

Body shape of true flies ranges from slender to corpulent, and they are typically soft, pulpy insects. From the fly dresser's viewpoint most important terrestrial Diptera are on the plump side, and fat bodies of fur, peacock herl, polypropylene, or deer hair will make a like imitation. Wings of many flies are hyaline and are held over the back where their visibility to trout is minimal. However, other flies have smoky gray or mottled wings, and these may be visible to the fish where they extend over the body.

In spite of their seemingly hefty, solid appearance, many of the land-born true flies such as the common deer- and houseflies float remarkably high on the surface film. I was first made aware of this ability one spring day while fishing Clarks Creek in Pennsylvania. Deerflies were present in the shoreline foliage, and several mating pairs fell clumsily to the stream. Here they floated down—high and dry and seemingly unconcerned with their dilemma. They buzzed about and almost strode across the water's surface on their padded feet. Trout eventually stole several of these insects from the surface.

At the time I thought surely their bodies must be at least partially breaking through the surface film, though it didn't look like they were. Later I found out they do not penetrate the meniscus—not during the initial landing on the water, at any rate. I was on the porch photographing several winged ants in a basin of water at the time. Suddenly a buzzing object swept by my head and landed in the small bowl. A fly! Cashing in on the sudden opportunity, I clicked away the remainder of the film and watched the fly. The insect remained high on the film; its feet made the tiniest of impressions on the water's surface tension.

In a trout stream these flies might eventually sink lower into the film, but they float exceedingly dry when first entering the water. Imitations should follow suit, with the exception of a few large varieties such as the horsefly that sometimes float lower in the meniscus. Wet imitations of terrestrial true flies are clearly inappropriate, however.

Common houseflies have a well-earned reputation as disease carriers. But even these flies have their positive attributes. Their most important function—one which we could little afford to lose—is their role as scavengers. The insects clean up enormous quantities of vegetative and animal waste, especially during their larval stages. The true flies also pollinate more flowers than bees do and consume large numbers of harmful insects, particularly caterpillars.

LIFE CYCLE

Metamorphosis of the true flies is complete. The larvae, commonly termed *maggots*, vary in shape from slender to burly and lack legs. They are blind and rarely live exposed to the sun. Dark, damp areas, such as decaying plant and animal matter, are favored.

Larvae may hatch from eggs after as short a period as twenty-four hours during warm weather and be ready to pupate in five days. Since as many as five hundred eggs may be laid by a single housefly, it's apparent how flies could easily become frighteningly abundant if disease, parasites, and predators did not keep their numbers in check.

The larva of the housefly changes into a pupa after reaching a size of 8–12 mm. Three to ten days pass before the adult emerges. The life span of the adult typically ranges from two weeks to a month, and up to fourteen generations of houseflies may occur in one summer in the mid-Atlantic area, eight in New England.

FISHING THE DIPTERA

Diptera patterns cannot be classed with the ants or beetles in order of importance, but there are situations where trout will come readily to these imitations and ignore most others. Deer- and horsefly patterns are best during hot summer months, with deerflies especially prevalent along woodland streams. Horseflies are often found where livestock grazes near the water. The housefly is common along pasture streams where cattle manure provides prime breeding ground for the insects. March flies have on several occasions been the prevalent food form on eastern rivers early in the spring.

TRUE FLY STRUCTURE AND FLY DESIGN

Though most true flies appear rather chunky, they generally land gracefully on the water's surface. Sometimes it appears as if that's exactly what they wanted to do. Unfortunately for the flies, few are able to take off as easily as they set down.

Imitations should follow the lead of the naturals—alight gently and float softly over the fish. I've rarely had luck manipulating these flies. Long, scrutinizing looks from trout are common when using true fly imitations since the insects are not as familiar a food form as say the ants or hoppers. Realistic patterns and light tippets are the order of the day.

Polywing Housefly

PATTERNS

In keeping with my penchant for simple flies, I devised this basic pattern to represent the common housefly as well as stable flies, blue bottles, deerflies, March flies, and other common Diptera. It consists simply of a plump fur body with clipped, palmered hackle and a sparse wing of polypropylene tied flat over the back. The size, color, and precise shape of the body can be altered to match specimens prevalent along the water at any given time. A body of gray rabbit fur with a bit of dull yellow or rust mixed in is best for the housefly; this pattern is effective in sizes #14 through #22.

Aesthetically, the fly leaves something to be desired, and it was without great expectations that I tied it onto my tippet for the first time on Pennsylvania's Antietam Creek. A deep-bodied, 18½-inch brown trout that I had caught the year before was still there, hovering in a foot of water in a long, flat pool. Cautiously I worked out the line and dropped the fly above the poised fish.

The current was slow, and the fish also rose slowly beneath the fly, drifting under it until his nose nearly touched the hook. As my nerves neared the breaking point, he stabbed hard and vengefully at the polywing fly; a sharp snap of the wrist set him off on a brisk run.

1 Attach a 3X fine wire hook (Mustad No. 94833) in vise and wind thread onto the shank. Bind a dun hackle in just in front of the bend of the hook; barbules should be one and one-half times length of hook gap.

2 Dub on a plump fur body of appropriate color, stopping slightly behind eye of hook.

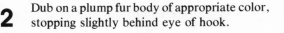
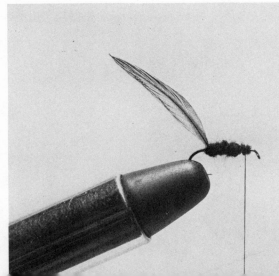

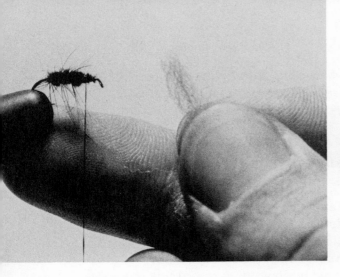

3 Wind hackle forward, palmer-style, and tie off where body ends at front of hook. Trim hackle from top of fly to allow placement of wings.

4 Select a small parcel of polypropylene for wings, ranging in color from grey to white depending on the opacity of the naturals' wings. Avoid using too much polypropylene; the wing should be quite sparse. Bind the polypropylene on top of the hook shank so that fibers extend slightly out to the sides and over the back of the body. The wings should come even with the end of the body; if necessary, trim them to form the tapered shape of the naturals' wings. Wrap thread to form fairly prominent head and whip finish. Trim a V-wedge from the bottom of the fly and the Polywing House-fly is complete.

Lively's Horse Fly

Chauncy K. Lively has carved a niche for himself as one of the most astute and creative fly tiers practicing the craft today. His patterns are fresh, realistic, and often innovative in design. The Horse Fly, which he described in his February, 1977 column in the *Pennsylvania Angler*, is an example of just such a tie. It is simple to construct, uses just a single bunch of deer hair, and presents a realistic image of this outsized insect to the trout.

As Lively notes in his piece, it is also adaptable to many true fly forms other than the horsefly. "I call it a Horse Fly, but the pattern, in sizes #10 down to #22, is adaptable to many representations, from the Robust Bot Flies to the little Blue Bottles. All share a squat appearance, with prominent eyes and wings folded flat over the back."

1 Fasten a hook in the vise (Mustad No. 94833 or 94840) and wind the thread over the hook to a point one-third of the shank length back from the eye. Select a bunch of black deer hair and even the tips in the hair stacker. The hair should be three full hook lengths long from the tips to tie-in point.

2 Holding hair on top of hook shank, tie in and spiral thread in tight wraps around hair and shank back to the bend.

3 Next, wind the thread back over the wrappings to the tie-in point. Trim the deer hair butts at the front of the hook.

4 Grasp the deer hair by the loose tips and pull it forward, binding it with thread between the initial tie-in point and the eye.

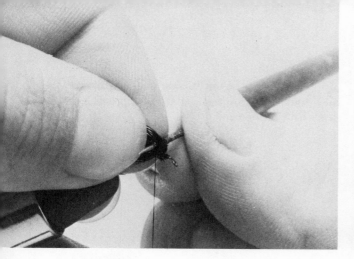

5 Place a dubbing needle crossways on the hair at the tie-in point. Fold the hair back over needle and hold it there with left hand. Withdraw the dubbing needle and make a tight loop of thread over the hair. Half-hitch or take several more turns of thread.

6 For legs, take three pieces of deer hair from trimmings and fasten underneath body. Wind the thread between the legs to separate them.

7 Whip finish head and apply drop of lacquer and the Horse Fly is complete.

SOME COMMON TRUE FLIES   **MARCH FLIES** (Bibionidae). The flies in this family have short, thick legs, and females are often stout in the abdomen. The insects are usually hairy and dark, though they may have red or yellow markings. The common name *March fly* derives from the appearance in early spring of the species *Bibio albipennis* in large quantities. Charlie Fox has seen these flies more than once along trout streams, and he says, ''The orange-legged March fly is highly cyclic, but when in abundance a floating imitation, like the right size John Crowe beetle, is just about necessary.'' March flies are typically 8–11 mm and hook sizes 14–18 are usually appropriate.

HORSE- AND DEERFLIES (Tabanidae). These vicious flies are common in woodland habitat and appear in greatest numbers during the hottest seasons. The females live on the blood of man and beast, while the males eat the nectar of flowers and sap. The larger horseflies belong to the genus *Tabanus* and feature large heads, protruding eyes, and stout bodies. Two hundred species are contained in this genus.

Deerflies belong to the genus *Chrysops*. They are smaller than horseflies and often are active during rainy weather. Some sixty species are found in the eastern portion of the U.S.

HOUSEFLIES (Muscidae). The housefly (*Musca domestica*) may be the most well known and least welcome insect in existence. Its filthy habits also make it a potentially dangerous insect: Each housefly carries an average of over one million bacteria per insect. Eggs are laid on manure or decaying vegetable matter in clusters of 75 to 100.

The family Muscidae contains numerous other species that closely resemble the housefly, such as the stable fly (*Stomoxys calcitrans*). Size varies greatly, from 2 to 10 mm. Most are gray or brown in color, though yellow and black are sometimes present. Males of the common housefly have a brownish yellow tint on the underside of the abdomen; females are tinted reddish here.

LACEWINGS (Neuroptera)

The Neuroptera is a small order of aquatic and terrestrial insects that includes the dobsonflies, alderflies, lacewings, antlions, dustywings, mantispids, and snakeflies. Dobsonflies and alderflies are aquatic; the others are terrestrial.

There are three hundred forty species of lacewings in North America. The name *Neuroptera* comes from the Greek words for "nerve" and "wing" and describes well the four delicately veined, membranous wings these insects have. Though I have found dustywings and mantispids on trout waters, lacewings are the most likely land-born insects in this order to end up in the gullets of fish. Even these are not particularly common insects in most areas, and appropriate-sized caddis patterns from the angler's fly box will usually do the trick should lacewings appear along the stream in significant numbers.

At rest, lacewings hold their wings folded tentlike over their backs and appear very similar to caddis flies, to which they are closely related. Two of the most common species are the brown lacewing (*Hemerobius pacificus*), a western variety, and the green lacewing (*Chrysopa oculata*), found east of the Rocky Mountains. Both feed heavily on leafhoppers, and the larvae have been known to consume as many as sixty aphids per hour. Lacewings are usually seen near twilight on summer nights as they venture out to feed, mate, or lay eggs.

Ronalds treats the lacewing ("Gold-Eyed Gauze Wing") in his classic work, *The Fly-fisher's Entomology*. The delicate, apple-green insect, he says, is present until September along English streams and "affords great sport."

TERMITES (Isoptera)

The termite order is not of major importance to the fly fisherman, simply because these insects seldom venture out into the open, avoiding both light and dry air as they live out their lives in subterranean habitats. The only time the termite might enter the trout food picture is during its mating flights, which occur in spring and early summer. At this time winged sexuals with dark, hardened bodies take off in great numbers. The termites do not mate in flight, as many ants do. They land a short distance from their colony, and a king and queen pair up as mates for life. They break off their wings, and then they find a nesting site; weeks later, mating occurs. If some termites did fall into trout streams during these flights, they may well be mistaken for ants by many fishermen.

Actually there are important differences between the ants and termites. The name Isoptera translates as "equal wings" and applies to the two pairs of opaque, equal-sized wings that are held flat over the back of sexual termites. Ants, as sexuals, have two pairs of unequal-sized wings that are often transparent and usually much shorter in proportion to the body than those of termites. Another major difference between the ants and termites is that the latter lack the thin petiole, or waist, seen in ants.

In spite of these structural differences, ant patterns usually suffice in the event that termites set down on the trout stream in numbers. This is simply not a common enough occurrence to warrant devising specific patterns.

CENTIPEDES (Class Chilopoda)

These long, flattish animals feature hollow claws which they use to paralyze their victims. Different species vary widely in form, though most varieties feature prominent legs. There may be as few as fifteen pairs of legs on a centipede or as many as one hundred seventy-three. One pair protrudes from each body segment.

For imitating centipedes I prefer either a dry woolly worm dressed on a long-shank hook or a turkey quill trimmed to shape with a considerable number of feather barbules left extending from the body to mimic the prominent legs on these critters. Brown and grey are good colors for all patterns.

MILLIPEDES (Class Diplopoda)

These are the so-called "thousand-leggers." Chunkier than centipedes, their mode of travel is as slow as the centipede's is fast. A favorite strategy of this animal is to curl up into a ball and play 'possum' when disturbed. Decaying vegetable matter is their principal food, and millipedes are common along woodland streams, particularly in damp, shaded areas.

These arthropods, not really "insects," are often large and call for imitations tied on 2X long shank hooks in sizes #6 through #10. Two pairs of legs protrude from each segment of the animal's body, but these do not figure prominently in the trout's view of the millipede; I rarely include them in imitations. Cork, clipped deer hair, or turkey quill type imitations of caterpillars serve well to mimic the long, cylindrical forms of these creatures, and brown is the most common color. Millipedes generally enter the water rather clumsily, and a cast that makes a bit of noise is often appropriate.

SPIDERS (Class Arachnida)

Next to the Insecta, this is the largest class of Arthropoda, containing fifty thousand described species. Also included in the Arachnida are mites, harvestmen, and scorpions. With few exceptions, these creatures are terrestrial in habits and feed on other animals, mainly at night. The head and thorax are united in spiders to form a cephalothorax. While they vary widely in external form, the two body segments are characteristic of virtually all spiders. Adults have four pairs of legs.

Spiders are of minor importance in the diet of trout, but some specific patterns made of clipped deer hair and cork have worked well on occasion, particularly along forested stretches of water. For cork spiders I like thread legs; with clipped deer patterns a few strands of hair are left extending from each side to mimic the eight legs. These flies work best in grays and browns on hook sizes #14 through #18.

The spider pattern that's most well known is not a truly imitative dressing at all. The common "spider" fly actually serves as more of an attractor than a realistic imitation of the spider form. Like the Neversink skater it is used to provoke rises from anger or curiosity as much as from hunger. Spiders differ from the skater in having a body—usually of tinsel, floss, or quill—and sometimes tails; the hackle is also shorter than that found on skaters. These patterns are tied on short-shank hooks.

John Atherton was perhaps the strongest proponent of the powers of the spider. In his classic work, *The Fly and the Fish*, he wrote: "if I had to be limited to one dry fly it would be the spider, without any doubt. . . . It can be used in so many more ways than the conventional fly . . . and best of all, it brings up the large fish." (p. 53.)

Like skaters, spiders can be fished dead drift, inched upstream in subtle twitches, raced across the water with hard jerks, or dapped downstream with a greased leader and buffeting hindwind. Trout often come to the fly with a rush of enthusiasm, leap over top of it, and nab the offering on their downward lunge—antics that are sure to send chills down the angler's spine.

Variations of spider patterns: spider with tinsel body, spider with no body, spider with floss body and no tail.

chapter
ten

EPILOG

It is autumn in the Shenandoah Valley. Dry leaves, broken loose from the hardwoods on the Massanutten Mountain Range have started to gather around the foundation of my cabin. Through the window I can see wood ducks preening themselves along the shores of the river, flaunting their brilliant plumage in the falling light. Silently, I hope for a few flank feathers.

Outside an almond-hued ant scurries in and out of the patchwork of sunlight streaking through the Chinese elm in the yard. An American field cricket, enfeebled but not yet silenced by the first frosts, creaks out his last message from the stone walkway. As I pass, the familiar summer music stops altogether, and I feel a twinge of sadness.

The Japanese beetles that ravaged the elm tree earlier in the summer have disappeared completely, but I know their offspring are under my feet right now. Next year the larvae will hatch and continue the species. Beetle fishing will resume. I can almost see their copper-green backs in my mind as I inspect the few decrepit leaves the beetles' appetites and the hard frosts have left clinging to the tips of the tightening branches.

Their swift-footed relatives in the Coleoptera order, the ground beetles, still have a hunt or two left in them. Tonight, under the mask of darkness they will stalk through their hunting grounds in the woodlot. Prey is growing scarcer as winter approaches, but the predators will find a few caterpillars and ants for a final autumn repast.

Some hoppers, too, have survived the first frosts of fall. But they are slower now, their bounding foreshortened by the lowering temperatures in the Valley. Over by the water, the treehoppers still leap with summer's quickness, though. Like a midget frog, the tiny brownie catapults itself through the air to flee my nudging fingertip. And most delicate of all, the hair-covered caterpillar clutches the gray bark of an oak. Somnolent in fall's cool grip, it seeks only a suitable nook in which to spin its cocoon and work the dazzling magic of metamorphosis. Even the houseflies soar more slowly now, and for that, at least, I am grateful.

The rods are cleaned and cased; my reels put away. Even as the terrestrials wind down their activities I have been half-heartedly closing out my fishing season. The fly boxes have been sorted through and filed for the winter. But even while snows cover my yard and the river flows ice-white and silently, there will be a few insect stragglers ranging about—cold-resistant species that venture out on warmer days. And if I break out the gear on a sunny January afternoon, I may find a willing fish or two that will take my ant or beetle imitations. Just a thought.

BIBLIOGRAPHY

Atherton, John. *The Fly and the Fish*. New York: Freshet Press, 1971.

Baker, Whiteford L. *Eastern Forest Insects*. Washington, D.C.: United States Department of Agriculture, Miscellaneous Publication No. 1175, 1972.

Barker, Will. *Familiar Insects of America*. New York: Harper & Brothers, 1960.

Barrett, Peter. "The Magic 40 Degree Mark." *Field & Stream,* May, 1977, p. 76.

Bashline, James L. *Night Fishing For Trout*. New York: Freshet Press, 1973.

Bergman, Ray. *Trout*. New York: Alfred A. Knopf, 1976.

Boyle, Robert H., and Whitlock, Dave, eds. *The Fly-tyer's Almanac*. New York: Crown, 1975.

Brooks, Charles E. *The Trout and the Stream*. New York: Crown, 1974.

Brooks, Joe. *Trout Fishing*. New York: Harper & Row, 1972.

Chauvin, Remy. *The World of an Insect*. New York: McGraw-Hill, 1967.

Comstock, John Henry. *An Introduction to Entomology*. Binghamton: Cornell University Press, 1920.

Costello, David F. *The World of the Ant*. Philadelphia: J.B. Lippincott, 1968.

Cotton, Charles, *The Compleat Angler*. London: Oxford University Press.

Crowe, John. "Approach." *Pennsylvania Angler,* August, 1975, p. 16.

————. *Modern ABC's of Fresh Water Fishing*. Harrisburg: Stackpole, 1965.

Dalton, Stephen. *Borne on the Wind*. New York: Reader's Digest Press, 1975.

Dean, Jim. "The All-purpose Fly." *Field & Stream,* August, 1975, p. 76.

Engerbretson, Dave. "Tackle and Tactics for Low-Water Trout." *Fly Fisherman,* July, 1977, p. 32.

Evans, Glyn. *The Life of Beetles*. New York: Macmillan Publishing Inc., Hafner Press, 1975.

Fanning, Eleanor Ivanye. *Insects From Close Up*. New York: Thomas Y. Crowell Co., 1965.

Farb, Peter. *The Insects*. New York: Time Inc., 1962.

Flick, Art, ed. *Art Flick's Master Fly-tying Guide*. New York: Crown, 1972.

Fox, Charles K. *This Wonderful World of Trout*. New York: Freshet Press, 1963.

Frost, S.W. *Insect Life and Insect Natural History*. New York: Dover Publications, Inc., 1942.

Gerlach, Rex. *Creative Fly Tying and Fly Fishing*. New York: Winchester Press, 1974.

Gerlach, Rex. *Fly Fishing The Lakes*. New York: Winchester Press, 1972.

Glick, Perry A. *Collecting Insects by Airplane, with Special Reference to Dispersal of the Potato Leafhopper*. Washington, D.C.: United States Department of Agriculture, 1960.

Grove, Alvin R. *The Lure and Lore of Trout Fishing*. New York: Freshet Press, 1971.

Halford, F.M. *Dry-fly Fishing*. Reading, England: Barry Shurlock Co., 1973.

Harvey, George W. *Techniques of Fly Tying and Fishing*. Harrisburg: Pennsylvania Fish Commission, 1976.

Heacox, Cecil E. *The Compleat Brown Trout*. New York: Winchester Press, 1974.

Heckman, Bruce H. "The Coachman and—the Moth Hatch?" *Fly Fisherman* April/May, 1973, p. 56.

Henkin, Harmon. *Fly Tackle*. Philadelphia: J.B. Lippincott Co., 1976.

Hewitt, Edward R. *A Trout and Salmon Fisherman for Seventy-five years*. Croton-on-Hudson: Van Cortlandt Press, 1972.

Hocking, Brian. *Six-legged Science*. Cambridge: Schenkman Publishing Co., 1968.

Hoffman, Ben. "A New Twist on an Old Worm," *Pennsylvania Angler*, July, 1974, p. 26.

Jennings, Preston J. *A Book of Trout Flies*. New York: Crown, 1970.

Jorgensen, Poul. *Dressing Flies For Fresh and Salt Water*. New York: Freshet Press, 1973.

———. *Modern Fly Dressing for the Practical Angler*. New York: Winchester Press, 1976.

Kirk, David. "Resting and Feeding Behavior of Brown Trout." *Trout Magazine*, July 1976, p. 18.

Koch, Ed. *Fishing the Midge*. New York: Freshet Press, 1972.

La Fontaine, Gary. *Challenge of the Trout*. Missoula: Mountain Press, 1976.

Lanham, Url. *The Insects*. New York: Columbia University Press, 1964.

Larson, Peggy P. and Mervin W. *All About Ants*. Cleveland: World Publishing Company, 1965.

Leonard, J. Edson. *The Essential Fly Tier*. Englewood Cliffs: Prentice Hall, 1976.

Lively, Chauncy K. "An Upwing Ant." *Pennsylvania Angler*, Harrisburg, May 1977, p. 26.

Lively, Chauncy K. "The Carpenter Ant Revisited." *Pennsylvania Angler*, Harrisburg, November 1974, p. 26.

Lively, Chauncy K. "Hewitt's Venerable Skater." *Pennsylvania Angler*, Harrisburg, January 1978, p. 26.

Lively, Chauncy K. "The Horse Fly." *Pennsylvania Angler*, Harrisburg, February 1977, p. 26.

Lively, Chauncy K. "The Japanese Beetle." *Pennsylvania Angler*, Harrisburg, May 1973, p. 26.

Lively, Chauncy K. "Lake Erie King Mystery Fly." *Pennsylvania Angler*, Harrisburg, November 1970, p. 24.

Lively, Chauncy K. "The Single-Hank 'Hopper.' " *Pennsylvania Angler*, Harrisburg, November 1977, p. 26.

Lively, Chauncy K. "Tying 'Wonder Wings'." *Pennsylvania Angler*, Harrisburg, March 1973, p. 34.

Lutz, Frank E. *Field Book of Insects*. New York: G.P. Putnam's Sons, 1918.

MacAloney, Harvey J. *The Hemlock Borer*. Washington, D.C.: United States Department of Agriculture, 1967.

MacAloney, Harvey J. *The Saratoga Spittlebug*. Washington, D.C.: United States Department of Agriculture, 1971.

Marinaro, Vincent C. "Secret of the Neversink Skater." *Outdoor Life,* New York, 1977, p. 75.

Marinaro, Vincent C. *A Modern Dry-fly Code*. New York: Crown, 1970.

––––––. *In the Ring of the Rise*. New York: Crown, 1976.

McClane, A.J. *The Practical Fly Fisherman*. Englewood Cliffs: Prentice-Hall, 1975.

––––––. *Fishing with McClane*. (George Reiger, editor). Englewood Cliffs: Prentice-Hall, 1975.

–––––– ed. *McClane's Standard Fishing Encyclopedia*. New York: Holt, Rinehart and Winston, 1965.

Meck, Charles R. "The Cork-Bodied Ant." *Pennsylvania Angler,* September, 1977, p. 26.

Needham, Paul R. *Trout Streams*. San Francisco: Holden-Day Inc., 1969.

Newman, L. Hugh. *Ants from Close Up*. New York: Thomas Y. Crowell Co., 1967.

Niemeyer, Ted. "A Handful of Hoppers." *Fly Fisherman,* June, 1977, p. 59.

Oldroyd, Harold. *The Natural History of Flies*. New York: W.W. Norton Co., 1964.

Oldroyd, Harold. *Collecting, Preserving, and Studying Insects*. New York: Macmillan Co., 1958.

Ostrander, Robert L. "Fall Browns and Yellowjackets." *Pennsylvania Angler,* September, 1973, p. 12.

Ovington, Ray. *Basic Fly Fishing and Fly Tying*. Harrisburg: Stackpole, 1973.

Parker, Barry. "Looking Into the Trout's Window." *Fly Fisherman,* March, 1976, p. 90.

Reinholdt, William N., Jr. "The Calcaterra Ant." *Fly Fisherman,* Feb/March, 1973, p. 56.

Romoser, William S. *The Science of Entomology*. New York: Macmillan, 1973.

Ronalds, Alfred. *The Fly-fisher's Entomology*. London: Herbert Jenkins Limited, 1921.

Schwiebert, Ernest G., Jr. *Matching the Hatch*. New York: Macmillan, 1955.

Schwiebert, Ernest. *Remembrances of Rivers Past*. New York: Macmillan, 1972.

Shiner, Don. "Beetle Baits." *Pennsylvania Angler,* June, 1974, p. 26.

Slaymaker, S.R. II. *Simplified Fly Fishing*. New York: Harper & Row, 1969.

––––––. "Terrestrial Tricks for Low-Water Trout." *Outdoor Life,* New York. September, 1977, p. 78.

––––––. *Tie a Fly, Catch a Trout*. New York: Harper & Row, 1976.

Solomon, Larry and Leiser, Eric. *The Caddis and the Angler*. Harrisburg: Stackpole, 1977.

Sosin, Mark and John Clark. *Through the Fish's Eye*. New York: Harper & Row, 1973.

Stefferud, Alred, ed. *Insects, The Yearbook of Agriculture 1952*. Washington, D.C.: United States Department of Agriculture, 1952.

Swan, Lester A., and Charles S. Papp. *The Common Insects of North America*. New York: Harper & Row, 1972.

Swisher, Doug, and Richards, Carl. *Fly Fishing Strategy*. New York: Crown, 1975.

———. *Selective Trout*. New York: Crown, 1971.

Teale, Edwin Way. *The Insect World of J. Henri Fabre*. New York: Dodd, Mead & Co., 1949.

———. *The Strange Lives of Familiar Insects*. New York: Dodd, Mead & Co., 1962.

Vesey-Fitzgerald, Brian. *The Worlds of Ants, Bees, and Wasps*. London: Pelham Books, 1969.

Walton, Izaak. *The Compleat Angler*. London: Oxford University Press, 1956.

Wigglesworth, V.B. *The Life of Insects*. Cleveland: World Publishing Co., 1964.

Wilson, Louis F. *Variable Oak Leaf Caterpillar*. Washington, D.C.: United States Department of Agriculture, 1971.

Wright, Leonard M., Jr. *Fishing the Dry Fly as a Living Insect*. New York: E.P. Dutton & Co., 1972.

Zim, Herbert S. and Cottam, Clarence. *Insects*. New York: Golden Press, 1956.

INDEX

233